The Furnace

Engineering Income, Asset and Tax Based Systems of Representation

By

J.D. Weisinger

INFINITY
PUBLISHING

ISBN 978-0-7414-9747-5 Paperback
ISBN 978-0-7414-9748-2 Hardcover
ISBN 978-0-7414-9749-9 eBook

Printed in the United States of America

Published July 2013

INFINITY PUBLISHING
1094 New DeHaven Street, Suite 100
West Conshohocken, PA 19428-2713
Toll-free (877) BUY BOOK
Local Phone (610) 941-9999
Fax (610) 941-9959
Info@buybooksontheweb.com
www.buybooksontheweb.com

Table of Contents

Introduction

Chapter One

The most efficient form of democratic government is one where representation is based upon population. Population is naturally correlated to GDP, Tax liabilities, and includes a diversity in incomes, asset accumulations, and occupations and therefore carries the most diverse electorate. Representative governments provides security and stability which translates into economic growth and political power. However, truly representative governments are hard to manufacture. Most democracies don't spontaneously form during peace time to form representative democratic government. Most are hard fought over and involve significant concessions to powerful brokers and demographic groups. This is why most democracies are inherently flawed from the start and the test of time determines whether the citizens can negotiate more power sharing and political compromises protecting their own political franchises. Democracy is based upon cooperation and mutual benefit and often those already enjoying the privileges of power and wealth want to protect their entitlements.

The result is imbalanced representation in the legislatures, overly empowered executive branches, and dependent judicial branches. It is within this domain that parsing representation into GDP, tax liabilities, population is more acceptable with more stringent eligibility requirements based on incomes, assets, and enlistment more appropriate. If completely representative government is made impossible due to institutional powers unwilling to relent the solution may be to engineer more sophisticated systems based on more specialized representation where the deficiencies in one institution are accommodated by enfranchise within another. Even those nations that are initially incorporated with horribly imbalanced systems of representation have an opportunity over the course of decades and centuries to reconfigure how their representation and elections are apportioned permitting itself to provide its citizens more accurate representation, more stable political environments, and longer periods of higher economic growth.

Taxation is the primary enabler of government and principle duty of government. This intuitive and intimate relationship is evidence that tax based representation will be of the most profound improvements to political science. Tax based representation provides political franchise to those individuals actively participating in the funding of the organization or government. The premise of tax based representation invites new schedules of voter entitlement with proportional representation based on the amount of taxes paid (liability), segregating tax liabilities in brackets similar to income gradients, or correlating the amount of representations to a jurisdiction's aggregate federal liability in terms of gross or net amounts. It is even possible to attaché voter franchise to specific taxes remitted which opens the possibility of entitling corporations with representation based on their tax liabilities or enfranchising specific demographic segments.

Taxation is a potent mode of representation due to the fact that it correlates political power with government funding; by incentivizing the behavior of paying taxes it guarantees the nation or state access to more capital which often translates to greater economic and military powers. Taxation is a critical issue for most constituents which can result in terrible problems for nations during crises in public finance and economy. It is speculated that increasing taxes can limit economic growth and recovery as much as decreasing government spending as most economic activity is conversed with complementary contractions in opposing sectors. By associating tax liabilities with nationalist sentiments it can diffuse potentiated circumstances where economic duress seriously strains the population, its businesses, and a government's ability to navigate treacherous domestic political realities and dangerous external geo-political environments. A fully funded government is a more secure government. When modes of representation are dependent on tax values and tax liabilities these attributes are more guaranteed.

In previous eras of human development politics and economics were not separate domains but rather one called political-economy. Modes of representation are generally coupled to population as a means to cover all of the necessary variables of economy, tax liability, and popular sentiments. Indexing representation to GDP captures values from economy and is highly correlated to population and tax liabilities and might be a more efficient substitute. GDP is a derivative of population and can account for many of the same properties captured. GDP used in tandem with other systems of wealth representation or popular representation might provide significant improvements over those that are one dependent on a single mode of representation. Economy is such a dominant theme in politics and society that using GDP as an index for representation should implicitly be accepted if not openly advocated for.

Political systems can be engineered to produce more representation for those jurisdictions which have more economic power. This way better economic policies can be exported from the better performing jurisdictions with an increased number of representatives and more political influence. It is a relations already present in domestic relationships and international relations. The states or nations with stronger economies and more capital typically exert much more influence than those with lower weaker economies and fewer strategic assets. Attaching voter representation to GDP reinforces this relationship and can be a significant motivation for capturing higher GDP's with more exact economic modeling.

Attaching the voter franchise to bond assets is one of the most versatile modes of wealth representation for manufacturing new governments, economic unions, erecting international institutions, and enfranchising those investors and citizens making contributions to the nations public finance. Bond holder voter franchises will contribute to the immediate competitiveness and durability of the nation-state. The contributions provide capital useful in the administration or defense of the state. Each contribution is enumerated with specific values and dates which dictates the exact parameters of political representation. The fact that the number and value of bonds can be controlled allows the state to manage voter franchise and protect against monopolization or abuse.

Wealth representation is a mechanism that empowers conventional states maintaining taxing powers with the advantages in capitalization typically reserved for public stock companies. The premise is remarkable in its application for insurrections and rebellions as the emergent government has a greater chance of success due to the improved funding capabilities. In one stroke of finance it could form allegiances with populations and alliances with other states or nations. It maximizes its access to the resources necessary for waging war or rebellion. Financing war efforts is critical to both fledgling states and established nations and any government which can expand its base of support and revenues by offering bonds with common stock properties at fair market values.

Bonds are more appropriate only because the wealth based representation is a partial entitlement and not all of the states equity will be captured by the release of the instrument. Bonds represent a liability rather than equity but can still carry voting privileges. These voter franchises can be associated with only one chamber of the legislature or one branch of the government ensuring that a majority of representation is still monopolized by residents or citizens within the state's jurisdiction. Common stock denotes value with implications of profit for the organization. Although the organizations liabilities and assets could be calculated most governments don't seek profits and access to taxing powers would be a dangerous implement and might subject it to claims of illegitimacy. Common stock also denotes complete ownership of all equity which is incompatible with mixed systems of representation by unfairly denying other stakeholders (nonfinancial) access to the equity.

Coupling voter entitlements to treasury bonds is probably the most effective way to establish international institutions as it attracts investment, rewards contributions, but more importantly is adjustable year after year and can accommodate different political conditions. Bond based representation is correlated to commitment but operates exclusive of economy and population despite the correlation; with greater motivation a participant can overcome shortfalls in population and GDP. Economic Unions can be predicated on the mutualization of debts with voter franchises attached as incentive. This can be accomplished by the nations or by the citizens who can all participate in the consumption of bonds. If carefully coordinated institutions can be vested with political influence proportional to population or some other index and then assume proportional representation within the member nations legislatures by persistently investing in bonds. Other strategies might involve manipulating social security or retirement programs as a means to moderate the political franchise provided by bond based representation; this would be useful in offsetting an improved franchise for institutional investors by permitting government treasurers to leverage public pensions and public programs.

As a least common denominator bond representation can be used in reparations or empire formation when the conquering nation sets repayment conditions and demands political representation through those conditions. Under these conditions democracies could be subjugated to a dominant power where the population maintains many of its former privileges but where another nation makes substantial contributions to how it regulates and governs itself. This mode will operate at higher efficiencies when more than a single conquering nation is granted voter franchise; with two or three nations gaining a majority of representation in the legislature it permits the conquered populations to triangulate between the occupiers to gain political advantage and more successfully navigate the dire consequences of the failed war effort. Obviously if the conquering nations are all democracies themselves the net impact of this form of reparation or occupation will be more favorable than if the offending nations are autocratic or colonial. In fact over time and if the representation is reciprocated it presents an opportunity to forge a union or federal system rather than an empire.

Bond based systems of representation are also likely to be the first acquired as government financiers in the private sector are more likely to earn this concession due to the high incidence of public finance crises. This is important for established governments as it will likely be the only opportunity to reform its democratic system. Most nations suffer from a sclerosis and actively resist even the most practical of reforms. Most of the other wealth based systems of representation require the incorporation of a new state or new institution. Both are far less frequent than the number or wars and financial disasters that occur every few decades. Bond based representation is almost inevitable after the concept is more widely distributed as the opportunities for it to be used for reform or power concession are fairly regular.

The first democracy in nearly 2000 years had all of its representation indexed to landed estates. Not only did a citizen need to own an excessive number of acres in order to be eligible to hold office but a moderate amount of acres were needed just to vote. The herald of modern democracy had more similarities with an aristocracy as huge portions of urban citizenry and poor were excluded from the political process; the disenfranchised could only pay taxes and enlist in the military. Obviously it did not result in a fair system and was quickly reformed after several rebellions and revolts by dissatisfied enlisted and peasantry. Shortly thereafter the land requirements were dropped and direct voting access to a second legislature was granted.

Land requirements should not be the principle determinant for voting franchises but with more precision applied to the apportioning of powers it can still play an important role in politics. Not only can residential real estate be segregated from commercial real estate but values can be dissected into gradients very similar to income and tax liabilities (such as the property tax which implicitly includes all land owners). Including gradients permits non land owners and renters to participate as they can be provided voter franchises in opposition to or as a complement to the landed classes. Land can also be used in value voting systems where the number of votes are equivalent to the cost of the property. Segregating residential from commercial properties allows for representation to imitate normally distributed systems when commercial assets are excluded.

Equity based representation will eventually be the most useful way to index voter franchise within both public sectors and private sectors. Not only does it attach voting powers with assets but many securities grant representation on corporate boards. The combination of direct political access through voting and indirect political access through corporate boards and lobby makes equity representation the most versatile and ultimately the most durable system for representation. The next era of economy and public finance will be dominated by permanent funds and sovereign wealth. Equity representation is the perfect implement as most jurisdictions will gain tremendous influence on public stock companies which can serve as a means to interface other economies, other permanent funds, and other political unions. Securities are even more useful as device for construction of unions and economic empires as they impart a voter franchise, exact a return on capital appreciation or a dividend which can be equivocated to taxes or reparations, and can be considered permanent collateral in building intuitions and coalitions. Equity representation may also be made more useful by virtue of granting corporations voter franchises through tax liabilities or other indices which will naturally be extended to the private or public investor through corporate governance.

Income can be used in a similar respect tax liabilities are used to index representation. Income can be measured in pre-tax and post-tax values split into brackets or between median and below groups or median and above groups. Income representation is means for individuals, corporations, and jurisdictions to gain segregated representation or proportional representation. Many citizens typically work for salaries or earn returns on investments and both sources are legitimate. Corporations can be weighed in similar respects with profits equivalent to income. Jurisdictions typically don't earn income or profits but their tax revenues can be considered as income. However, income based representation isn't implicitly accessible to all adult citizens if they aren't working. Regulation can accommodate this defect by splitting family income in half so that each partner is entitled to vote in the system.

In systems that tallies incomes for representation it might be necessary to offset corporate representation with governmental representation as wealth is not distributed evenly in most economies and where the richest segment is naturally a composite of corporate owners. Double counting income by enfranchising the governments could be a spoiler as democratic jurisdiction introduce an aggregator of interests and uncertainty in leadership. Their leadership is certainly normally distributed among competitive parties under most conditions. Government incomes can be augmented with the proliferation of permanent funds. The assets contained within them can produce incredible incomes to supplement the tax revenues which implicitly account for between a moderate proportion of all incomes.

Democracies are less effective and competitive with public finance systems burdened with excessive debts and unfavorable ratio's in stimulus. However if they were to update their systems of representation in regards to asset classes and incomes they might be able to spread imperial economy to less sophisticated regions and nations with commoditized representation and offices earned as concessions and improvements upon the more ubiquitous autocratic or poly-autocratic systems of government. Most Democracy form as a result of occupation or revolt and in this process most form incredible inefficiencies in representative government due to the conflict of self interests and the lack of time to negotiate. Democracy based upon wealth representation should predispose more unstable nations to democratization efforts that also include greater economic compatibilities for economic union formation and empire building. No doubt corruption will be a constant threat for the next era in political economy be it wealth representation or state capitalization but it certainly compliments a period of history rife with environmental threats from climate change and security threat from the proliferation of data and information.

Other topics previously covered include tax unions and voter unions. Tax unions are agreements between state benefit providers and corporations seeking lower cost access to healthcare and retirement benefits. The companies pay the jurisdiction for access to the benefits which ultimately rewards resident tax payers with improved government services or lowered taxes. The real efficiencies gained are in economies of scale where companies from distant or foreign jurisdictions can pay the city or state for access to their benefits infrastructure communicated by private service providers but where the sums produce incredibly large incomes for the governments.

A terrible defect of Globalism and the dominance of large multinational conglomerates is the lack of fidelity to one state or nation. This method of integration also aids in cementing more concrete financial relationships and obligations between states and corporate entities Synthesizing benefits for more cost effective labor and payroll management will produce more profits and fundamentally alter the corporate-government paradigm for interdependence. States don't only gain access to revenues they are granted access to larger business networks which include more companies, more professionals, more labor unions, and more markets. Eventually these syntheses can impart a voter franchise for corporate residents which can culminate into much more political influence for the individuals and equity owners.

Tax Unions will undoubtedly benefit from methods of re-presentation which are correlated to tax liabilities or incomes where the recipients are corporations. Corporations can be granted representation in more complex political systems which make possible more critical interface between economic unions and the participating states and entities. Integrating corporate and political representation will be much more important in the future as companies continue to acquire market share and economies of scale. Multi-national companies are likely to become titanic in size after merging with the state capitalist infrastructure found within the larger economies in the world. Permanent Funds and Sovereign Wealth Funds will dictate which states and nations are successful as they impart representation on corporate boards and predispose the jurisdiction to lower taxes and higher government revenues.

Minor deviations and improvements upon even a small number of attributes can provide an incredible amount of variety in political systems. They can improve function and relieve a large number constraints on productivity. They can contribute to better oversight and less waste. One relatively minor change to campaign finance laws can have profound consequences years or decades later. One of the most primitive human instincts is to resist change citing the terrible risks involved. Often there are more risks in preserving the current political system than in changing it as most inefficiencies are ruthless exploited over generations resulting in terrible consequences. Most people cant recognize the risks engineered into the current system as they are inured to the threats. This does not mean they aren't endangered and the neglect can result in more severe crises.

Humans inexplicably agree to future circumstances that are not in their own interests. Often a hostile environment is used to coerce the concessions but other times premises are more profound then their application. Take for example the proliferation of unrepresentative senates within many state and national legislatures. A Senate typically deviates from an Assembly in that the number of representatives is not correlated to the number of residents located with a jurisdictions. This dilutes political representation as smaller populations are disproportionately represented and where a demographic minority must be negotiated with to pass legislation accepted and advocated for by the majority. It's a defect in reasoning where citizens equate the rule of the majority with mob psychology. The overwhelming desire to protect the rights of a minority leave nations exposed to exploitation.

The engineering flaw rests in legislation requiring both parts of a bicameral legislature to pass the measure. By promoting obstruction in one of the chambers its greatly reduces the likelihood that both chambers will successfully produce legislation. The number of bills passed are reduced and so is the quality. The majority party is constantly making concessions to a minority party which compromise regulation and other necessary components of the states. During public finance crises or other critical moments in history it is less likely that the politicians can successfully navigate the dangerous circumstances. A failed state will result where the apparatus of government cant regulate industry adequately nor tax its citizenry. Political instability rises and opportunities to unwind the original democratic entitlements are made available.

Nation building is a monumental task where those currently enfranchised through politics and economy are often asked to make concessions in conjoining otherwise disparate territories. In order to form a Union one must subrogate one's ability to govern oneself. This is a terrifying prospect considering most of politics is the ruled by self interests and those interests aren't always aligned. Nations are built from states and states are built from communities. It is hard to demand that citizens submit to the majority rule of those with different interests then them. That is why it is often only accomplished during periods of such terrific danger and instability. Most democratic governments form as the result of insurrections, rebellion, and revolution be they accomplished slowly over the course of several decades or centuries or at once after a successful military campaign. Harsh conditions act to intensify the drive to form alliance and allegiance while simultaneously reinforcing self interests and optimal representation. Power sharing is such a complicated premise that often the majority succumbs to poisonous council and installs cumbersome and imbalanced legislatures that marry one representative chamber with a second unrepresentative chamber.

Political science is a relatively new science. For the vast majority of human history autocratic governments reigned supreme and their reliance on dictum precluded any serious evolution or improvement. It's the source of contemporary executive branches which are the vestigial organ of the dictator. There is no reason why the majority of government apparatus must be under the rule of one elected official. The hierarchy already distributes responsibilities among a several other officials without depreciating its overall function. Legislators could easily assume many of the functions through committee leadership. There is less reason and worse argument that the principle powers of the executive branch couldn't be split into only two or three departments each elected and independent of the other. These topics haven't been fully explored because the half the race is terrified with subrogating power to others while the other half is terrified of abdicating the powers they have already assumed. It's a matter of extreme dysfunction and an utter lack of communication.

The same is true when contemplating different modes of representation. Obviously the race still fears rule of the majority evidenced by their supporting senate structures on state and national tiers of government. It is true that GDP representation accommodates many of the same variables contained with popular representation and it is also true that GDP representation is profoundly more accurate than senatorial representation by almost every measure. It continues to reflect population, tax liabilities, and economy where as a senate structure completely counteracts precise representation. Political architects should place more trust in the population to successfully govern itself – including the legitimacy of majority rule. More of the outcomes would be positive if there weren't artificial obstructions engineered into the systems producing the gross imbalances in power and providing access for excessive exploitation. Representational government will fail the people less often than those governments purposefully crafted to elicit argument and contradiction between the different demographic groups and economic classes.

The device of imbalanced representation is not likely to be abandoned despite the rational against its continued use. With that premise in mind a much more diverse landscape of political systems can be entertained. It makes more sense to create a larger number of integrated branches and chambers to coordinate more power sharing with greater ease. A more modern version of the senate is value voting. Value voting is naturally irregular and uneven in the distribution of representation which typically favors one demographic or class above another but it can be employed similar to the senate with the intent to make government function less predictably. Offsetting majority rule with minority enfranchisement will have dramatically different consequences depending upon the environment and participants.

Designating a voting franchise attached to bond consumption accomplishes the same check on majority rule but a different segment of the population is enfranchised. Instead of rural states having a political advantage over more populous state the investors class will more access to more proportional votes.. The value voter franchise can be moderated by the deployment of state sponsored retirement programs. This can check the growing influence of the investors class while there exists no simple solution to remedying the institutional advantage provided to less populated states permanent access to a disproportionate amount of representation. The value voting has significant advantages over senatorial representation in that bond consumption is promoted which should result in faster economic growth and lower future borrowing costs for the state and nation. State based senate representation offers no additional advantages to the body politic

There are two primary means to manipulate representation. The first is to moderate the number of representative provided to a jurisdiction or segment of the population. The term employed is representational coefficient and it is the proportional difference between jurisdictions along the selected index (GDP, Population, etc). The second is to attach a varying degree of representation based upon some asset or attribute. This is exemplified by value voting or some equivalent method that bases a number of votes on the value of some asset class or liability. The two can be used independently or in tandem but each has an incredible impact on net representation for the individual or state.

More options can be engineered into systems to dramatically change the power dynamics within the nation or state. Whether or not representation is determined by jurisdiction or by district can have a tremendous effect on representation by providing the individual access to multiple politicians, and possibly making the value voting much more potent. Even more sophisticated political devices can be used that make individual politicians eligible for multiple seats in multiple chambers or consolidate a states proportional amount of representation into only one office and election. Political science is still in its infancy with a huge number of innovations and inventions still waiting to be uncovered and unlocked.

Politics is the most important form of organization as it is a fulcrum for harnessing and managing the economic and natural resources of a nation. It is not acceptable to weather current inefficiencies out of fear of uncertainty. Inefficiencies in the political system compound into dramatic losses and significant institutional threats to sovereignty and prosperity. Political innovations have the opportunity to provide significant advantages in wealth and power. For most of the modern era the concept of democracy and wealth went hand in hand with the expectations that successful economy was dependent on personal freedoms and open elections. Free markets were thought to be the offspring of democratic privilege with unrestricted trade benefiting economy with faster growth and more stability.

Federal systems and Economic Unions have one advantage in that the individual states or nations don't need to necessarily abandon or alter their current institutions they can simply manufacturer newer ones. Inter-regional or Inter-State institutions can accommodate for many of the inefficiencies of older democratic systems, especially during periods of unprecedented instability in economy and demography. Multi-state authorities can operate almost identically to federal agencies with authority and impact with the opportunity to redistrict its own representation within the larger union or federal system. Redistricting can save incredible amounts of capital resources on government infrastructure. It can refine and regulate previously individual market economies more efficiently providing faster growth and more prosperity. They should be able to leverage their combined representation more effectively through collective bargaining.

It is within this aspect that the different aspects of wealth representation can be experimented with. Populations will already have access to demographic based representation on the state and federal levels and might be more accepting of asset based value voting or on the number of representatives being indexed to GDP or Tax liabilities. Politics moves more like tectonic plates and a people can experiment with single institutions with limited responsibilities first and develop broader based and more universal reforms later. Inter-state infrastructure can be installed over the course of several generations as an added measure of security and efficiency. Creating these systems provides a redundancy for cooperative government where other tiers might fail due to public finance crises and crises in leadership.

Having immediate access to a fully representative and more modern form of government to replace another failed or failing government could be instrumental in providing the necessary protection required for the constituents and residents. Federal systems can only be rebuilt and re-organized with dramatic intervention and the state which devote more money resources and intellectual capital to interim government prior to an event are much more likely to be the government charged with the responsibility to re-engineer the union or federal system. Enacting new institutions present the only opportunity for democracies to implement wealth representation by reform.

New modes of representation along wealth indices or other specialized demographics might prove instrumental reviving the modern democratization movement especially if a larger number of demographic and economic segments can be coerced into power sharing and profit sharing positions based on incomes, assets, and tax liabilities. Wealth Representation will likely be an inducement for participation in Republican governments especially in environments of incredible economic and political duress. Wealth representation will serve as an incentive to democracy while reinforcing capitalist economy. Support for theses initiatives will be found in a larger cross section of the population with popular sentiments as well as elite segments.

Wealth representation is tremendously versatile and can be used towards the formation of international institutions – and albeit only discrete portions of the population will have suffrage the powers and privileges might induce others into agreement. Exhaustible bonds are the perfect instrument for use in wealth representation as the confer a fixed unit of representation for a fixed period of time in exchange for guaranteed funding for the institution. The same principles apply to tax representation which might be pivotal in founding new governments with principles and principals. Although imperfect, wealth representation may be the anchor to secure future democratic reforms based on more uniform and universal political enfranchisements.

Most of the wealth based systems of representation require a more mature computer science and information technology infrastructure. The reforms require the collection and correlation of massive amounts of incredibly personal information. Trust is a requirement as ordinary citizens can not evaluate their peers qualifications and quantifications. Popular representation is an efficiency because participants can be better assured of more accurate representation and more equal access. However, some of the wealth based reforms can be implemented immediately without concerns of compromise. Most of the institutional based wealth representations are more secure due to the labor and capital resources already available to the aggregate. The easiest wealth based reforms to enact are those that determine the number of representatives apportioned to a jurisdiction. Voting can still proceed through the mechanism of one person equals one vote but the representation can be correlated to tax liabilities, GDP, or revenues. Where there is a will there is a way and there should be no doubt that certain aspects of wealth representation will almost certainly become political reality – economy is our immediate environment pervading most aspects of life and liberty.

Engineering

Chapter Two

Modern political systems are complex and dynamic institutions but they can still be reduced to a relatively small number of fundamental attributes. These characteristics can be recombined into a large variety of more specialized or more practical systems. The refined systems can then be engineered for integration within even larger Unions. Power sharing and efficiency initiatives occasionally forcibly and abruptly installed which makes a survey of new systems structures, and institutions useful in engineering more responsive and adaptable governments prior to the economic and political crises that predispose their implementation. Although any new institution or political power will have both advantages and disadvantages they will change the prior political calculus that precipitated the crisis or event leading towards reform.

This chapter lists all of the most relevant and useful of attributes in outline form and briefly describes each one. The order of the attributes is arbitrary but the outline still serves a purpose in making a quick translation of property to code for more efficient substitution and re-organization. Although disparate and seemingly unconnected when presented within the individual system designs they will coalesce to form the most important themes contained within the other chapters. Most of the attributes are self explanatory but in case of ambiguity the term and definitions can be referenced with ease in this chapter.

The most fundamental aspects of legislatures are listed with the number of chambers qualified after its status as unicameral, bicameral or multi-cameral. All three types of legislatures have both advantages and disadvantages. Unicameral Legislatures are the most efficient where laws can be passed with less effort and with greater frequency. It is the most basic and fundamental form of majority rule. This speed allows the nation or jurisdiction to adapt to critical environments quickly and with implied consent. The velocity at which legislation can be passed might also be viewed as a negative; changes may be made too hastily and require reversal. However, reversals are also much easier to achieve due to the fact that only a simple majority in one chamber is necessary to unwind previous legislations.

Bicameral legislatures definitely accommodate this defect by actively inhibiting reversals but the pace at which new legislations are passed is much slower by virtue of two majorities are needed within two chambers that are often occupied with majorities form opposing parties. Bicameral legislatures are a factor of 3x more conservative in this respect. Its actually much more likely that legislation fail passage in both chambers than be affirmed. This can have a terribly corrupting effect. The regression will produce ample opportunity for institutional powers to monopolize market share in politics and economy.

1.) Legislative

- i. Organization
    - x) uni-cameral
    - xx.) Bi-cameral
        - z. 1st camera
        - zz. 2nd camera
    - xxx.) Multicameral
        - z. 1st camera
        - zz. 2nd Camera
        - zzz. 3rd Camera
        - Zzzz 4th Camera
    - xxxx.) Abolished (usurped by executive, administrative laws only)

Bicameral Legislatures are slow and ponderous and can be unresponsive during crises. They are easily exploited by institutionally enfranchised as voting down progressive legislation is incredibly easy unless predicated on some natural disaster or horrible consequence.

Multi-legislatures combine the disadvantages of both unicameral and bicameral chambers by virtue of their ability to assume the responsibilities of other branches and reserve powers from each other. A multi-legislature, or complex legislature, could combine a unicameral structure for the chambers assuming executive or judicial powers with bicameral structures for those retaining legislative powers. Complexes permit multiple segments of the population to be individually enfranchised which offers opportunity for concession as well as specialization. Multi-cameral structures are more compatible with Reserve system structures, triangulation powers, and legislative equivalents to Tripartite Executive structures all of which will be explained in more detail in subsequent chapters.

The entry of abolished legislatures is useful for manufacturing political systems where the executive branch or judicial branch usurps the legislative primary responsibilities. During emergencies it offers significant efficiencies. Nearly half of the laws governing a nation and its economy are administrative laws derived from executive authority. With a more specialized Executive department it might be able to develop the entire legal canon. This is especially true with configurations where there is no unitary order within the executive branch but rather discrete and independent parts that act as checks on the other parts for a more distributed and balanced structure.

For the contemporary history of democracy certain executives have had veto powers over the legislature. This reinforces the dictatorial aspect the original founders intended. They modeled the Presidential office on a Monarchy burdened by Parliament. However, this has conspired to produce some of the worst outcomes for democracies when employed with bicameral legislatures which already inhibit regulatory initiatives and reform movements. The odds of passing a significant piece of legislation are already minimal and made much less frequent with expected opposition in party occurring in a moderate amount of instances.

It is unlikely that Executive officers will abandon Veto powers but there is a more appropriate substitute. Macro-political votes allow the executive branches to interact with legislatures and other branches and triangulate between multiple legislatures to confirm one version of legislation over another version. Instead of inhibiting the frequency of successful legislation the Macro-political vote would increase the number of passed bills. Its simple a much more productive power than the Veto, especially if it doesn't apply to the repeal of legislature, acting like a one way valve towards more progressive regulatory and civil rights environments. The bony politic still has the opportunity to repeal legislature but it requires the cooperation of all of the legislature. In cased of Tripartite Executives structures the Macro Political vote would offer confirmation of the legislation created through agency laws in order to check each individual Executive branches accumulation of power over the others.

Another important qualifier for legislative branches is whether they are representational or tyrannical. If another branch or chamber appoints legislators it qualifies as tyrannical. It is expected that terms continue to apply to the officers serving in the chamber. Tyrannical appointments can come from any number of executive, judicial, or legislative branches from the same tier or adjacent tier of government. The term representative implies that the number of representatives elected are correlated to a proportion of the electorate generally being population size but also qualifies when parsed by economic criteria and other qualifying measures.

Non proportional representative criteria has its uses but is the weaker of the two forms of eligibility criteria in that it always produces an imbalanced system of representation which is more easily exploited by minorities or the politically enfranchised. Imbalanced systems of representation can still work but they require offsetting powers between demographic or economic criteria so that more segments of the populations are empowered than those disenfranchised. This is the primary source for political concession during moments of crisis.

ii. Attributes

- x. Representative
- xx. Tyrannical
  - z. Appointed by exec
    1. Unitary
    2. Legislative
    3. Executive
    4. Judicial
  - zz. Appointed by leg (stipulated)
  - zzz. Appointed by judicial
  - zzzz. Appointed by retired members
    1. Legislative
    2. Executive
    3. Judicial
    4. Reserve Branch

Tyrannical systems are qualified by the branch or tier making the appointments and produce the political levers for manufacturing extra-national tiers of government (central, federal, or economic unions). Tyrannical appointments are also useful for emergency governments and for configurations that demand greater control over a specific tier or branch of government.

Tyrannical systems have practical use but otherwise introduce many of the same flaws non proportional representative appointments endure, unless they are indexed to the population or some other gradient criteria. Appointed legislatures can be representational of population in the same respects that elected legislatures can be which will impart more legitimacy to the institution as the individual senators will be accorded a proportion of power equivalent to the scale of part:whole in regards to population, GDP, or tax liabilities paid.

Atomized configurations dictate that the members of lower tier legislations appoint by consensus the members of the higher tier legislature. Terms will insulate current higher tier legislatures from political turnover occurring too quickly and too often. The original structure for the U.S. Senate was for members to be appointed by the U.S. House Representatives. The Atomized structure imitates this mechanism but operates across tiers rather than chambers. The Atomized attributes permit appointments to be made by either the Executive branch or the Legislative branch which will be incredible useful for constricting extra regional or extra-national governmental institutions like Economic Unions and Satellite systems.

xxx. Atomized (lower tier governments dictate representatives in higher tier, lowest tier elected by popular vote)

1. Council members appoint representative
2. Executives (mayor) appoint representatives

Most contemporary Democracies are actually Republican forms of governments but modern technologies in communication and information distribution might accommodate True Democratic reforms. The term True Democracy typically implies the an entitlement for citizens to vote directly on the issues in front of the legislature. Historically this has had disastrous consequences but the Greek Empire did persist for hundreds of years and thrive for much of it. Corruption set in and an endless period of warfare followed. Only then did the empire recede. Modern economy, society, and technology is much more complicated than the ancient era of Greece but citizens are much more capable of appreciating the difference and accommodating their inadequacies. It might be prejudicial to suggest that a True Democratic structure for legislature isn't effective to be used in a complex of legislatures or more sophisticated political systems.

True Democracies can be implemented in a popular form with no restrictions on access or voting based on rigid economic or demographic criteria or True Democracies can be improved with a auxiliary chamber meant to filter the legislation for popular voting. These filters can be subjected to eligibility criteria and refined with procedural rules to ensure the locus of power remains with the larger voting body. More mature postal systems, telephone systems, and internet systems provide the necessary communication infrastructure permitting the True Democracy structure to be distributed among a much larger population over a much larger area. Independence from a physical building allows for larger populations to participate efficiently with enough checks on voter fraud. True Democratic formats might be more acceptable within Multi-legislatures where the correct number and magnitude of responsibilities can be delegated to the popular chamber without diluting the specialized leadership professional politicians provide.

xxxx. True Democracy (non-republican)

1. Structure
    a. Monochamber
        i. Straight
        ii. Leverage
    b. Monochamber with Auxiliary (Filter)
        i. Straight
        ii. Leverage
2. Components
    a. Monochamber (all functions usurped by referendum)
        i. Referendum weekly
        ii. Referendum biweekly
        iii. Referendum monthly
    b. Auxiliary Chamber
        i. Presentation (acts like filter, tabling issues and bills)
        ii. Deliberation only (Public Con science, details bills for public

referendum)

2. Powers
    a. Authoring Legislation (Auxiliary chamber with presentation only)
    b. Confirms Legislation (Triangulation)
    c. Repeals Legislation (Reconciliation)
    d. Confirms Appointments (Triangulation)
    e. Confirms Treaties (Triangulation)

When professional politicians are abolished the legislature can still rely on committees formed by popular votes within the jurisdiction. No eligibility constraints would be permitted and terms must apply but committees allow for a more precise examination of issues prior to the public referendum. Instead of independent representatives they would be voting for committee members on a regular basis. This actually provides for greater specialization of candidates as each will be evaluated on the merits of their argument and not prescribed individual powers outside of debate.

The auxiliary chamber can be delegated presentation powers where they dictate which legislation is tabled for popular voting. Procedural rules will protect the franchise of the public in their responsibility for voting on the most important issues. A filter will only allow for more order with issues prioritized and emphasized according to the needs of the nation or state rather than the individual. If necessary, auxiliary chambers can be relegated to deliberation only with the tools necessary to research and argue the issues prior to a popular vote but where no filibuster controls are authorized.

The Democratic votes can be organized as straight votes where only those voters which turn out for the vote count towards the tally of votes to decide the issue. In a system with a slower frequency of referendums this can result in tremendously fewer voters and votes. A leveraged vote tallies only the votes casts but the winning measure is then able to allocate all of the votes from eligible voters in the jurisdiction towards a vote including the results of surrounding jurisdictions. This effectively doubles the number of possible votes the issue or measure would ordinary get, and depending on voter turnout produce a net effect in multiples of votes earned more than votes cast. Versions can restrict the block vote to only those votes cast relegating the leverage but the premise remains the same.

All of the powers of a True Democratic legislature imitate those of a Republican legislature except they are much more limited and specialized. The fact that most powers are predicated on triangulation makes it a powerful partner for other government branches with legislative responsibilities including appointment powers, treaties, and laws. Future evolutions and improvements to the True Democratic chamber can include powers over budgets and taxes but they can produce more disastrous results more quickly where a span of misallocated budgets and ill conceived taxes can cripple a nation or states within just a few years.

Oversight is another typical legislative power that isn't readily compatible with True Democratic chambers as no discrete committees are formed with the intent to scrutinize over the executive branches agencies. It is possible that the appropriate infrastructure is created and that oversight powers can be earned but then the chamber begins to blur its structure with that of more conventional Republican chambers. The fact that legislative powers are restricted to confirmation or triangulation rather than authoring is also testament to the fact that the True Democratic chamber satisfies a more specialized role than conventional Republican legislatures enjoy and that the difference should be respected.

The powers of the Legislative branch are also enumerated within the list so they can be delegated between the chambers. The powers are;

i. Powers

- 1. Laws
- 2. Oversight
    - a. Unitary
    - b. Judicial
    - c. Tripartite Presidential
    - d. Tripartite Attorney General
    - e. Tripartite Treasury
- 3. Ratification (Treaties)
- 4. Executive
    - a. Foreign (President/ Military/ Intelligence/Alliances)
    - b. Domestic (Attorney General/

Law enforcement/ General Administration)

   c.. Commerce (Treasurer/Central Bank & Banking/Insurance Agencies, Commerce).

   d. Fractal (all executive functions assumed by separate committees)

5. Appropriation (Budgets)
6. Judicial
7. Appointments
8. Role
   a. Presentation (Filter)
   b. Deliberation only
   c. Ratification (within the same branch)
9. Triangulation
   a. Stipulated (Powers apportioned to the camera)
   b. General (Powers apportioned to the other cameras.
10. Taxing
11. Appointments (Direct, by Majority leader)
12. Elections

Enumerating the different powers is really important for all systems that maintain more than one or two chambers. The separation of powers is also necessary for instances where the executive branch is divided into multiple branches or fractal (departmental) structures. Executive powers can easily be assumed by committees within legislatures with the chairperson acting as CEO and the remaining legislators acting as a corporate board. This permits the most interesting and possibly most useful combinations and intersections of power within democratic systems of representation and governance.

Another potent improvement in legislative power is the opportunity to adopt Judicial review and judicial responsibilities. The part:whole structure of a congress split into two or more parties does mitigate many of the concerns the ability to author legislation will translate into a monopoly when combined with the power to adjudicate over the laws. Each individual legislator's power would be constrained to an individual court and limited number of cases with appellate courts and internal regulatory procedures making the synthesis sounder and safer. Many legislators naturally acquire legal educations which makes them more acceptable substitutes although terms will natural impede in the accumulation of experience. It is not the soundest of powers but neither is the contemporary unitary executive with appointment and veto powers.

There are fewer options for Executive branches but most combinations are more potent in regards to changing the function and essence of a government. Most executive branches emphasize top down control which means considerable power is concentrated within a single individual. Executive Branches have direct access to military assets and law enforcement officers which makes them more powerful than legislatures which are typically divided by region and party without immediate access to emergency equipment and personnel.

2.) Executive

i.) Unitary (standard) – Primary determines subordinates

The most common, earliest, and simplest of configurations is the Unitary structure where one executive maintains complete and unchallenged command over the entire executive branch. This permutation offers incredible efficiencies in regards to coordinating internal policing with external intelligence and actions, especially in regards to foreign policy and treaties but also between commerce and economy. Efficiencies come at a cost with no significant internal check on the abuses of power. This can occur within the domain of economy as regulatory agencies and or legal through policing agencies. One of the most frequent abuses is the refusal to enforce regulations and previously enacted laws. This is exacerbated with free market ideologies which in limited party systems produces an environment where regulations are ignored or enforced for periods of equal length resulting in unpredictable markets.

To mitigate this natural flaw in political science Executive branches can be separated into multiple parts to preserve the net advantage of the branch while introducing some internal checks on power. The simplest division is into three parts with a President maintaining control over foreign policy, militaries, state departments, and intelligence agencies; an Attorney General maintaining control over internal domestic law enforcement and regulatory agencies; and finally a Treasurer General to focus on the Federal Reserve, economic stimulus, permanent funds or sovereign wealth, sciences, R&D, and infrastructure. The divisions mitigate accumulation in powers during states of emergency or in erosions of system balance between the legislature and executive departments.

More complex systems can marry one Tripartite branch with another so combinations of Presidential/Treasurer, Presidential/Attorney General, or Attorney General/Treasurer occur to introduce some efficiencies in coordination without devolving back into a Unitary structure; these structures can be labeled bipartite or bifurcated and may offer more flexibility when married with more sophisticated legislature or judicial systems. Not only can the powers be assigned on a permanent basis but more complicated multiple executive systems can manufacture for themselves a system to delegate or auction executive powers between the executives during or between election years, possible as a system of competitive budgeting or corporate governance.

ii.) Divided; all individually elected, primaries determine subordinates

x.) Tripartite

c.) Treasurer/Central Bank, Science, Permanent Funds, Commerce,

cc.) President/ Military/ Intelligence/ State,

ccc.) Attorney General/Law enforcement/ Regulatory/ General Administration

cccc.) Delegated or auctioned powers (use fractal sub routine, xx.)

The third option is a Fractal structure (departmental) which provides an opportunity for the public to elect each agency or department director independently. It should be noted that this differs from a Executive Legislature because the agencies are not governed by committees but rather specific individuals. The Fractal structure eliminates almost all concerns of individuals assuming too much power during states of emergency. A Fractal system permits leadership to me tailored to the agency rather than the party allowing for a more flexible election process. In contemporary liberal versus conservative political divisions, it would permit the electorate to install more conservatives within the military and law enforcement agencies with liberals retaining executive control over the regulatory and economic agencies. This might result in significant advantages for the state.

With staggered terms the nation can engineer itself a system where leadership is rotated in odd years to ensure that the public can elect directors to counter unpopular policies enacted by other agencies. Appointed Fractal executive branches are efficient in regards to permitting different legislative committees access to government functions which should be displaced across the multiple parties and multiple chambers of the Legislature. This would imitate a Prime Ministerial form of government unless the independent legislative committees are afforded the opportunity to appoint their own directors of fractal agencies. It completely subrogates the executive branch to the legislative but circumvents scenarios where a majority leader might otherwise appoint all of the agencies directors.

xx.) Fractal – each department elected or appointed individually

c. Powers;

1. Central Bank Appointments
2. Banking and Insurance Regulatory agencies
3. Industry (Non Agriculture/Pharmaceutical/Health) Regulators
4. Economic advisors and research
5. Trade Treaties
6. Commerce Departments
7. Domestic Law enforcement
8. General Government Operation
9. Agriculture/Pharmaceutical/ Health Regulators
10. Scientific Research (Space Agencies/ Oceanic, General Science)
11. Peace Treaties (military)
12. Intelligence Agencies
13. Military Branches (Reserves)
14. State Departments
15. Laws (Legislative)
16. Confirmations of appointments
17. Infrastructure/Monuments

Executive branches can be abolished with the powers and responsibilities usurped by legislative or judicial branches where the function will be dictated by the powers prescribed to the branch within that section's options. Executive legislatures are just one possible solution with executive powers able to be apportioned to judicial branches or reserve branches as well. Less mature federal systems and economic unions may incorporate legislatures and court systems without an independent executive branch. It would then be the responsibility of the member states and nations to enforce any of the laws and regulations established by the legislature.

iii.) Abolished (Congress assumes responsibilities and internally determines agency chairs or department secretaries)

iv.) Hybrid (stipulated number of divisions and powers)
  x. Three (fractal subroutine)
  xx. Four (fractal subroutine)
  xxx. Five (fractal subroutine)

Judicial Branches need not necessarily maintain the contemporary structure of interlocked and hierarchical circuits. Instead, Justices can be appointed or elected to Congresses, representative of population or some other criteria, with an annual internal vote determining which judges are appointed to which committee, with those committee replacing the different hierarchical circuits within the court system. This permits the Judicial Congress to rotate individuals within committee to minimize abuses of power, be it on a annual basis, a term basis, or life tenure basis (i.e. permanent). It also guarantees more power sharing between parties and ideologies with a greater likelihood that the Congress and all committees appointments remaining evenly distributed among the parties actually in office.

3.) Judicial
  A. Structure
    i.) Independent Circuits (like family/ criminal/ superior/ supreme)

ii.) Congressional structure with internal votes forming committees

x. subject to yearly rotations

xx. subject to terms, and vacancies

xxx. Permanent (life tenure)

B. Powers.

i.) Judicial

a. General

b. Individual Circuits

i. Family

ii. Civil

iii. Criminal

iv. Superior

v. Appellate

vi. Supreme

ii.) Legislative Sub Routine

iii.) Executive Sub Routine

iv.) Reserve Sub Routine

The number of justices can be determined by population and resemble other elected institutions like the U.S. House of Representatives or they can be enumerated by a constitution or made representative of some criteria other than population (like number of states or counties, GDP, or a jurisdictions tax liabilities). A larger number of justices do not dilute the prestige of the court system. In fact, it makes deliberation more effective and minimizes the impact of outlier verdicts and opinions. It reduces the negative consequences of a bad appointment or an ineffective judge. It naturally allows for more points of view from more demographic groups and more facts to be presented, with more research performed. More judges within larger populations will speed up the time it takes for civil and criminal matters to be processed with due diligence. More importantly, a larger number of judges allow more specialization within the courts for more precise and accurate verdicts.

Most judicial branches will be pre-occupied with discharging the typical responsibilities of justice and law but there will be times that they assume individual responsibilities from the other three branches and the attribute matrix provides the flexibility to attach powers through subroutines. This can occur during periods of emergency, the powers can be prescribed at the inception of the institution, or they can be bestowed by some other branch by amendment. Many of the tripartite executive branches assume appointment powers over the Judicial which might legitimize justices assuming more specialized executive functions. In other instances the Judicial department should be granted access to traditional legislative powers like oversight as it falls within similar domains of authority

C. Transmission

i.) Elected

x. Representative of population (like House) tethered to individual jurisdictions

xx. Unrepresentative (like US Supreme Court, or Senate) with a stipulated number of justices untethered to jurisdictions

After the number of justices is determined, whether the group is elected or appointed, and if appointed, appointed by whom must be stipulated. With more complicated political systems come more sophisticated appointment powers. Specific circuits and committee can be appointed by specific executive or legislative branches. This is especially useful in Tripartite executive structures where judicial appointment powers can provide a check to domestic policing powers with the Presidential or Treasurer General delegated authority while excluding the Attorney General from the process.

ii.) Appointed

x.) By executive

1. Unitary
2. Presidential
3. Attorney General
4. Treasury
5. Determined by the committee/ circuit (stipulated)

xx.) By legislature

Elections for judges do mitigate the threat of conflicts of interests within political appointments. They also guarantee that the court's ideology keeps pace with the general populations ideologies. Both impart a measure of stability that is lost when other elected officials appoint judges for indefinite or permanent terms which cause a dislocation in representation and execution with government institutions.

Reserve branches offer a government the invaluable opportunity to recycle previously elected officials and preserve their years of experience within the government within an institution with abbreviated powers. Reserve branches can be relatively simple with all public officials maintaining eligibility or they can be partitioned into separate parts for different party or branch members. Admitting all retired officials is the easiest method to immediately constitute a Reserve body for a new government institution. A greater numbers of participants do imbue greater legitimacy as it is harder for one party or one generation of officials to dominant the dialogue or powers of the branch. For maximum utility, the Reserve branch can be composed from previous elected officials from different tiers and branches of government so that more precise checks and balances can be installed.

Even more sophisticated reserve branches can be self admitting with current members authorizing new memberships based on terms. This better ensures the highest quality of official is admitted within the Reserve branch rather than opening membership up to one term retired officials who demonstrated no particular affinity for politics or integrity. Reserve branch members can even be appointed so that the number is naturally measured and the participants can be vetted.

4.) Reserves (continuing to use retired political representatives)

- i.) members
  - a.) all retired elected officials
  - b.) self admitting (internal party vote)
    - i. Terms
    - ii. Permanent
  - c.) appointed (determined by previous position, speaker, whip, president)
    - i. Term
    - ii. Permanent

Reserve branches offer an incredible opportunity to continue regulating political officials after their terms expire. With Reserve branch responsibilities come restrictions on employment and permanent salaries. This can mitigate the more corrupting forces within a democratic government where private sector companies can coerce politicians with lucrative positions after they are unelected from office. The incentive to forward the agenda of powerful corporations is diminished with the permanent salary and permanent oversight over politician finances. The fact that Reserve branch members are no longer elected will remove other inhibitions to their representation creating an interesting check on the other elected branches of government.

There are powers that are indigenous to Reserve branches and those that can be borrowed from the other branches. The traditional Reserve powers are the power to Repeal, Excision, Excommunication, and Triangulation. With a consensus between a two chambered Reserve branch, a simple majority in a unicameral structure, or a majority of chambers within multi-cameral structure the Reserves can employ the Repeal, Excise, or Excommunication powers. These actions should not occur at a high frequency and require a bi-partisan effort among different chambers and retired party members. The Reserve Branch acts as the rear guard and protects the body politic from outlier political maneuvers or unwarranted pieces of legislation. The Reserve Branch should have considerably more experienced career politicians within its ranks which justify their high caliber powers.

If the traditional powers of the Reserve branch are not adequate new powers can be prescribed to the Reserve branch or it can assume those of other chambers and branches. Most executive and legislative powers can be delegated on an individual basis or in lots of traditional groupings. The Reserve branch can more easily assume legislative powers with the ability to confirm appointments, write and confirm legislation, oversight, ratify treaties, and the other responsibilities ordinarily delegated to similar bodies. Judicial powers aren't transferred too easily but in moments of crisis concessions can include Reserve branches with access to appellate courts or lower level circuits.

ii.) Powers

a.) Executive (sub routine)

b.) Legislative (sub routine)

c.) Judicial (sub routine)
d.) Exclusive Reserve
x.) Repealing; Legislation
xx.) Excising; Executives, Legislators, or Judges
xxx.) Excommunication; Politicians from Parties (and Reserve Branch Eligibility)
xxxx.) Triangulation (in Bicameral Legislations); where consensus between the two Reserve Houses can be used as a substitute to one of the Elected Legislatures

Repealing legislation is a powerful check on the Legislatures authority. Repeals can occur immediately after the passage of a bill or years later after the consequences have been deemed dangerous or detrimental. This will make the overall political system more conservative with the number of passed bills and legislations subjected to the threat of repeal from both the Reserve chamber and General Legislatures. A more accessible repeal process might contribute to economic and political stability in representative governments. Executive branches with triangulation powers instead of veto powers would accelerate the rate of passed laws warranting a more mature repeal process and allowing the two to offset each others advantages.

With a super majority within one chamber or consensus between multiple Reserve chambers the institution can Excise currently elected or appointed legislators, executives, or justices from office. Reserve branches should not be in agreement very often considering the natural split in party or regional affiliation so when consensus is earned it implicitly authorizes the severe actions. Fear of retaliation should limit the number of unjustified excising attempts with the other party or parties likely to gain consensus in a counter-movement and orchestrate similarly aggressive maneuvers.

According to a sum over histories explanation of history for prediction of behavior these episodes will be unavoidable but that doesn't mean they can't be checked by a Veto by the Executive. The instances where an opposition party maintains a supermajority in the Reserve branch will be small and the frequency will be even less when the Executive branch wont be able to defend against these episodes with a Veto. Most excised legislators will immediately gain access to voting within the Reserve branch which inherently diminishes the majority abusing the excise power. There are a number of self limiting attributes which make the Excising powers more acceptable than first impressions typically impart.

Excommunication is a similar power to Excision although it only concerns members of the Reserve branch. This allows the chamber to self regulate itself and disjoin members guilty of crimes or misdemeanors that embarrass or threaten the body politic. This power must be restrained to super-majority proportions as well to help ensure that one dominant party does not overwhelm a smaller less relevant party and exclude them unjustly from the Reserve system. This is true even in cases where one political party has been relegated to history with no active members in the General Legislature or Executive branches to defend them. Most of the members of a Reserve system can be considered relics of the past from the onset so it would be unnecessary for older less powerful parties to be single out for elimination.

Triangulation is a power that permits one branch to confirm the actions of another branch but where there are multiple chambers or branches each vying for confirmation in competition with the others. Generally, this pertains to legislation with an executive branch or reserve branch confirming legislation passed by one chamber of a multi-chamber legislative branch at the expense of dissent from the other chamber or branch. Repeal powers might slow the pace of legislation but Triangulation powers will accelerate the number of passed bills.

This power allows Presidential systems to imitate Parliamentarian systems by increasing the likelihood that the elected executive can negotiate agreement and pass the legislation that it wants. It also has the ability to offer a powerful check on Parliamentarian systems by placing the power in the hands of a Reserve branch rather than the elected Executive branch which offsets the immediate power of Presidents.

iii.) Structure

a. Bifurcated by party (multi-Cameral);
b. Unicameral (indiscriminant)
c. Fractal; organized by decade (or increments that

produce odd numbers, singularly or in tandem
by position within boards and legislatures (with a
delay in activation of the reserve body politic until
the imbalance is achieved if necessary to perpetuate the ordinary progression of politics).

Consensus is necessary to deploy any of these powers and that completely depends on the structure of the Reserve branch. Unicameral systems allow for a more dynamic interface between retired politicians and currently elected government with less of a check on the powers of the Reserve Branch. Unicameral structures should be used more often when the Reserve branch assumes those powers of other conventional branches of government and less often when apportioned the special Repeal, Excise, and Excommunication powers.

Chambers of Reserve branches can be dedicated to individual parties (or coalitions of parties) so that its members with self admitting or appointment powers primarily influence their own parties Reserve powers. Multiple chambers for Reserve Branches provide innate checks on the powers of the branch by making it much less likely that consensus is reached. The Reserve branch should be an auxiliary part of the government with its most important powers used during crises or where a majority of retired officials agree they should be used.

Fractal organizations allow for multiple chambers to be engineered around decades, parties, branches, or other indices to produce an off number for convenience in authorizing Reserve powers or for a more precise control over the Reserve Boards. Increasing the number of Reserve components might actually improve the likelihood of achieving the consensus necessary to implement any of the powers. Different generations of the same party may have different intentions which imparts some flexibility within the branch. Peer pressure is always a factor and a majority should be easier to earned with smaller and more distinct groups of retired politicians.

It is very important to stipulate the exact pool of retired officials which are eligible for election or appointment to the Reserve branch. The specific branch and tier of official can be determined in accord with the apportioned powers so that a pool of retired state level governors acquire powers to check an executive branch or a pool of state legislators can apply continual oversight over the currently elected federal Congress. Retired officials need not be constrained to the same branch they served in and it might be more useful to have retired legislators provide oversight over a judicial circuit, retired Executive officers oversight over specific chambers of the Legislatures, or retired judges oversight over currently elected Executive branches.

iv.) Pool
  1. Tier
    a.) National
    b.) State
    c.) Local (county + municipal)
  2. Branches
    a.) Executive
    b.) Legislative
    c.) Judicial

When necessary the Reserve Branches can be engineered with a parameter or time frame requiring a confirmation from the legislature for continued use; this would permit governments to experiment with different combinations of Reserve branches knowing they are temporary in nature unless re-confirmed. This allows for older nations to introduce the Reserve Boards within the framework of its constitution or government without disrupting the current checks and balances within the system. A system of temporary authorizations will increase the number of different Reserve Boards created within the Reserve Branch maximizing the likelihood of successfully integration and minimizing the occurrences of failures due to abuses in powers.

Most governments are composed of municipal tiers, state or regional tiers, and then federal tiers. Later evolutions of government might also include corporate tiers (direct representation), with divisions into nonprofit self regulators (industrial), resident owned commercial governments (socialist), and hybrid systems based on Permanent Fund assets for more sophisticated modes of representation (incomes, assets, and liabilities). Nonprofit self regulators are democratic associations formed by the industries participants who are charged with regulating their own services in regards to labor, market share, and other competitive facets. Employees will be represented as will residents but there will be no professional political class dictating policy and law.

More complicated systems can include resident owned businesses and commercial governments deploying permanent fund assets as measures for influence and control over industry; representation can be a function of the number of shares or convertible bonds owned. Eventually tiers might only relate to the public sector services an individual receives with the representation gained by virtue of stock in state capitalist securitized service providers or public stock private sector providers. In outlier circumstances traditional governments may be absent with Corporations acting as surrogates. Eligibility criteria can be used to permit certain public stock companies with a plurality of owners to be prescribed limited statehood with the representational powers based on the number of employees and management working for the entity. These companies will be public utilities with ownership distributed among a larger cross section of individuals, retirement programs, and permanent funds.

Economic Unions are a tier of government which other governments earn representation through. Many federal systems start off as economic unions and over time consolidate regulatory powers, taxing powers, and law enforcement powers. There should be no doubt that larger single currency, single language markets are a major accelerant to economy when a universal regulatory system is applied. In many instances the number of governmental and nongovernmental tiers can change depending upon location and access.

5.) Tier

- A. National
- B. State
- C. Municipal (and County)
- D. Corporate
    1. Industrial Nonprofit Regulators
    2. Employee Owned (Resident Owned, Socialist)
    3. (Permanent Funds) C-G/Private Finance Initiative
- E. Economic Unions

Conventional governments can retain control over the more sensitive aspects of policing and military but private/public finance initiatives can also accommodate these domains with local and state permanent funds providing the natural check on power accumulations. Permanent Funds permit unprecedented integration between public sectors and private sectors permitting access to satellite formation and making union formation easier. Not only can the permanent funds be used to integrate two public sectors but public sectors can be merged with corporate boards. Modern Corporations are often much larger than contemporary governments with more personnel at their disposal and much more capital resources. Public sectors from any tier can gain tremendous power and influence by making consistent and regular investments into eligible public companies. Governments typically have longer life spans than corporate entities providing a significant advantage when investments are made over 50 year or 100 year periods. Public sectors can amass significant voting shares within their permanent funds which also produce revenues making them more secure and powerful.

Permanent Fund investment can reciprocate or stymie the tremendous influence corporations and wealthy individuals have on politics through campaign finance and other modes of control. Potential corruption is not a viable counter argument as most modern governments are steeped in corporate welfare subsidies, economic stimulus initiatives, private finance lobby, and other compromising business practices. Permanent Funds introduce a self limiting check on corporate influence by permitting the governments to exercise control over the system. In a best case scenario corporations would be more limited in their lobby and campaign contribution efforts while in the worst case scenario they can better ensure the process distributes donations more evenly between the competitive parties.

Nonprofit industry regulators can assume most government agency and department responsibilities with Democratic appointments set up by stock contributions, permanent bond contributions attached to representation, or by governmental decrees. These nonprofit institutions must accommodate labor and other contributors to economy and not focus exclusively on the wealth drivers and owners classes. By installing Union representation and consumer representation on the boards, the par-governmental infrastructure retains more legitimacy and integrity while gaining more functionality.

Without the majority of consumers, laborers, employees, and owners willing to participate within this government system it will fail. Laborers and Consumers are 98 percent of an economy as the middle and lower classes contribute the effort to produce most the goods and services offered in the economy and then the consumption and demand that generates the wealth and profit. Most corporate profits are the difference between labor costs and product costs. Communities can better leverage their ability to manage the nonprofit industrial model of government with permanent funds as the average professionals, laborers, employees, and consumers will also be able to employ stock positions to influence the corporate boards who install a significant portion of the representatives on the nonprofit industry regulator boards. There should be no doubt that permanent funds and sovereign wealth are an evolution in political economy that will provide invaluable improvements to representation and economic growth by conserving profits and increasing velocity of transactions.

The spectrum of asset ownership obviously encompasses fundamentalist capitalist systems where no permanent funds are employed and a majority of government operations is dependent on corporate cooperation but the foil to this condition is an environment where the majority of large business are community owned after generations of compounded investment through permanent funds. Even when community ownership outweighs private stock ownership a significant portion of the wealth of a nation will still be securely anchored within the professional classes and the small business owners who continue to vote in elections for corporate boards while discretely managing their services and private companies without undue interference from the regulators or government.

6.) Term limits

- a.) max length of term
  - i.) 2
  - ii.) 4
  - iii.) 6
  - iv.) unlimited

Term limits are a necessary component of all functional democracies. If any of the major components of government do not have term limits it will be easily exploited by political parties competing to secure and maintain positions of institutional power way beyond any measure of legitimate representation. This applies to all executive branches, all legislative branches, and all judicial branches. The deleterious effect of the abbreviated length of terms for U.S. Representatives is evidence that terms should be longer than 2 years especially in competitive election systems that require significant effort for re-election and involve deregulated campaign finance. The short term predisposes members to way too much undue influence from wealthy contributors and corporations. It has an incredibly corrupting force on contemporary politics with members often required or incentivized to neglect voting constituency interests in favor of corporate or wealthy donors.

The consequence of corporate lobby on shorter and less predictable terms is a greater reliance on incomes earned post public service which naturally favors large corporations who are promised high salaried and low effort company positions as repayment for the unprofessional and untrustworthy representation. Terms of only 2 years also depreciate the labor involved in performing the public service as half of their appointment is spent campaigning for the next election which imposes serious constraints on time and effort.

It can be argued that the proportion of campaigning also contributes to political instability with frequent vacillations in control which could be moderated by only slightly longer term limits. Terms of six years are more adequate for managing the time and effort constraints installed within election based systems of representation. They also mitigate some of the undue influence corporations have over the chamber by making the election more infrequent. However, the U.S. Senate is often an example of how representation can be dislocated with a public's expectations not being realized.

Longer terms are beneficial to democratic legislatures but if the chamber is not representative of population it can introduce serious deficits. Longer terms are more defensible and naturally less responsible; it exaggerates the ability of an election system not to accommodate the prerogatives of the majority of voters and it enfranchises minorities from certain demographic and income classes at the expense of the majorities who expect representation. Lengths of four years are a decent compromise between 2 year and 6 year terms especially when the number of consecutive or total terms served is regulated and where there are multiple chambers acting in concert.

Those national representatives sitting on intelligence committees or armed services committees should have years of dedicated experience to maximize benefits to the country in regards to national security and regulatory experience. However, establishing a maximum number of terms makes it harder and more costly for corporation to unduly influence politicians with lucrative post career positions for large sums of money. Corporations will have to make more investments into new campaigns for more members unlike successful career politicians who can leverage institutional election advantages to minimize corporate campaign donations by attracting a larger number of donors.

Not only are the numbers of politicians increased which will burden the companies with more salary expenses but they will also have to employ more of the less knowledgeable and less influential politicians. The civil servants who acquire decades of specific task orientated experience and who are more insulated from the corrupting force of corporate campaigns accomplish the bulk of government work. Oversight is much less expertise intensive than the performance of the service or duty which means shorter terms lengths would not seriously depreciate the quality of service provided by the country.

Legislators should not have unrestricted access to terms as it predisposes the nation to terrible generational imbalances in cultural and ideology. Labor environments change, demographic environments change, and economic environments change. All of which makes one representative more qualified and more useful than another. This exposes the nation to imbalances in representation despite numerical parity or accuracy. Instead, a system should be developed to encourage politicians whose careers end due to limits to pursue other chambers or offices within the federal, state, or local tiers. Reserve Branches adequately conserve the political capital (experience) while enforcing the pertinent restraint on accumulated power.

b.) max number of terms

- i.) 2
- ii.) 4
- iii.) 6
- iv.) unlimited

It is possible for a politician to acquire significant expertise over the course of 8 - 16 years or longer with moderate term lengths and term number limits. The typical length of service for a working adult from age 25 to retirement is only 40 years which sets an ordinary ceiling or threshold for maximum term length and numbers. Most citizens are only eligible for election at a more advanced age, which is appropriate considering the maturity or experience necessary to author legislation, and provide oversight on executive functions. This gives legitimacy to the argument that shorter terms and fewer consecutive terms are more appropriate. It is also precedent for establishing a ceiling or retirement age for politicians.

c.) constraints on number of terms

i.) Lifetime Maximum (sum)

ii.) Intermittent (reset after absence)

iii.) Unlimited

There is an important distinction between consecutive terms and total terms. Consecutive terms are only those were re-election is earned immediately after the preceding term. This usually determines institutional advantages, which makes a lower number of consecutive terms safer in regards to maintaining accurate representation between demographics and generations. Establishing a threshold for total terms allows an elected official to leave office after defeat or a switch between government roles and then return but with an extension of maximum number of terms. Establishing controls on both consecutive terms and total terms so that officials can be forced out of office for a few terms to return with only a slightly higher threshold of remaining terms of eligibility is appropriate to conserve political capital and expertise while mitigating the threat of excessive accumulation of institutional power.

d.) restraints on terms

i.) Sum of both elected and appointed

ii.) Sum of all elected

iii.) Per individual office/region

The structure of the election is incredibly important for determining how the government is modeled. Democratic elections involve a large number of variables including campaign donation regulations, election coordination (Presidential or Prime Ministerial), and whether or not they are popular elections, or are more insulated with electoral colleges or appointed representatives. Most elections involve competitive campaigns with multiple opponents pitted against each other in public debates and T.V. advertisements. Whether or not these contests are funded by public sources with prescribed tax contributions or by private more competitive sources determines how susceptible the system is to corruption.

These attributes can make one system magnitudes more conservative than other systems. They affect how quickly the government apparatus adapts to crises and circumstances, how fast it progresses towards labor rights and more civil rights. They can also dictate how susceptible they are to corporate money, government money, or foreign money. Most citizens make policy choices based exclusively on how popular the options are in their immediate vicinity and culture. They are in fact mirrors of either restrictive or progressive policies meaning that they conditioned by exposure to favor either political inclination.

7.) Elections
- a.) Campaign Donations
  - x. Publicly Funding
  - xx. Privately Funded
    - i.) citizen only
    - ii.) citizen and corporate
    - iii.) government (corporate equivalency)
    - iv.) open (citizen, corporate, and foreign entity)

In order to fund these events the politicians require political donations from other citizens, corporations, or governments. Regardless of whether or not the donations are regulated in terms of maximum amounts, the eligible parties must first be determined. The least common denominator is permitting citizens to make campaign contributions while determining either or both corporations and governments to be eligible is a more serious assertion. Corporations can be both privately owned or publicly owned and those that are listed on the stock exchanges or have multiple owners should take the diversity of those owners' political beliefs into question prior to donating to a particular party or candidate. It should be unlawful for management to transfer corporate dollars to political candidates unless they are in proportion to the listed affiliations of stock holders with management shares redistributed by the same proportion a second time. There should be no concessions made on this issue as executives incentives aren't completely aligned with shareholder preferences especially if they come from different demographics, income brackets, and where a nearly half of all securities are typically owned by pension funds including public pensions.

In order to fund these events the politicians require political donations from other citizens, corporations, or governments. Regardless of whether or not the donations are regulated in terms of maximum amounts, the eligible parties must first be determined. The least common denominator is permitting citizens to make campaign contributions while determining either or both corporations and governments to be eligible is a more serious assertion. Corporations can be both privately owned or publicly owned and those that are listed on the stock exchanges or have multiple owners should take the diversity of those owners' political beliefs into question prior to donating to a particular party or candidate. It should be unlawful for management to transfer corporate dollars to political candidates unless they are in proportion to the listed affiliations of stock holders with management shares redistributed by the same proportion a second time. There should be no concessions made on this issue as executives incentives aren't completely aligned with shareholder preferences especially if they come from different demographics, income brackets, and where a nearly half of all securities are typically owned by pension funds including public pensions.

Politicians construct tax policies, trade policies, and regulatory systems which make any political donation more potent than the initial intent of the corporation on any single issue. The use of shareholder equity to forward the designs and ambitions of company executives is unwarranted and closer to theft than any legitimate representation of interests. The best examples of this are public and private pension fund investments into companies favor candidates that don't synch up with pensioner beliefs. Most pensioners are not aligned with management in regards to the labor policies they enforce, the fiscal policies they advocate for, and the misuse of natural resources, and especially the forceful deregulation stance posited. When political contributions are involved the fiduciary duty encompasses more than profits as the costs include tax penalties, subsidies, and remediation and often accumulate in amounts greater than the original investment.

Private Campaign finance is an infinitely more complicated issue when the shares owned by pension funds are vested under the management of the investment banks who are leveraging the government assets to their own personal advantage when lobbying members of government. A larger portion of public pensioners will always diverge from the investment bank's management's political preferences and it is almost certain that a large number of government officials will be on the business side of those campaign dollars come Election Day

Unrestrained corporate campaign donations set precedents for state governments and local governments also making campaign donations. Most governmental donations will continue to be distributed normally in accord with the proportion of successful appointments and this imitates most corporate incentives to distribute campaign donations to all parties evenly encouraging corruption rather than decide election results. Public officials are elected as a product of the private or public campaign system and being such are eligible participants for redistributing the state or cities political capital through independent campaign donations. Governments typically adhere to a normal distribution between competitive political parties which contributes to an argument of implied consent. They can be effective force multipliers for influence without disrupting the natural tendency to vacillate between available parties. Government campaign finance contributors may create momentum at critical junctures in the national or state wide elections but it's unlikely they will have an exaggerated impact when compared to the volume of corporate or civilian private campaign donation.

If policy architects maintain that financial and commercial markets must be freer and under-regulated then political markets must grant equal access between citizens, corporations, and governments. Corporations and Governments are both aggregators of populations but governments adhere more to popular political inclinations. This makes them more eligible as political donors than corporations which are a natural fulcrum of economic activity but are far from representative of the populations employed by them or which purchase their products.

Obviously, one must still enforce a framework for fair elections but if citizen and corporate donations are acceptable, contributions from governments must be viewed with similar legitimacy. If money is indeed an expression of free speech then government representatives are entitled to use tax dollars to coerce favorable or comparable policies from competitive jurisdictions in the same respects corporations and wealthier citizens do. Politics is the science of self-interests and democratic governments epitomize the coordination and organization of concerned citizens. Campaign donations will lay the foundation for increased cooperation between party members of even competitive parties and jurisdictions from outside the state or region. It is an intriguing dynamic that can permanent alter the trajectory of a political party or nation.

Many citizens don't recognize the difference between Presidential Elections and those with Prime Ministers. Presidents are typically elected independently from their legislatures resulting in scenarios where the President can win office but then face a Congress where the Opposition Party is a majority. When Prime Ministers are elected they implicitly have the support of the political party winning a majority of seats in the primary legislature. Prime Ministers can enact reforms more easily and have the political power to help enact laws that coincide with campaign promises and agendas. Coalition styled elections are much more efficient in that more legislation can be passed more quickly regardless of it reforming previous laws or enacting new laws. This efficiency helps conservative office holders as much as liberals.

Presidents can sit idle for years prior to earning the political support for a mandate. Inefficiencies in the system of representation are abused more easily as it is far easier to limit the rate of progress or reform simply by refusing to enact new legislation. Take for example a bicameral legislature in combination with a Presidential Veto. The likelihood of successfully passing reforms is minimal with a split congress occurring half the time, an antagonistic congress occurring one in four times, and majorities in both chambers having a frequency of one in four as well. of occurring in the lowest frequency. This contributes to a 1 in 4 chance to pass legislation before the Presidential Veto is taken into consideration. A Veto changes the frequency to 1 in 8 or approximately 15%. During crises this could spell doom for the nation but the worst consequence is expressed over extended periods of time where the missed opportunity for reform can seriously harm the economy and disrupt stability.

Coalition governments improve this ration to nearly 1 in 1 with only one chamber of congress and no self limiting Veto power necessary. There is no evidence that suggests that these systems are prone to frequent and disruptive repeals which would be the single best argument for maintaining an antagonistic bicameral legislature.

b.) Structure

i. System

x. Presidential (antagonistic or unsynchronized with legislature)

xx. Parliamentarian (majority in legislature determines executive officer)

Voting systems need not be relegated to one vote for every eligible person. Instead votes can be distributed according to the value of asset, number of stocks, number of acres, or in relationship of part to whole, or some other pre-set calculation. Changes to the voting system can be just as profound as those changes made to the structure of branches within a government or the modes of representation used for eligibility.

ii. Vote

x. Number (One stock or One Acre = One vote or Ratio)

xx. Part: Whole (Asset Value = Number of Votes, coefficient)

xxx. Combinational (Weighted Part:Whole)

xxxx. One Citizen = One Vote

Democracy is premised on one vote per citizen. It is an exceptionally good measurement for a legitimate and efficient government. More complicated governments with more branches and departments might actually gain efficiencies by introducing variations in voting systems for those particular parts. It might be more convenient to permit one chamber of a bicameral legislature to be determined by stock ownership and the value of bond assets in order to introduce significant corporate and economic interests into government while simultaneously eliminating private campaign finance and maintaining the standard one person one vote mechanism for the executive branch and second legislative chamber.

The same inefficiencies involved in senatorial representation can be achieved by manipulating the voting mechanism. Senates aren't representational of populations as each city or state is afforded and equal number of senators regardless of population. Obviously, the one person one vote rule is violated when comparisons are made in regards to ration of senators to represented citizens. All senate structures are direct arguments and contradictions of the primary premise of democracy as majority rule. Senates can be an effective hedge against abuses levied by a majority but are more easily abused by minorities gaining a disproportionate amount of influence in the nation or union. Minorities can be extremely effective at obstructing government and the progress of civil rights, economic rights, and developing well funded and strong public sectors. Political Systems with too many protections against majority rule are prone to extreme periods of dysfunction and susceptible to instability.

Value voting in both bond representation and equity representation can be reformed by introducing a scale of representation with brackets reflecting a static amount of representation. The premise is similar to how tax brackets are formed accept that rather than producing a percentage of taxes owed an integer is substituted for vote representation. This figure conveys a numerical value for voting. Those in the lowest voting bracket would maintain a one to one ratio for votes per person, those in the middle bracket would gain a two to one ratio of votes per person, while the the top income bracket would confer a vote multiplier of 3:1. No doubt this would skew voting powers to the middle classes but the middle class tend to be more representative as a class. The middle class includes professionals, union members, public sector employees, and small business owners. The higher income members would gain more parity with lower income citizens but the focus will remain on the middle class and provide them voting multipliers.

Value voting can also occur in ratios with the value used extracted from a dividend or amount and in some proportion of one whole vote. Thresholds can be enacted that stipulate a minimum amount of consumption prior to earning the franchise and maximum improvements in vote coefficients. The exact parameters of a bracket or ratio used in a value voting system will always be stated more clearly within the charter for the voter franchise specific to the unique system employing the device.

Combinational value voting typically requires integration within a hierarchy such as a corporation or military. It is similar to value voting but it provides votes equal to the number of persons living within the jurisdiction, under direct command, or within the department or agency. In a combinational voting system citizens would be afforded one vote apiece, their mayor would gain access to a number of votes equal to that of the town, a county executive would earn an equivalent number of votes as the number of residents in all of the participating towns, while the Governor would leverage an amount of votes equal to half the entire population of the state. The chief executive officer in the system is always relegated to half of the total votes in the system. Otherwise, combinational voting systems should be led by committees with equal votes or it will be dominated by the single executive wielding a huge margin of votes. In order for the executive to be outvoted an overwhelming majority of 65-70% of the other voters must contradict their position. The method is reminiscent of feudalism and can be applied to corporate, military, or governmental elections and appointments (confirmations)

Structure includes how voting is directed within the jurisdiction. The two most common methods are direct through popular voting and indirect through systems like the Electoral College. A more detached version than the indirect method is one that insulates elections from the public by relegating voting to the domain of the legislatures. By far the most appropriate and effective method for voting is the most direct through popular voting. It enfranchises the entire population with majority rule which should be checked by a strong alternating binary party system or a more functional rotation in a multiparty system. There is a more practical reason for permitting majority rule to govern a nation – the people must take responsibility for the actions of the nation unlike situations where minorities are vested with the principal political power. This implied responsibility is a burden to all descendants and all voters; it persists even in cases where a minority establishes political control and usurps all the benefits of the state or wages war in the name of the state. Maintaining the integrity of majority rule is extremely important as current administrations and cultures create legacy and history with mistakes often reverberating through history for the length of the states survival.

c.) Intimacy

x. Direct (Popular)

xx. Indirect (Electoral College)

xxx. Insulated (Legislative dictates)

i. Majority of seats in unicameral or multi-cameral

ii. Majority of chambers in multi-cameral (Macro-political Vote, lower tiers)

iii. Includes reserves as separate chambers

xxxx. Coalition (majority of lower tier executives determine higher executive officer)

Electoral College is an indirect method that produces inconsistent results for popular representation in elections which contributes to political instability and long lasting feuds. Electoral Colleges are scandalous affairs in democratic countries as they insulate legislatures or executive branches from popular control. Even inefficiencies as small as 4% differentials between electoral votes and popular votes between states will produce extremely divergent results in political economy over extended periods of time. As the sample size increases so do the outliers and deviance from normalized results. That figure of 4% represents an outcome of 4 times in 100 elections where the imbalance in representation likely results in an unpopular election of a politician to office.

That's only in an unadulterated system where party interference and political machinations of bureaucrats can introduce wildly inaccurate results frequently exploiting a class of citizen who would otherwise be in the majority and select the winning candidate. Examples include voter suppression efforts or manipulating campaign finance laws to dilute representation. Stability is engendered by votes dependent on accurate and popular elections. This does not mean there won't be failures in public finance or governance but it does mean that more of the population can expect to be held responsible for their errors and mismanagement during office. Where there is inaccurate representation and excessive amounts of waste in the political markets there is less culpability and a greater likelihood of secession, insurrection, civil war, or occupation. At the very least, inefficiencies in the political market produce imbalanced wealth concentrations and poverty which can't be cured as power accumulates within the institutionally wealthy.

Insulated elections occur when democratically elected legislators hold a quorum and reach consensus on electing the chief executive officer for that tier. It's not a direct election but it's not an indirect system like an electoral college either. It is very similar to how parliamentarian systems elect their prime ministers except that the legislators are already elected and the election pertains to a branch external from their own. Macro-political votes between the chambers of a multi-chamber legislature can also be used as a substitute to the individual votes by electors. In this case each chamber votes and records the majority verdict. The majority verdict from each chamber is then tallied with the other chambers and determines the winner of the executive election.

Methods involving macro-political votes permit chambers with lower number of representatives in ratio to population or other indices to maintain the same elective powers as chambers with larger number of representatives. One of the more interesting ways the macro-political votes can be used is by subrogating election powers to the lower tiers of an office. Instead of permitting the legislatures within the federal tier to determine the federal executive the macro-political votes can be distributed to the state legislatures within the participating jurisdictions. Likewise, a coalition of governors can be bestowed election powers over the chief executive of a federal tier in the same respect the state legislatures are given macro-political votes. The Governors hold a quorum and the majority verdict determines the outcome of the presidential election. This is another form of insulated election that is neither direct nor indirect but which must be considered as valid as the elections held for those individuals participating in the insulated election.

Appointment powers have been enjoyed by executive branches since they were first authorized through popular elections. A legislature typically maintains traditional oversight with all appointments conditional on a conformation process. In more complicated systems of government, more precise declarations must be made in regards to which executive branch is permitted to exercise the appointment power. This book deal primarily in Tripartite and Bipartite structures which divide the executive branch within two or three principle branches which is the main reason why three options are offered.

- d.) Appointed
  - x. Tyrannical
    - 1. Executive
      - a. Presidential
      - b. Attorney General
      - c. Treasury General
    - 2. Legislatures Majority Party
    - 3. Judicial
  - xx. Discretion
    - z. Mechanism
      - 1. Commoditized (market price)
      - 2. Inherited (1st Born, board succession)
      - 3. Decree (personal selection)
      - 4. Any

Appointment powers can be wielded by legislatures just as effectively as executives with a majority leader allowed to install the directors of their choice. When Executive Legislatures usurp all of the previous responsibilities and charges of a unitary executive branch it will obviously need to delegate authority over the apparatus of government. In other instances, a Judicial branch might have domain over an agency requiring appointment with confirmation from another branch. The delegation of appointment and confirmation powers are necessary checks and balances between the various branches or chambers. A government can fall into complete dysfunction with the abuse or neglect of either appointment or confirmation powers and all efforts must be made to ensure they are accessible during even the most dire or stressful of circumstances.

Power transmission can completely avoid elections under different processes. A tyrant can simply dictate a successor or the change can be at the discretion of the previous office holder. Discretion can take the form of decree, inheriting, or commoditized sales or transfers of political office. These methods sound like dastardly autocratic mechanisms but it can be a more complex and sophisticated systems of financial representation that supplements a primary form of demographic representation. Most political systems are imperfect with the flaws ruthlessly exploited by opposition parties but this can be incredibly important in recruiting support for fledgling democracies in previously autocratic or despotic nations.

Multiple chambers of legislatures and several distinct executive branches with specialized powers introduces the diversity needed to make the necessary concession to attract the elites willing to risk overthrowing the current institutional power. More importantly, any power transmission method can result in democratic elections despite autocratic origins; jurisdictions can purchase commoditized seats or positions and provide their own rules for democratization, inherited positions can result in popular elections if lineage is interrupted or left vacant by a lack of heir, and any transmission by decree can name the jurisdiction as recipient thus permitting popular elections to commence afterward. More leniency in discretion might provide more flexibility during extended periods of crisis with pre-established routines, rituals, or histories predisposing the redistribution of political power through different methods.

Even more interesting and useful combinations are possible when dealing with permanent funds, sovereign wealth, and integration between multinational corporations and labor companies. Tyrannical appointments can be institutional powers for Executive offices, Legislatures, or Judicial branches as long as they are clearly stipulated within the constitution or framework for government administration. Most governments couldn't function appropriately if appointment powers were not available as elections are capital intensive and resource intensive operations which can be extremely burdensome to coordinate across a large number of tiers or branches.

By making individuals, corporations, and governments all eligible as consumers of commoditized representational offices it enables conventional governmental hierarchies to fully integrate corporate hierarchies. Smaller nations may benefit from making representation available to corporations which extend their soft influence into a increased number of larger nations and economies. Representation can be constrained by extremely large occupation fees which permit the government to expand their public sector (military spending, welfare, or law enforcement) while maintaining lower taxes in the private sector. There will obviously be a gradient in influence and complete reciprocity will likely never be achieved but democracies could become vastly more competitive in foreign markets. Corporations headquartered in their nation can earn representation in another nation's political systems and economy. Corporate boards are typically governed by stock ownership making them much more accessible to other governments and permanent fund managers.

zz. Eligibility
- 1. Individual
  - A. Citizen
  - B. Resident
  - C. Alien
- 2. Corporate
  - A. Nonprofit eligibility criteria
    - i. Charity designation;
    - ii. Non Charity Designation;
  - B. Conventional Incorporations
    - i. Employee owned;
    - ii. Public;
    - iii. Private
    - iv. Indiscriminant
  - C. Incorporated
    - i. Domestic Corporation – same state
    - ii. Domestic Corporation – different state
    - iii. Foreign corporation

Eligibility for discretionary power transmission mechanisms can be dictated with a charter or constitution to determine which institutions or persons can barter and trade for the privileges of office. Individuals, corporations, and governments can all independently be authorized as recipients or consumers of non-democratically transmitted offices. On the individual basis eligibility can be made more exclusive by citizenship constraints, residency requirements, or alien entitlements.

The alien entitlement can be combined with the citizenship option so that nonresident citizens can hold office. None of the attributes are exclusive and from these three option come an almost infinite number of combinations when systems are engineered with the access provided for specific tiers and branches. Resident aliens might gain representation on the local tier but be prohibited from voting or holding office in state and federal tiers. Nonresident citizens could be an instrumental resource for governing reconstruction or occupation efforts. Other combinations might aid in imperialism and other efforts to engineer empires between otherwise disparate jurisdictions.

By designating difference between citizenship requirements, residency requirements, and alien entitlements one system can coerced into compatible with other foreign systems and larger economic unions. All of these attributes can be toggled independently to manufacture different variations of *demicratic* governments (hybrid word from demi meaning half and democratic meaning rule by the people). Governmental tiers can be dissected into city, county, state, and federal with the domains restricted by executive, representative (legislature or reserve), judicial, or by agency in either domestic or foreign jurisdictions.

3. Governmental
    A. Tier
        i. city
        ii. county
        iii. state
        iv. Federal
        v. Indiscriminant
    B. Domain
        i. Office
            x. Executive
            xx. Representative
            xxx. Judicial
        ii. Agency (Fractal)
    C. Jurisdiction
        i. Domestic
        ii. Foreign
4. Any

Available options also include such mechanics as term length and units. Term lengths can be determined as willful terms based on transitions during or between sessions or years so that the office can be sold or bartered at will. The terms can also be stipulated by the office with all parameters established by a municipal charter or constitution. A generational term allows the office to be bestowed for the lifetime of the recipient which imitates monarchial transmissions between principals and heirs. The added advantage is that a city, state, or nation can reclaim the seat after one generation as a means to eliminate familial accumulation of power.

Units refer to the number of seats permitted to be owned or managed by a single individual, department, or company per jurisdiction. A company could acquire multiple legislature positions within a single jurisdiction if it was represented within multiple districts. The same is true for governments and individuals. This characteristic does not limit any Legislative Broker entitlements if they are already permitted by the branch and chamber. The Poly Bureaucratic option allows for the accumulation despite other inhibitions in any of the independent chambers or branches.

zzz. Mechanics
- 1. Terms
  - a. Willful Terms (transactional)
  - b. Stipulated Terms
    - i. Office term
    - ii. Single Year
    - iii. Generation (Life)
- 2. Units
  - a. Exclusive (Singular)
  - b. Poly-bureaucratic

A more accessible system of representation permitting governments to purchase seats or inherit them promotes bloc formation and integration between public sectors. It is a nonviolent means for one jurisdiction to consolidate power temporarily or longitudinally. In the same respect mergers and acquisitions can create or protect market share in the private sector integration within the public sector has the best opportunity to radically redefine and redistribute geo-political power. Two jurisdictions in separate systems (be they states or nations) could organize their representation offices in a parallel manner to provide each other access or reciprocity. The gradient would obviously benefit the larger jurisdiction which has more proportional seats to spare but empire formation premised on the exchange of representation will ultimately benefit both partners as they more easily re-organize both of their economies along similar regulations, currencies, or languages.

If any specific quality defines a democratic nation it will be the eligibility requirements for voting. The very fabric of the society and soul of the nation is found in which demographic groups are empowered with representation, in what proportion, and combinations. Most modern democracies don't discriminate between criteria when it comes to administering a popular vote for legislatures, executives, or judges but with more refined and exact systems of representation stricter regulation of voting hierarchies can produce more efficient systems.

Certain governmental powers can exercised with more precision and expertise from legislatures exacted from more practiced and knowledgeable legislators and voting constituents. Manipulating voting rights is a treacherously dangerous power to exercise but political engineers can ensure that powers and privileges are delegated responsibly with adequate checks and balances. More mature and successful systems to accommodate power transfer mechanisms so that voter rights and eligibility criteria can be re-organized according to contemporary social and economic pressures. More sophisticated governments with multiple executive branches and multiple legislative chambers will accommodate the extra specialization necessary to administer larger economic unions and empires.

8.) Eligibility Constraints

a.) Criteria

x.) Military

x branch

i. Army
ii. Navy
iii. Air Force
iv. Marine
v. Coast Guard
vi. National Guards

xx) Indiscriminant

There should be no doubt that one of the most potent eligibility requirements for political office is prior military service. Although most state don't make this a pre-requisite many citizens overwhelmingly favor retired soldiers and war heroes during election campaigns. Within the scope of more complicated and more varied political systems segregating between the different branches may be appropriate to hedge against the consolidation of political power within a particular tier or branch.

Conscription has long been a reluctant liability for the majority of citizens but in modern political caste systems they can be most effective way for civilians to be granted election powers in government. During periods of threat or economic instability the trend is for greater enlistment which produces a naturally more diverse electorate for the competing parties. Leadership takes courage and discipline and citizens can acquire these attributes in the armed services. They certainly can demonstrate them better than citizens who haven't served.

A significant portion of the governments most important responsibilities are military and intelligence giving the politician more acquainted with the community and details more familiarity. There is a major difference between setting voting criteria and determining candidate eligibility. Setting candidate eligibility will permit the non veteran citizenry to vote in elections despite their inability to be elected. When voting rights are attached to veteran status it is less likely that the cohort will vote for a non veteran even if they are still allowed to entertain candidacies.

In specialized systems of military eligibility each army, navy, and air force branch could be apportioned a separate chamber in a legislature. Other variations include occasions where the Army and National Guards are permitted to elect the Executives while the Air Force and Coast Guard elect the Legislators with the Navy and Marines electing the Justices. These permutations can apply to governments in reconstruction, occupation, or in instances where enlistment is mandatory in order for all citizens to retain their political franchise. Universal service will make the all political systems structured around branch eligibility more legitimate and ensure that a pool of adequate candidates remain available. The premise behind permitting the entire armed forces to democratically govern over recently conquered jurisdictions is to immediately manufacture a democratic process to transfer to the occupied nation as well as to discourage imperialism (or corporatism) within the victor nation.

Evolutions of universal suffrage for enlisted and veterans might include the opportunity to vote in nonresident jurisdictions within the political union; so that a retired marine in Texas could vote online for the Governors of all of the other states holding general elections that term. This entitlement is especially useful for periods of reconstruction after a civil war but military styled cultures might elect to impose these rights under normal conditions. Premises and powers like these help political integration between states while promoting voluntary enlistment. Technological advances in computers and communication will permit more interesting and effective ways to enfranchise specialized segments of the population.

Military eligibility criteria are much more useful for engineering non-democratic systems, corporate systems, or hybrid systems. One possibility is installing a contemporary feudal system or a purely mercenary version by combining Military enlistment with autocratic transmission mechanisms such as inherited or commoditized so that the jurisdiction can imitate earlier forms of political economy without actually abandoning democracy completely.

Maintaining inherited position or commercial acquisitions protects the previous political franchises of the elites within the new jurisdictions recruited into the Union or empire. Commoditized seats or positions make it especially easy to integrate with Multinational or national corporations. Eligibility criteria can be as exact as to dictate the specific military branch permitted to vote within the election or hold the office with specific governmental branches or tiers which makes for extremely specialized systems especially when mandatory enlistment requires the majority of citizens to serve in the military.

Throughout human history there are occasions where one dominant political party manages to wrestle control away from the other factions and is able to dictate all policy and procedures for the new government. One example is Communism. It was intended to be a system of complete political economy with the nonelected government presiding over all aspects of economy. It typically operates with one dominant party dictating policy between all of the tiers and jurisdictions. Fundamentalist capitalist systems can sink into this inefficient form of governance and economy. Corruption blurs the differences between parties and market solutions start gaining popular support despite their gross inequities. There is not much variety or use in single party systems and the option is only included as a means to construct satellite systems.

ii.) Political Party (i.e. single party systems)

x. branch specific

xx. tier specific

xxx. indiscriminant

Poly-Autocratic systems invite distributed systems for blame and for burdens in leadership. A committee always provides better leadership than a single individual over a course of several generations as a strong and principled autocrat can always be followed by a weak and morally bankrupt leader. Internal party mechanism will generally keep members in line with party ideology regardless of the integrity or quality of those ideas but more contributors will aid in the experimentation or development of those ideas. Poly-Autocratic systems based on party committees also limit the degree of intense competition for power within nondemocratic systems. It is harder to remove a group of seven leaders rather than just one, where any conspiracies to remove a small number of party members won't result in a dramatic of a change in ideology or political engineering. Larger more inclusive parties with more leadership positions also distributes power in a more effective way which dispels many of the conventional tensions within autocratic states.

A more specialized version of party governance actually empowers the governmental caste with all voting powers without abandoning a multiparty system. Extending the voting franchise to all government employees maintains some of the autocratic efficiencies in caste systems but provide such a large and diverse sample size of voters within the Demi-Republican system. Multiple parties with divergent political ideologies and governing styles provide the system many of the benefits of democracy. The world already has examples of systems based upon extremely exclusive membership and voting criteria. They cannot be confused with democracies or Republican forms of government but they will be much more effective than autocratic regimes.

iii.) Caste

x. Governmental Caste; maintaining employment in the public sector is the pre-requisite for voting in governmental elections.

1. Specific branch
    a. Executive
    b. Legislature
    c. Judicial
2. Specific Tier
    a. National
    b. Regional
    c. County
    d. Municipal
3. Indiscriminant
4. Status
    a. Active
    b. Retired

The government caste only represents the elected or appointed government officials. There is another more exact subdivision in political eligibility criteria. The occupational caste represents the non military civil servants includes law enforcement agencies, intelligence agencies, space agencies, and all of the other state or federal tier government employees. Government employees typically represent only 6.0% of the total population making any systems designed with these entitlements Demi-republican rather than Democratic.

When the total number of local, state, and federal employees are tallied up with elected officials and military enlisted the final value should incorporate a wide variety of political prerogatives and beliefs to help accommodate the nonvoting populations or for more specialized experience in voting for the elected officials within the narrow domain within their franchise. A government caste does model the civilization for a more nationalistic social-political hierarchy with the voting franchise. With a more precise application of the voter eligibility criteria a nation can better delegate resources by dictating which branches of government in which tiers benefit from this specialization.

xx. Occupational Caste; maintaining employment in a foreign military or law enforcement agency is the pre-requisite for holding office or voting.

1. Law Enforcement (FBI, SS, IRS, etc) equivalent
2. Intelligence (NSA, CIA, FBI) equivalent
3. Regulatory (SBA, EPA, OSHA, etc) equivalent
4. Scientific (NASA, NOOA) equivalent
5. Commercial-Economic (Labor, Commerce, Fed)
6. Corporate (Imperial, Departmental, or self regulating)

Wealth offers the greatest opportunity to enact voter eligibility criteria as a huge variety of different indices can be used which accommodate most citizens of the nation. Representation can be conserved within the system which makes it the perfect substitute for universal suffrage contributing to the specialization in both governmental branches and tiers.

iv.) Wealth (employee/employer, aristocratic

- A. Asset based
    - 1. Grade
        - a. Lower third
        - b. Middle third
        - c. Higher third
        - d. Above Median
        - e. Below Median
        - f. Inclusive
    - 2. Class
        - i. Capital (Equity and Cash)
            - 1. Private
            - 2. Public
            - 3. Governmental
        - ii. Land
            - 1. Commercial
            - 2. Residential
        - iii. Bonds
            - 1. Private and Corporate
            - 2. Government
        - iv. Any

Representation based on wealth should use multiple axes of differentiation within the same wealth class. For instance, if an asset based system is employed then multiple chambers or multiple bands of voter classification should be derived from the single asset class so that a larger cross section of the same population gains proportional representation from that single derivative. Otherwise, it would be too easy to construct a system from outliers and exclude large segments of the population be they the wealthy and owners' class or the unemployed and labor classes. Using income as an example with the typical bands being low, middle, and high it would be exploitative to only offer representation to high income earning citizens and exclude middle or lower income citizens.

Bifurcating the measure into above median and below median segments is one of the most effective means to create distinct populations from one pool of eligible voters. It ensures that all segments of a population are represented and share economic interests and pressures. The more egregious forms of economic oppression through wage suppression and duress modeling must be more forcibly argued in the prism of wealth and class differences. The differentiation of population based on economic criteria will provide the specialization the chambers need to focus more intently on their own economic interests.

Asset based representation such as those focused on stock ownership grant individuals simultaneous representation within the institutional political system as well as the private sector. Most equity based investments provide voting shares within the corporate boards of the nation's best performing companies. The majority of equities are typically owned by the top 10% of income earners within the nation. There is a remedy to this gross imbalance. Pension funds and community permanent funds would help smooth out the averages and accommodate the differences in values for systems of representation incorporating all bands of the asset based representation. Otherwise, the system would likely produce a colonial or auto-colonial form of representation. Equity representation through personal assets and pensions might be one of the most important foils to an imbalance of income or asset representation favoring the elite and wealthy classes. Corporations themselves are a fulcrum of economic and political power with tremendous influence within government Permanent Funds will focus on corporate board representation and reciprocate this influence.

For centuries land barons dominated medieval Europe and although there was no voting with ballots, the aristocracy voted with pledged soldiers and promised military support in exchange for maintaining titles and access to taxes and income from the land. The Magna Carta was an important development towards Democracy and it was a revolt staged by the landed aristocracy within England that demanded representation in the Monarchy through a Legislature. This would be the basis of future democratic reforms despite the fact it was not a popular form of representation. The United states premised its initial democratic representation on land requirements. It was an aristocratic republic for the first few decades until protesting veterans earned universal suffrage for Caucasian adult males. This can be the premise of other more contemporary forms of land based wealth representation. Asset qualifications can be differentiated into commercial and residential based eligibilities. Most entitlements should be focused on residential properties to capture popular representation but industrial representation may have its uses.

Public Sector bonds offer an incredible opportunity for the debt holders of a nation or jurisdiction to gain direct access to a chamber or branch of government. This will be especially useful for assembling allied nations into economic unions or integrating corporations into political empires when influence is reciprocated between parties and sectors. Bonds are quite possibly the most useful form of asset representation. Most bonds come with predetermined time frames and values providing government engineers an instrument that provides an instrument with predictable impact on elections.

Other eligibility criteria and exclusivity attributes can be judicially applied within chambers or through offices where the responsibilities are more constrained and less critical. This would be a successful strategy in a system composed of a large number of different bands from a large number of different wealth tiers and classes although the net or average focus of representation should still be concentrated on the middle to working classes to accommodate the most voters. This type of specialized representation would be more effective in regards to regulating certain sectors of the economy as well as integrating different governments within a Union or Empire along commercial and wealth based indexes; reaching the broadest base of an electorate typically results in success with numerical advantages earned through self interest often proves insurmountable to opposition parties.

Income based representation can be just as varied as Asset based representation with the source qualified in addition to the proportion. Small business owners have different skill sets than employees or corporate board members. Income from working or investing can be segregated so that employers and employees are granted different rights than minority interest owners and equity traders. This helps specialize which citizens gain access to the regulators and legislators governing the different aspects of economy generating the incomes used to determine representation.

In most instances where income based representation is used the options will be used in constellations. Income from employers be they small business, professional, or employee should all be grouped together. Investment revenue can include the leisure class and corporations but may have more use in the future when governments manage permanent funds and assume other commercial responsibilities.

B. Income based (regionally adjusted)
- i. Source
  - a. Employer (Small Business)
  - b. Self Employed (Professional)
  - c. Employee
  - d. Investments (minority ownership, other instruments)
  - e. Tax Revenues
  - f. GDP

Tax Revenues can be justified as income for jurisdictions but must be segregated into those paid into the general fund or paid into a higher governments general fund. Most cities, states, and federal systems levy their own taxes which produce recordable incomes for use towards representation but they must be tallied separately to maintain accurate values. A state government would tally the money it collects in taxes for the federal system and then earn representation in proportion to the other states within the union. The tax revenues actively support the government granting the voting entitlements. This operates under an identical premise for bond based representation with financial support proportional to the influence earned within the institution.

Basing external representation on a states own ability to tax itself also better guarantees a better environment with more military and police spending, more spending on education and welfare, and more subsidies for businesses and innovators. Nations which spend more money on themselves and their residents typically develop sounder economic policies and sounder communities prone to less violence and less extreme political ideologies.

Correlating representation to GDP captures a fair proportion of representation by population but has extracurricular benefits by exporting the region's more successful economic policies through the increased political influence. Large population bases can have lower GDP than small efficiently managed population bases. GDP representation is a measure of the differential and a way to distribute the efficiency across jurisdictional borders. There is the danger that a jurisdiction will vote in accord to its own self interest and take advantage of other cities, counties, or states but that gross behavior already occurs in most contemporary political systems. Senatorial representation has propagated within most democratic systems and is predicated on disrupting majority rule and providing inaccurate representation.

The term political-economy predates both modern democracy and modern global economy and was used specifically to illustrate the very intimate and intricate relationship economy has with politics; Modern states should employ more precision in defining the roles and powers of the different facets of government in accord with the powers and privileges of the classes of individuals working as legislators or voting for representation within the chamber or branch. The species entertains most ideologies in binary opposition with unchecked capitalism rivaled by ominous communism where both are extremes within one spectrum of political economy. Generally, neither satisfies all that the citizenry require. However, they still introduce significant themes that ultimately benefit the growth of theory and practice which will help leaders and voters navigate the tumultuous exchange of sacrifice and service across generations and national borders. The dynamism between the owner class and the labor class has entertained the race for hundreds of years and more specialized systems of political economy will empower both segments with democratic franchise through the refinement of government institutions and the reinforcing of roles.

Imagine the potential of an entire chamber representative of only employees and laborers offset by another chamber dedicated to the interests of the owners class and leisure class (institutional wealthy and investors). Normally labor and the owners' class represent opposite positions and it would be fairly easy to predict non cooperation between two specialized chambers acting in opposition but if both chambers also included the professional class or middle class as a bridge in interests it increases the likelihood that moderate policies will be passed by both chambers. One chamber will admit only low income and middle income and the other will admit only middle income and upper income; this prevents cross corruption from intermingling of campaign donations or other means of influence. The middle class typically votes in larger numbers (with a component unionized) which will be competitive with the upper class which has the capital advantage but not the advantage in votes.

When the legislators more readily recognize the class they represent and suffer the same economic stressors they will be better advocates for their constituencies. There will be more transparency when everybody appreciates their designated roles. There will be less incentive and less opportunity for ambitious legislators to leverage their votes for another income or asset class without the camouflage of one or two ambiguous national parties with ideologies based on coalition rather than specific interests in economy or society. Multi-party systems can accommodate asset/income representation better especially in cases where multiple chambers are employed as the parties can specialize their platforms within a chamber devoted to a specific economic class and their associated legislative powers.

The grade of income is a threshold which must be met prior to earning eligibility. Brackets can be set by statistical modeling to capture lower income, middle income, and higher income. The Median value can be used as a divider between two primary classes with one below and one above the most frequent income range earned. Incomes can remain inclusive with the number of representatives determined by a tiered system similar to a progressive tax. Net and gross figures can be calculated with pre-tax values and post tax values which are the best means to incorporate fiscal policy as a means to regulate representation and voting systems. The same mechanism preventing wealth from accumulating within one segment of the population can be used to stymie the concentration of political influence. The two generally go hand in hand and any attempt to modulate one is an effort to manipulate the other.

ii. Grade

a. lower bracket
b. Middle bracket
c. High bracket
d. Below Median
e. Above Median
f. Inclusive
g. Net (post taxes)
h. Gross (pre taxes)

Political representation based on taxes paid can be one of the most successful variations of wealth based democracy as it rewards those classes or individuals who pay more taxes. Not only should this result in a better funded and stronger government but it should continue to distribute representation in a proportion that imitates contemporary voting trends. This method actively discourages corrupt tax policy where the wealthier classes refuse to pay significant taxes by empowering the segments that pay more. Not only should the imbalanced tax policy be slowly corrected with fairer distributions of tax liabilities but it incentivizes base populations to accept paying more in exchange for more political power. The promise is that different classes and demographic segments will compete with pledged taxes to gain more representation. Small businesses and corporations, have the opportunity gain tremendous political representation with an increase in taxes paid into the government regulating them.

Segregating incomes based on pre and post tax amounts presents an interesting opportunity to relocate individuals from one class to another. This can have major effects on the middle class band but an even greater impact on the top 10% which is often subject to higher income taxes and where adjusting the capital gains tax will have an immediate and pronounced effect. Toggling the tax status would be an effective political tool for parties or chambers to adjust their own representation year after year to accommodate different climates in political-economy.

Tax based systems of representation can be facilitated by three primary mechanisms. The first is where the individual is granted access to specific democratic institutions with eligibility determined by their tax liability bracket. The second method divides a single population into above median and below median so that all individuals and entities are represented. The third method is based on value voting tax where with the amount of representation gained by the individual, city, or state is based on the gross or net taxes paid into the system. Enumerating voter representation by taxes may be the most appropriate venue to permit direct representation of corporations within government sectors.

C. Tax liabilities

- i. Threshold
  - a.) above
    - x. lower bracket
    - xx. Middle bracket
    - xxx. High bracket
    - xxxx. Median
  - b.) Below
    - x. lower bracket
    - xx. middle bracket
    - xxx. higher bracket
    - xxxx. Median
  - c.) Straight (value voting and other methods)

The representation is dependent on the type of instrument being measured. Most states use sales taxes, property taxes, income taxes, and capital gains taxes. There are plenty of other taxes not represented in this matrix and they can all be fairly easily introduced or substituted. The point is more that the representation can be tailored to a specific instrument. Many governmental tiers specialize in a tax and it would be more appropriate for the jurisdiction to utilize only that measure. Sometimes it is more appropriate for a jurisdiction or tier to tally all applicable tax liabilities. Any number of instruments can be listed with the values averaged or tallied. All of the public records and prior histories should be available to aid in organizing the voter entitlement.

ii. Instrument

a.) sales
b.) property
c.) income
d.) capital gains
e.) Total (Combined)

The domain of the tax, or its source, is a major component of the index. Taxes can be segregated by personal taxes or corporate taxes. The amount of money paid into a tier or system should be compensated for by a discrete measure of representation and making the distinction between person, thing, or place is an important part of the process. Many corporations pay the same taxes paid by individuals in addition to the corporate tax substituting for income tax. It will be necessary to designate government taxes so that the jurisdiction can earn representation in economic unions or federal systems.

iii. Domain

a.) Personal
b.) Corporate
c.) Governmental (Remits)

A representational index related to asset and income is incorporation status. Within this index professional classes with S type incorporation can be distinguished from the owners class with C type incorporation. It also allows Non Incorporated Labor to be distinguished from Unionized Labor while Nonprofit Corporations get their own designation. All of the primary components of economy are represented and correlated to the superstructures they belong to. Nonprofit Companies include Universities, Think Tanks, and the typical welfare and progressive service providers, C type incorporation empowers the owners' class. And employees are classified as either Unionized or Nonunionized labor. Self employed and the professional class will make up an extremely large section of representation as it includes those with S type incorporations and professional designations that elect not to vote with other segments (denoted in the registration process). The unemployed and retired makes up the last portion of incorporation dependent classes.

D. Incorporation status

a. Class

i. S Type (Professional)

ii. C Type (Corporate Board Members)

iii. Non Incorporated Labor (Non licensed employee)

iv. Unincorporated Professional License (Electrician, Plummer, Accountant, lawyer, Doctor, etc)

v. Unionized Labor (Representatives)

1. Represented by Board Members

2. Direct member votes

vi. Nonprofit Corporation (Board Members)

v. Unemployed and Retired.

As long as incorporation privileges are not over-regulated and made exclusive the barriers segregating the population will permeable enough for the population to adjust its own participation in the differentiated institutions or chambers. A system of representation will be determined to be fair if it extends access to all segments of the population; this obviously includes those based on asset ownership, different tiers of income, and of course different incorporation statuses. A nation and culture defines itself with self interests and those democracies that provide more specialized roles for politicians will earn for themselves a more sophisticated society and history. It is a means to accelerate typical labor and capital movements, to manufacture new class motivations, and to engineer newer systems of incentive to model future generations.

With greater role identity the individual and group will explore more thoroughly the opportunities and responsibilities of their own class and form expectations of the other classes and segments represented in the system of political economy. It must be self evident that it is the efficiencies within political economy which mold the society and its economy and with greater diversity will come new social and financial innovations. Supply and demand occurs within political economy and maximizing production is often a function of disseminating the correct information and permitting a population enough time to appreciate the consequences and opportunities the information provides.

For more intimate wealth representation the attribute eligibility is based on can be amended by more precise qualifiers. There are significant differences between the incentives and motivations for employees and employers from the healthcare sector that oppose the interests of employees and employers from the finance sector or consumable products sector. This conflict in self interests will contribute to a more competitive system when those individuals have opportunity to defend themselves by voting and apportioning taxes for oversight and regulation. Unregulated finance sectors contribute to systemic risk of financial collapse while unchecked health insurance sectors cause massive inflation in the healthcare sector and divert consumption away from the real economy. If the owners and employees of the other sectors were more aware of the mixed interests they might be more open to regulating those industries and companies.

b. Employee number

i. Micro (1-10)
ii. Small (10-200)
iii. Medium (200-10,000)
iv. Large (10,000+)
v. indiscriminant

There are significant differences between employers ranging in size from a micro business of under 10 employees to a national corporation of more than 10,000. Not only are there different motivations but there are varying degrees of access to capital and expertise which must be accommodated within the system of representation to ensure the interest of one sector or company class does not eclipse the interest of another. Mechanical and procedural amendments can be made when distributing representation and powers to ensure that the chambers and branches accommodate multiple perspectives.

c. Specified within

1. Specific branch
2. Specific tier

When political engineers gain direct access to apportioning sector representation to specific regional jurisdictions it will provide a means to economically model the country for specialization of sector headquarters and infrastructure. In many nations, there is typically one epicenter for finance with a majority of the largest providers located within the same city or states. That region has access to more specialized knowledge for producing regulation and oversight over the industry translating into significant economic efficiencies for employees, employers, and residents. State governments can elect to engineer their own representation to promote industrial relocation within the jurisdiction to foster this concentration and specialization. Regional representation can be determined by a top down decision or by the residents themselves; it should also be appreciated that introducing small imbalances within the domain of wealth representation should not contort or derange the entire system as the enfranchised sector should remain a minority population within the larger demographic. The proportion of unaligned voting citizens should continue to outweigh the population of employed citizens providing continued integrity for the democratic system.

Most nations already control their borders with enough precision so that access is only granted to approved individuals. With this rigid control on the type of person admitted and the numbers accepted a government can feel more assured when granting limited representation to either temporary or permanent resident aliens.

v.) Domicile

a. Resident Alien
b. Citizen
c. Non resident Alien

The resident alien criteria would be useful for providing limited access to government. Voting rights can be relegated to certain lower tiers or specific agency representation. Obviously, states participating in an economic union with other states could elect to empower resident aliens with special suffrage while the other states in the Union are protected by continuing to exclude the alien from federal elections or their own state votes.

The governmental caste was previously relegated to other federal enlisted, regulatory, or elected officials but should be expanded to include regional and municipal police, fire, EMT, and other civil emergency servants. Their representation can be specific to the tier their work and domicile in or they can be included within a specialized democracy only permitting the government caste from all eligible tiers to elect officials and dictate domestic and foreign policy.

vi.) Emergency Professionals (all federal and civil police, militia, fire, and EMT.

x. tier specific (certain military branches are only eligible for certain tiers of government)

c. municipal

cc. regional

ccc. national

xx. indiscriminant (any Emergency branch and any political branch)

An important demographic to consider when reo-organizing representation is lawyers and judges. Many contemporary politicians secure law degrees as a means to demonstrate their capabilities for office and prepare them for the legislative process. This demographic represents a large pool of potential public employees to draw from which includes municipal judges, prosecutors, and public sector regulators. In political systems with much more specialized roles, these law enforcement professionals would contribute exceptional knowledge and dedication.

vii. Judicial (only Judges and lawyers)

a. judges

b. lawyers

x. public sector lawyers

xx. any licensed lawyer

c. judges and lawyers

A judicial election system might produce more qualified candidates and appointments if law and justice experience was necessary to vote for judicial elections and both public sector and private sector lawyers were included. Lawyers have a more intimate perspective and can evaluate candidates better.

Education is a demographic which can be used to tailor representation in a myriad of ways and with more exact systems of election within governments it permits the most experts and specialists the most powers of appointment. There would be incredible gains in efficiencies if Economics, Finance, and

Accounting majors from either undergraduate or graduate schools were a pre-requisite for electing executives charged with Treasury responsibilities or regulators overseeing banks and finance companies.

Physicists, Biologists, and Chemists would provide exceptional benefits when electing industrial regulators or science and exploration agencies. Likewise, Anthropologists, Sociologists, and Psychologists likely have more insight when electing welfare agencies or other community centric efforts. For most contemporary college graduates, a system of specialized representation is most likely the only benefit they will extract from their education as most economic opportunities are not correlated to major but otherwise help produce adults with sounder social-political beliefs.

viii. Education

- c. Associates
- cc. Undergraduate
  - x. Differentiated
  - xx. Undifferentiated
- ccc. Graduate
  - x. Differentiated
  - xx. Undifferentiated

Before these limitations on voting can be exercised education must first be made accessible; the easiest and best method would be creating a mandatory military enlistment law and then tethering education and healthcare benefits to performance. Not only could representation be premised on military experience but then extended for more specialized elections for certain executive agencies and branches. Political engineers can start modeling society and form a more flexible caste system based upon education and experience but where the different facets of industry and government all work to check the other demographic powers. Social-Industrial differentiation over time occurs where there is restricted class mobility and where excessive duress exists within the general economy; traditionally this has occurred through wealth transmission, education, and occupation but precedent could be set for transmission based on such criteria where representation is also guaranteed within a wealth/education based democracy.

Federal systems and Economic Unions typically involve concessions made to states and nations in exchange for participation. Communities are already organized into units of unequal population and varying economic strength. Depending on the need of the new union, representation can be metered out by demographics but where the smaller number of cities, counties, states, and nations are involved rather than the larger numbers of gross populations. All of these variables are aggregators of demographic and economic information making them more accessible for the anchoring of representation. It is a means to smooth out an average of disparate net populations while also manufacturing the levers of political control.

ix. Jurisdiction (per unit; index equivalent to population, taxes, or GDP)

- i. cities
  - a. Above median index
  - b. Below median index
  - c. Straight
- ii. counties
  - a. Above median index
  - b. Below median index
  - c. Straight
- iv. states
  - a. Above median index
  - b. Below median index
  - c. Straight
- iii. regions
- iv. nations
- v. corporations
  - a. Above median index
  - b. Below median index
  - c. Straight

Reorganizing popular representation into jurisdictional representation is a means of incorporating nation-states into larger economic unions by reducing the importance of previously established state or national boundaries and placing focus on city or state based interests within new economic bloc boundaries. Using cities, counties, and states as a unit can be qualified by other criteria rather than population. The other wealth and demographic representation criteria can be attached as descriptors so that more appropriate or useful indices of representation are used when configuring the new political union or institution.

Interstate agreements for block voting can significantly redistribute the political influence and strength of a region already engaged within a larger super-structure of an economic union or federalist nation. States entering into individual agreements with each other may be the only recourse to re-negotiate representation within a Union without earning amendments to the over-arching system. The typical indices for representing jurisdictions (senatorial organization); Population, GDP (income), Numerical Units (Cities/counties/States), Tax Revenue, Feudal (Military Units pledged), and Wealth (Commoditized representation; where the economic union sets value and auctions off positions annually/term). All are applicable to economic unions as well as voting blocs with federalist systems.

There really is no difference between federalist systems and economic unions but for practical purposes federalist systems are defined by their concentration of tax dollars to a community military including intelligence at the exclusion of the participating states or nations which maintain limited or marginal armed forces. Federalism is nation formation where as an economic union has more flexibility in terms of regional law enforcement and individual armed forces.

Defining whether jurisdictions are constrained by proximity and borders in block or union formation is important but that attribute can limit the frequency or union formation and the likelihood. Boundless attributes actually impart more durability in federal super structures as the joining of disparate jurisdictions, or those in remote locations with no shared boundaries, increases the cooperation necessary to maintain those relations within the economic union. Forcing involuntary unions is only a method of last resort when normalized relations have broken down between states and counties (or provinces) and where a reorganization of representation is necessary to maintain order and the semblance of cooperation. In these instances, coerced unionization can be used to mitigate regional antagonism by merging interests and mitigate regional political strength by fracturing the representation with lower orders of non proximate organization. Modern communication technologies and transportation free political engineers from the conventional proximate distance over time calculations for political representation.

Most of the criteria previously enumerated and explained can be applied to either voting or eligibility for holding office, and in most cases both. In fact more sophisticated systems of representation can have independent criteria for each entitlement creating more balanced or more specialized political markets. The fastest way to destabilize a state or nation is to enact anti-democratic legislation that removes the voting franchise for a specific demographic within the community. Eligibility criteria shouldn't be updated or improved without the consent of the segment losing the entitlement however political architects can negotiate with demographics by bartering and rearranging representation so the same segment which loses voting eligibility for one branch or chamber of government gains more representation or special privilege in another aspect of governmental administration.

Providing voting franchise to a community that previously was bereft will ultimately benefit the international community and its neighbors in the long term despite any short term turbulence or initial conflict. Republican government tends to distribute intellectual capital better than autocratic governments in problem solving and have the tendency to preserve peace rather than exert imperialism within its immediate environment.

b.) Action

i.) to vote

ii.) to hold office

There will definitely be times when it is appropriate for legislators or executive from different tiers of government to appoint the officers of other branches. This is true in instances of colonial or imperial ruelrship but also has uses for integrating more efficient command hierarchies between federal and state tiers or within local jurisdictions. Appointed officers can occur within the same jurisdiction which has the potential to maximize efficiencies in governance without depreciating the franchise of democratic rule within the jurisdiction. Political engineers should consider both top down control and bottom up control where elected municipal officers appoint state officials or where state officials appoint federal civil servants. Appointments can occur through the consensus of legislators which would imitate a parliamentarian mode of elections or executive from lower jurisdictions can vote to install the executives within higher jurisdictions. There are a myriad of different combinations that can be explored in theory prior to implementing for self governance or union management.

c.) domain

i. exclusive

ii. non exclusive

Eligibility requirements can be independent or they can be accumulative. Independent attributes are non exclusive which means permits citizens satisfying one component of the eligibility criteria to vote or hold office when multiple attributes are listed. Exclusive domains require voters or candidates to maintain all eligibility criteria listed making the population of possible voters or candidates much smaller. More complicated systems of representation will attempt to index divergent qualities as a means to hedge or check the influence or power of any single segment of the population. An example of this would be maintaining a domicile requirement with an income requirement. Neither are related but in exclusive systems both must be satisfied in order to qualify.

An example of non exclusive attributes would be indexing one legislative chamber to income earners within the lowest bracket along with income earners from the highest bracket. Obviously one resident couldn't possibly satisfy both requirements. This has an important effect on representation because it conjoins the political power of the lowest income earners who occur in large numbers with the highest income earners which occur infrequently. By offsetting this chamber with another devoted exclusively to middle class income earners it dilutes the richest segment and emphasizes the middle class without mitigating the poorest. This might be an effective check to the corrupting power of private campaign finance which overwhelmingly benefits the highest income earners.

9.) Appointed by

a.) municipal

x. legislature

xx. executive

xxx. judicial

xxxx. reserve

b.) regional

x. legislature

xx. executive

xxx. judicial

xxxx. reserve

c.) national

x. legislative

xx. executive

xxx. judicial

xxxx. reserve

Voting isn't a right it's a duty and a responsibility. Advocating for mandatory or compulsory voting for citizens is an appropriate response to the expected malaise that typically overtakes democratic societies and governments. The danger in contemporary governments is that special interest groups and other outlier populations are more likely to vote than average or lower class citizens. This pressures government engineers into satisfying the demands of minorities rather than the base and contributes to the polarization of political-economy. The product is an unstable government, dangerous to itself as well as its neighbors and others community members.

10.) Voting

a.) compulsory

b.) voluntary

Making voting mandatory is complementary when specializing eligibility criteria for voting and holding office; with greater privileges come greater responsibility. Voluntary voting is the standard for contemporary democracies but the mode of representation and political governance is relatively new and it can be expected that as political systems evolve more will demand compulsory voting from their eligible citizens.

Most democracies won't function correctly if an oligarchy of political parties constricts the political choices voters can make. Every opportunity must be taken advantage of to ensure that binary political systems do not dominate the political markets. Multi-party systems promote more cooperation and coalition building and reduce the deleterious byproducts from peer pressure and lack of diversity. Political Parties can be regulated by size so that smaller units of similar parties exist but their leadership is individually determined with bureaucracy limiting how efficiently they can market and organize their efforts.

If size is not an adequate limit then each state or provincial jurisdiction must organize its own party with its own leadership and work to negotiate the regulations governing the marketing of the individual parties so that one brand name does not exist and a national initiative is harder to organize. Most state representatives and parties have wildly different and often antagonistic interests that compete for funding and legislative priority. Requiring different party names will help identify reoccurring patterns in power distributions and profit sharing. Political parties vary within distant regions with their own conservative and liberal spectrum differentiating the members from one state and another.

11.) Political Parties
- a.) Primaries
  - i.) closed
  - ii.) Open
- b.) Endorsements
  - i.) Two Party System
  - ii.) Multiple Party Endorsements
  - iii.) Endorsement Parties

A more interesting structure for forming political parties is enfranchising the special interest groups by patenting the issues and permitting those groups to extend or retract endorsements based upon performance. The special interest group can then dictate how all endorsed politicians vote on any measure tabled regarding their interest. This will disrupt the any command hierarchies within a two party or multi-party structure while infusing more integrity within the legislature by limiting politicians abilities to claim endorsement while bargaining votes on that issue for other issues.

Endorsement party structures enables open primaries with multiple candidates to satisfy more individualized constituent groups with more specialized representation. The endorsements are individually tailored and demand performance which means voters will have more accurate representation on the issues the care most about. The endorsement parties themselves should be able to dedicate more resources to debating and deliberating the issues voted on by the professional politicians with less conflict in policy. More sophisticated endorsement systems will permit the endorsed politicians to hold a practice vote prior to the real vote with the result dictating the endorsements party formal and public position on the issue. The era of computer technologies will grant the access needed for more highly organized voting.

Jurisdictions or districts typically define a legislator's constituency. Jurisdictions tend to encompass a whole state, city, or county. For example, if a state is permitted two senators all of the resident citizens are permitted to vote for both offices. The senators are both responsible for representing the same constituency. Districts reduce the State or city into distinct regions with a dedicated constituency. If the state has three districts and three assembly members each is only responsible for representing only one jurisdiction.

The difference is access with jurisdiction wide candidates required to satisfy a larger cross section of interests and district wide candidates allowed to specialize within a smaller cross section of interest. One produces a regression to the mean (or average) while has polarizing tendencies. Both have their individual merits, however, the two methods are not equal; jurisdictions tend to promote more cooperation within a state or city while districts tend to invite political abuses like Gerrymandering.

Although contrary to most critical beliefs, a smaller number of representatives should be accorded to district representation with a greater number allotted to jurisdiction representation; this will permit faster and easier political reorganizations with more binary or symmetrical areas of representation while also dedicating more resources to the representation attempting to satisfy the averaged interests within the jurisdiction.

More complex forms of representation including Legislative Broker and Executive Representation are more accessible with jurisdictional organization which must be considered when engineering a political system. A third qualifier is presented as a means to integrate commercial interests and accommodate corporate statehood if it ever applies. When and if corporations are granted suffrage they may need more specialized representation which does not necessarily correlate to either Jurisdiction or District but rather Industrial sector or market.

12.) Jurisdiction;

a. Jurisdiction wide (Senators)
b. Districts (Representatives)
c. Sector (Commercial)

After the criteria is established to determine eligible voters and candidates each system of representation must have a method to determine the number of representatives provided to each jurisdiction. Most Democracies correlate representation to population as it is the reasonable and balanced way to organize democratic government. The number of representatives can be correlated to other measures that have important functions within the nation state. For instance, representation based on GDP typically aggregates population with productivity producing a more practical form of representation because it can help transmit the economic ideologies that contributed to the higher economic product. Correlating representation to taxes is an even more sophisticated measure for representation because it combines population, with economic productivity, and fiscal policy. It can help ensure that one subset of the population does not exploit another through unfair gradients in tax policies or exploitative economic policies. It also positive reinforces tax collection by associating political power with the surrendered moneys.

13. Number of Representatives

a. Population
   i. Jurisdiction
   ii. Employees
   iii. Enlisted

Most democracies are built around the concept of proportional votes between jurisdiction which are based upon the size of the population in each. The premise of democracy is inextricably associated with popular representation. A least common denominator is calculated and then each population is divided by it to earn the representational coefficient. The coefficient equals the number of politicians prescribed to that region or state. This process results in representative government with all citizens earning an equal ratio of representatives to residents. It is by far the fairest and most accurate way to structure representation. Population naturally accounts for economic figures, demographic figures, and civil figures and is the basis for majority rule. The same process can take into account the number of employees found at one employer and the number of enlisted in a Military organization for more specialized forms of government.

b. GDP

i. Straight

ii. Per capita

GDP and similar economic indicators are substitutes to population to establish the ratio of representatives distributed among the various jurisdictions. There are two variants in the way GDP can be used in calculating the Representational Coefficient. The first is a straight calculation using a least common denominator. The raw GDP figure is divided by the LCD to determine the exact representative coefficient for each jurisdiction. GDP can vary from jurisdiction to jurisdiction with some states being much richer and earning much more direct influence within the system. Exceptions and outliers gain proportionally more or less representation. With the straight calculation of representation the wealthier jurisdictions can export their economic and political ideologies through the efficiency gained in representation. These are absolute terms which don't take population into account.

The second method is to average the value by dividing GDP by the population. The LCD is determined and divided into each result to calculate coefficient for representation. Using the Per Capita calculation there will be differences in the representation earned by each individual and each jurisdiction but the variance should be much smaller than the result of the straight calculation. A Per Capita calculation will result in a more equal distribution of representation between jurisdiction. A larger component of the population may be willing to accept this form of wealth representation making it more practical.

c. Taxes

i. Gross

ii. Net

x. Surrendered

xx. Minimum

Tax representation for jurisdictions can be a convenient means to establish tighter controls on federal or state budgets and check other imbalances within the system of representation. Tax representation can be based on net taxes paid or gross taxes paid. Net taxes paid are calculated from the previous year with the total federal or state rebates subtracted from the total remitted. This figure is not proportional representation and it is more than likely that certain jurisdictions will lose their representation due to receiving more federalist tax rebates than making federalist tax contributions.

Gross tax representation is based on the total amount of taxes remitted to the tier of government where the representation is earned The amounts assessed to each region are compared to each other to determine the proportional number of seats earned. The primary mechanism for establishing the comparative values is a ratio of taxes remitted to representatives. Each increment produces another representative. Each of the states or regions will be in ratio or proportion to one another

Federalist tax policy is necessary for stimulating lower GDP jurisdictions and should be a major component of fiscal policy. The idea is exceptional but its application is generally flawed. It is too easy to exploit wealthier jurisdictions where there is an imbalance in representation favoring the poorer and less populous states. A political union's measure of inefficiency is huge differences within taxes paid into a federal system and rebates received where a regional differential can exacerbate extreme political distrust or disdain over long periods. Economic Union and Federal government is based on cooperation and mutual consent; these extreme deficiencies are exacerbated over extended periods of neglect and can precipitate premature dissolution of the organization or entity.

Tax exploitation can be compensated for by introducing a tax representation based on net taxes paid so that those jurisdictions acting as net donors of federal taxes can leverage more political power within the system than the net welfare recipients. This will discourage the net welfare jurisdictions from perfecting their exploitative practices. It should condition them to think of the nation as a whole rather than focusing on their short term self interests, and develop macro-economic strategies based more on competition than federal government subsidy, specifically citing rebates for military manufacturers and universities, by reducing their net political influence and likelihood of earning future federalist government subsidies.

Due to the representation deductions due to tax rebates those that are welfare recipients won't have any representation in that specific chamber, branch, or tier of government which should be an extremely potent and effective means to discourage tax exploitation. In both scenarios, larger jurisdictions with more mature economies will have access to much more representation which is correlated to their extra contributions to federalist taxes. This will benefit the nation as population with the more specialized labor and more experienced professionals will have more representation. The regions with higher GDP and stronger economies will be able to export their economic practices and government theories. The net result of enfranchising those regions which pay more taxes should be faster economic growth and more competitive markets for export.

There is an option for regions or states with negative federalist tax contributions to continue receiving representation. It would be a bare minimum, a lowest common denominator set by the constitution, that would apply every time a state would normally lose representation in the chamber due to federalist tax policy. This is a significant concession but it will improve the chances of states agreeing to representational coefficients based on net taxes. Surrendering representation in exchange for increased federalist tax contributions might be to extreme a consequence for a conventional policy intended to build market economies and strengthen the pubic sector within poorer, smaller, or less capable regions.

d. Municipalities, Counties, States

i. cities
ii. counties
iii. states
iv. regions
v.. nations
vi. corporations

The number of representatives can also be based on population aggregators like municipalities, cities, counties, and states with a fixed ratio or arbitrary amount assigned to each unit. Using the U.S. Senate as an example an arbitrary number (coefficient) is assigned to each state and regardless of population the chamber of legislature is staffed with a number of senators equal to twice that of the number of states. This is one of the least effective weighs to distribute representation but it is popular as a means to protect minority populations and limit majority rule. A state with a population of 500,000 residents is provided as much representation as a state with a population of 36,000,000 residents. Obviously, the representational coefficient is much lower in the more populous states. This can introduce tremendous representational inefficiencies and significant political instability with grosser examples of inequality. It is a major concession that might be reproduced during the democratization process and must be considered as circumstantially valid as other modes of representation.

However, this premise can lead to a slightly more complicated but fairer system when the political units are used in the same respect as population to calculate representational coefficient. Cities, counties, states, regions, nations, and corporations can all be used to determine the number of representatives allotted when the number of cities in one region is divided by the lowest common denominator of cities within all of the regions. The LCD determines the representational coefficient in a manner identical to how popular representation is calculated. Regions with larger cities wont earn the benefit of larger populations but statistically speaking the states with more cities will earn more representatives. A nation would implement this system if it wanted a regression in representation for a more equal distribution of politicians between the participating jurisdictions.

Corporate representation is a trickier and stickier subject requiring much more thorough debate. It is almost inevitable companies within an unfortunate nation will earn a modified form of statehood during some crisis after demanding suffrage and earning the concession. In many Republican nations, corporations have already earned massive amounts of political influence and leverage over conventional representatives with deregulated private campaign finance systems and the tremendous lobby they employ. Many politicians naturally prescribe to the belief that corporate interests are in the best interest of the state.

This is a false premise as employees and labor are generally under-represented within the corporation and actively oppressed in terms of compensation. If corporations are to earn statehood, they must accommodate the owners, the employees, and the consumers interests. This is not impossible but merely implausible. With reforms it may be possible to admit certain minority-majority owned public companies (plurality in leadership) to statehood especially if a larger proportion of the equity is owned by state permanent funds and state pension funds. Only then might it be considered a public utility for the benefit of employees and residents and empowered with representation in legislatures.

Corporate representation sounds more dangerous than its application will likely be when taking into account a huge portion of securities currently owned by pensions and mutual fund companies. The public has direct access to these instruments and with adequate reforms they can better guaranteed that their interests will be represented. Permanent Funds and Sovereign Wealth are also propagating through public sectors which make it even more likely that communities gain influence over the corporate boards of public companies earning the representation in government. Shareholder activism, on part of pension funds and mutual funds, might mitigate the natural tendency for asset managers to vote with management introducing an opportunity for more efficient transmission of interests other than simple profit motives.

If necessary, a second threshold for representation can be enacted based on employment dictating an exclusion for companies with more foreign employees than domestic employees; not necessary but prudent, for the express reason of limiting the ability of multinational companies gaining significant representation in a large cross section of democratic or republican countries. Most of the indices applied to states or jurisdictions can be used to allocate representation for corporations. GDP is equivalent to gross revenue, taxes are paid by both jurisdictions and corporations, employees (or investors) are equivalent to population, and companies can certainly donate security forces and financial support for units in exchange for moderated representation.

It is conceivable that Republican systems devoted exclusively to corporate representation are engineered to align management's interests with employee interests to provide adequate financial and martial security for all parties involved in the political-economic union. The most successful models of political economy will likely involve combinations of representation for conventional states, for commercial forms of government based on permanent funds and competitive government services, and also provide opportunity to include modern public corporations into the system for revenue enhancement and effective resource management. Political economy is highly competitive and success will be enjoyed by the nations or economic unions who demonstrate greater flexible and adaptability to their immediate environment – access to reforms and the opportunity to manufacture relationships with new modes of representation may prove a critical function for political architects.

f. Executive Representation

Executive Representation concentrates the amount of influence awarded from proportional representation within one elected office. If the popular representation would have produced 11 senators for the jurisdiction the single Executive Representative would wield the equivalent of 11 votes within the legislature. It combines the best attributes of representational government and focused government. Leadership is focused onto a smaller number of representatives without diminishing the proportional influence the jurisdiction should have. The administrative staff of executive representatives within legislatures will have to bulk up to accommodate the larger number of committees they must participate in considering the severe contraction in members. The executive representative appoints their surrogates on any committee they sit on. Executive representation can apply to population, GDP, and taxes and only requires that the ratio of representatives to the index property be equal to the entire amount or value within the system.

g. Combinational (Scale)

Scaled representation is an abridged form of democracy that can be used in occupations, empires, or for feudal variations. The population would continue to vote on a proportional basis with the majority of participants receiving a single vote but a coefficient is introduced to provide management more votes in an escalated scale. The manager or leader is granted representation equal to that of the number of employees or enlisted under their command. Authoritarian control is avoided by distributing votes among all levels of leaders so that the bulk of the votes remains with the lower level managers when combined with the free vote of all enlisted or employed. The top commander would have the most individual votes but the combined total of all votes including subordinates always maintains a majority requiring the individual to seek out coalitions within the institution or company.

e. Feudal

i. Military Units supported

ii. Military Units volunteered

Less exact but more practical ratios of representation can be based on the number of military units volunteered to support the central or federal government. This can be numbers of units with the necessary equipment, it can be purely financial support with dedicated funding of other units, or it can be a tally of enlisted serving in the federal military. Although most permanent systems of representation shouldn't be based exclusively on donated military support it can be a supplement to another index of representation which might otherwise produce deficiencies for smaller and less economically endowed jurisdictions.

Jurisdictions will be paying more into the federal government for greater representation which is an acceptable premise where tax payments and tax subsidies are exchanged. This mode of representation can be exported to foreign jurisdictions that are invited into an empire or union in a method resembling medieval feudal representation; extremely useful during emergencies of a martial nature where increasing conscription passed the natural limits is necessary.

h. Legislative Brokers

Legislative broker powers allow currently elected politicians to consolidate power by winning elections in other chambers of the legislature or by earning multiple seats in the same chamber. Each position permits an additional vote and access to more committees. In more sophisticated political systems this could entail access to a much larger and more diverse group of legislative chambers. Legislative brokers are paid for each position and can use that salary to hire the staff they need to administer to the new duties and powers. The salary can also be applied to campaigning for open seats which means a successful legislative brokers is more likely to win other seats adding value to the set of appointments and making the candidate more attractive for campaign donations. In most political systems the total number of eligible seats will still be restricted by location ensuring that the integrity is protected as one broker will typically only represent one state. Legislative brokers will vary in size, power, and party contributing to the overall competitiveness of the system.

i. Asset or income (ratio of land, stock, bond, or tax liability)

Assets can be used in the same regard population and other factors are to generate representation coefficients. Wealth representation may be more legitimate when citizens retain their privilege of equal voting but where the varying wealth still translates to advantages for the jurisdiction. Land is the single most prevalent asset found in most states and may be used to the advantage of larger states to gain more representation than smaller states regardless of a differential in population. Equities may eventually translate directly into voting common shares within permanent funds and public sectors and correlating the representational coefficient makes complete sense.

Bonds are the most useful asset when determining the representational coefficient. It is not a fixed amount permitting jurisdictions to allocate different amounts each year to gain more or less representation in the system. This will positively reinforce consumption of federal bonds supporting the federal government or union government. Tax liabilities and incomes are eligible for determining representational coefficients as long as an LCD can be easily extracted to form the basis of proportional representation. Any reasonable ration can be applied through some aggregator allowing the nation to express political influence through economic factors while preserving the traditional democratic attribute of one person equaling one vote.

14. Macro-political (Executive, Legislative)
   a. alpha (primary executive or legislator)
   b. agency heads, committee heads

When an Executive branch is split in multiple parts each one can be empowered with a macro-political vote for use in negotiating with legislators. Each Executive branch or agency would have a vote in whether or not legislation passes with each institution maintaining one vote equivalent with the final vote of the legislation. It is a more progressive form of a veto requiring legislation passes by a Legislature to be confirmed by the majority of institutions including the executive branch prior to being made into law. This is a progressive reform to the contemporary single executive veto power. Increasing the number of intuitional parties with a macro-political vote actually increases the likelihood of more legislation passing.

When the voting franchise is extended to cabinet members and agency directors it greatly increases the likelihood of a diverse response which is appropriate provided the many intricate ways even minor laws can impact the socio-economic fabric of the nation. In order for macro-political votes based on large numbers of competitive positions it should occur where the directors and managers have the most discretion and independence. Fractal organizations will benefit most from this power.

More attributes can be considered for more accurate representation and management of interstate unions, economic unions, tiered occupations and empires, and financial and commercial integration between private and public sectors with permanent funds. Representation within both political and corporate systems is the most important aspect within the economy and nation. Long term trends are extremely predictable based upon the balance and speed of systems.

Inefficiencies are exploited from within the system and occasionally external of the system making constituents very vulnerable to exploitation by individuals, corporations, and other nations. Imbalanced wealth concentrations and political representation produce an environment of instability and danger. The usual symptoms are present; extreme budgetary problems resulting from low taxes and sustained government expenditures in excess of revenues, and excessive corruption in the election cycles from lack of access or excessive moneyed interests.

More obvious imbalances are evident when public sector institutions like penitentiaries and security services are privatized, and where labor protections remain diluted and ineffective. Decay occurs over the span of years and decades and is often irreversible when the population accepts and even advocates for their degraded environment – the result is always the same in that it ends in rebellion, revolt, or war as body politics suffer the same threats of injury and death as its citizens due but in economies of scale.

Political systems that resist change or impede the rate of change are subject to more threats of insolvency and dissolution. It's only a matter of time until excessively complex or rigid systems of political governance are exposed to crises which require quick decisive action but where the awkward interaction of antagonistic legislative chambers or executive branches fail to resolve a critical issue and precipitate a system ending event. More cumbersome systems requiring more dedicated cooperation are the easiest to exploit economically as regulations will be irregular and infrequent with institutional powers protecting current market share and monopolies rather than producing economic opportunity and fair exchanges.

Under-regulated political markets also subjected to moneyed representation based on campaign contributions rather than fixed proportions of asset or income representation is the quickest way to destroy integrity and faith in the system. Most economies have steep natural gradients towards monopolistic market share and dangerous wealth concentrations. Moneyed influence accelerates this trend and makes it more resistant to reform. Within decades, a nation could be rendered noncompetitive and irrelevant within the global theatre of political-economy.

All of these deficits present opportunities for insurrection, rebellion, and reformation. Stability is the most valuable currency in political economy but when a nation or state is in decline maintaining the current trajectory is not productive. Order can be achieved by diluting civil liberties, inhibiting organization, and enforcing property laws but this is hardly sufficient in dispelling the potential instability. Democratic societies should thrive more often than autocratic nations simply because the communities can provide for themselves with political and economic reforms. They will naturally seek out more stability and more productivity. Autocratic nations can continue to suppress opportunities for self determination but it will be a persistent ambition and goal for the population, especially when the premise of democracy exists elsewhere and the ideas can be communicated through trade or example.

Master List of System Attributes

1.) Legislative
- i. Organization
  - x) uni-cameral
  - xx.) Bi-cameral
    - z. 1st camera
    - zz. 2nd camera
  - xxx.) Multicameral
    - z. 1st camera
    - zz. 2nd Camera
    - zzz. 3rd Camera
    - zzzz 4th Camera
  - xxxx.) Abolished (usurped by executive, administrative laws only)

- ii. Attributes
  - x. Representative
  - xx. Tyrannical
    - z. Appointed by exec
      - 1. Unitary
      - 2. Legislative
      - 3. Executive
      - 4. Judicial
    - zz. Appointed by leg
    - zzz. Appointed by judicial
    - zzzz. Appointed by retired members
      - 1. Legislative
      - 2. Executive
      - 3. Judicial
      - 4. Reserved Board
  - xxx. Atomized (lower tier governments dictate representatives in higher tier, lowest tier elected by popular vote)
      - 1. Council members appoint representative
      - 2. Executives (mayor) appoint representative
  - xxxx. True Democracy (non-republican)
    - 1. Structure
      - a. Monochamber

i. Straight
ii. Leverage
b. Monochamber with Auxiliary (Filter)
i. Straight
ii. Leverage
2. Components
a. Monochamber (all functions usurped by referendum)
i. Referendum weekly
ii. Referendum biweekly
iii. Referendum monthly
b. Auxiliary Chamber
i. Presentation (acts like filter, tabling issues and bills)
ii. Deliberation only (Public Conscience, details bills for public referendum)
3. Powers
a. Authoring Legislation (Auxiliary chamber with presentation only)
b. Confirms Legislation
i. Triangulation
ii. Bicameral
c. Repeals Legislation
d. Confirms Appointments
e Confirms Treaties
i. Triangulation
ii. Bicameral

xxxxx. Abolished
1. Executive assumes Legislative Powers
2. Authoritarian.

3. Powers
1. Laws
2. Oversight
a. Unitary
b. Judicial
c. Tripartite Presidential
d. Tripartite Attorney General

e. Tripartite Treasury
3. Ratification (Treaties)
4. Executive
a. Unitary
a. Foreign (President/ Military/ Intelligence/ Alliances)
b. Domestic (Attorney General/ Law enforcement/ General Administration)
c. Commerce (Treasurer/Central Bank & Banking/ Insurance Agencies, Commerce)
d. Fractal (all executive functions assumed by separate committees)
5. Appropriation (Budgets)
6. Judicial
7. Appointments (confirmations)
8. True Democratic Role
9. Triangulation
a. Stipulated (Sub routine, Powers apportioned to the chamber)
b. General (Sub routine, Powers apportioned to the other chambers)
10. Taxing
11. Appointments (direct, by majority leader)
12. Elections

2.) Executive
i.) Unitary (standard) – Primary determines subordinates
ii.) Divided; all individually elected, primaries determine subordinates
x.) Tripartite
c.) President/ Military/ Intelligence/ Alliances,
cc.) Treasurer/Central Bank & Banking/ Insurance Agencies, Commerce,
ccc.) Attorney General/Law Enforcement/ Administration)
xx.) Fractal – each department elected or appointed individually

c. Powers;

1. Central Bank Appointments
2. Banking and Insurance Regulatory agencies
3. Industry (Non Agriculture/ Pharmaceutical/ Health) Regulators
4. Economic advisors and research
5. Trade Treaties
6. Commerce Departments
7. Domestic Law enforcement
8. Government Operation
9. Agriculture/ Pharmaceutical/ Health Regulators
10. Scientific Research (Space Agencies/ Oceanic, General Science)
11. Peace Treaties (military)
12. Intelligence Agencies
13. Military Branches
14. State Departments
15. Laws (Legislative)
16. Confirmations of appointments
17. Veto (Macro-political)

iii.) Abolished (Congress assumes responsibilities and internally determines agency chairs or department secretaries)

iv.) Hybrid (stipulated number of divisions and powers)

3.) Judicial

A. Structure

i.) Independent Circuits (like family /criminal/ superior/ supreme)

ii.) Congressional structure with internal votes forming committees subject to yearly rotations

iii.) Congressional structure with jurisdictions assuming circuits rather than the judges being independently elected or appointed to them

B.) Powers

i.) Judicial

a. General

b. Individual Circuits

i. Family

ii. Civil
iii. Criminal
iv. Superior
v. Appellate
vi. Supreme
ii.) Legislative Sub Routine
iii.) Executive Sub Routine
iv.) Reserve Sub Routine
C. Access
i.) Elected
x. Representative of population (like House) tethered to individual jurisdictions
xx. Unrepresentative (like US Supreme Court, or Senate) with a stipulated number of justices untethered to jurisdictions
ii.) Appointed
x. By executive
1. Unitary
2. Presidential
3. Attorney General
4. Treasury
5. Determined by the committee/ circuit
xx. By legislature

4.) Reserves (continuing to use retired political representatives)
i.) members
a.) all retired elected officials
b.) self admitting (internal party vote)
c.) appointed (determined by previous position, speaker, whip, president)
ii.) Powers
a.) Executive (sub routine)
b.) Legislative (sub routine)
c.) Judicial (sub routine)
d.) Exclusive Reserve (supermajority)
x.) Repealing; Legislation
xx.) Excising;
i. Executives
ii. Legislators
iii. Judges

xxx.) Excommunication; Politicians from Parties (and Reserve Branch eligibility)

xxxx.) Triangulation (in Bicameral Legislations); where consensus between two or more Reserve Houses can be used as a substitute to one of the Elected Legislatures for conformation (making bicameral legislatures more competitive with either being able to earn a confirmation.

iii.) Structure

- a.) Bifurcated by party (multi-Cameral);
- b.) Unicameral (indiscriminant)
- c.) Fractal; organized by decade (or increments that produce odd numbers, singularly or in tandem by position within boards and legislatures (with a delay in activation of the reserve body politic until the imbalance is achieved if necessary to perpetuate the ordinary progression of politics)

iv.) Pool

- 1.) Tier
  - a.) National
  - b.) State
  - c.) Local (county + municipal
- 2.) Branches
  - a.) Executive
  - b.) Legislative
  - c.) Judicial

v.) Terms

- a.) single equivalent
- b.) double
- c.) triple
- d.) total equivalent
- d.) Permanent

5.) Tier

- a. National
- b. State
- c. Municipal (and County)
- d. Corporate
  - 1. Industrial Nonprofit Regulators
  - 2. Employee Owned (Resident Owned, Socialist)
  - 3. (Permanent Funds) C-G/ Private Finance

Initiative

e. Economic Union

6.) Term limits

a.) max length of term

i.) 2

ii.) 4

iii.) 6

iv.) unlimited

b.) max number of terms

i.) 1

ii.) 2

iii.) 3

iv.) unlimited

c.) constraints on number of terms

i.) Lifetime Maximum (sum)

ii.) Intermittent (reset after absence)

iii.) Unlimited

d.) restraints on terms

i.) Sum of both elected and appointed

ii.) Sum of all elected

iii.) Per individual office/region

iv.) None

7.) Elections

a.) Campaign Donations

i. Publicly Funding

ii. Privately Funded

x.) citizen only

xx.) corporate

c. domestic corporations

d. foreign corporations

xxx.) government (corporate)

c. constrained to jurisdiction (county, state)

cc. constrained to nation

ccc. no restraint (foreign government access)

xxxx.) open (citizen, corporate, and foreign entity)

b.) Structure

i. System

x. Presidential (antagonistic or unsynchronized with legislature)

xx. Parliamentarian (majority

in legislature determines executive officer)

ii. Vote

x. Number (One stock or One Acre = One vote)

xx. Part: Whole (Asset Value = Number of Votes, stipulated ratio)

c. straight

cc. ratio

ccc. bracket

xxx. Combinational (Weighted Part:Whole)

xxxx. One Citizen = One Vote

c.) Intimacy

x. Direct (Popular)

xx. Indirect (Electoral College)

xxx. Insulated (Legislative dictates)

i. Majority of seats in unicameral or multi-cameral

ii. Majority of chambers in multi-cameral (Macro-political Vote, lower tiers)

xxxx. Coalition (majority of lower tier executives determine higher executive officer)

d.) Appointed

x. Tyrannical

1. Executive

a. Presidential

b. Attorney General

c. Treasury General

2. Legislatures Majority Party

3. Judicial

xx. Discretion

z. Mechanism

1. Commoditized (market price)

2. Inherited (1st Born, board succession)

3. Decree (personal selection)

4. Any

zz. Eligibility

1. Individual

A. Citizen

B. Resident
C. Alien

2. Corporate
    A. Nonprofit eligibility criteria
        i. Charity
        ii. Noncharity
    B. Profit Incorporations
        i. Employee owned;
        ii. Public;
        iii. Private
        iv. Indiscriminant
    C. Incorporated
        i. Domestic Corporation – same state
        ii. Domestic Corporation– different state
        iii. Foreign corporation
3. Governmental
    A. Tier
        i. city
        ii. county
        iii. state
        iv. Federal
        v. Indiscriminant
    B. Domain
        i. Office
            x. Executive
            xx. Representative
            xxx. Judicial
        ii. Agency
            (Fractal)
    C. Jurisdiction
        i. Domestic
        ii. Foreign
4. Any

zzz. Mechanics
1. Terms
    a. Willful Terms (transactional)
    b. Stipulated Terms
        i. Office term
        ii. Single Year
        iii. Generation
        (Life)

2. Units
    a. Exclusive
    b. Poly-bureaucratic

8.) Eligibility Constraints
  a.) Criteria
    i.) Military
      x branch
        a. Army
        b. Navy
        c. Air Force
        d. Marine
        e. Coast Guard
        f. National Guards
        g. Reserves
      xx. Indiscriminant

    ii.) Political Party (i.e. single party systems)
      x. branch specific
      xx. tier specific
      xxx. indiscriminant

    iii.) Caste
      x. Governmental Caste; maintaining employment in the public sector is the pre-requisite for voting in governmental elections.
        1. Specific branch
          a. Executive
          b. Legislature
          c. Judicial
        2. Specific Tier
          a. National
          b. Regional
          c. County
          d. Municipal
        3. Indiscriminant
        4. Status
          a. Active
          b. Retired

      xx. Occupational Caste; maintaining employment in a foreign military or law enforcement agency is the pre-requisite for holding office or voting.

a. Law Enforcement (FBI, SS, IRS, etc) equivalent
b. Intelligence (NSA, CIA, FBI) equivalent
c. Regulatory (SBA, EPA, OSHA, etc)
d. Scientific (NASA, NOA)
e. Commercial-Economic (Labor, Commerce, Fed)
f. Corporate (Imperial, or self regulating)

iv.) Wealth (employee/employer, aristocratic

A. Asset based

1. Grade
   a. Low (0-300,000.00)
   b. Middle (301,000.00-1,000,000.00)
   c. High (1,000,000.00 +)
   d. Above Median
   e. Below Median
   f. Inclusive
2. Class
   i. Equity
      1. Private
      2. Public
      3. Governmental
   ii. Land
      1. Commercial
      2. Residential
   iii. Bonds
      1. Private and Corporate
      2. Government
   iv. Any

B. Income based (regionally adjusted)

1. Source
   i. Employer (Small Business)
   ii. Self Employed (Professional)
   iii. Employee
   iv. Investments (minority ownership, other

instruments)
v. Tax Revenue
vi. GDP

2. Grade
   a. lower bracket(s)
   b. Middle bracket(s)
   c. High brackets(s)
   d. Below Median
   e. Above Median
   f. Inclusive
   g. Pre tax values
   h. Post tax values

C. Tax liabilities
   i. Threshold
      a.) above
         x. lower bracket
         xx. Middle bracket
         xxx. High bracket
         xxxx. Median
      b.) Below
         x. lower bracket
         xx. middle bracket
         xxx. higher bracket
         xxxx. Median
      c.) Straight
   ii. Instrument
      a.) sales
      b.) property
      c.) income
      d.) capital gains
      e.) Total (Combined)
   iii. Domain
      a.) Personal
      b.) Corporate
      c.) Governmental

D. Incorporation status
   a. Classification
      i. S Type (Professional)
      ii. C Type (Corporate Board Members)
      iii. Non Incorporated Labor (Non licensed employee)
      iv. Unincorporated Professional License (Electrician, Plummer,

Accountant, lawyer,
Doc tor, etc)

v. Unionized Labor
   1. Represented by Board Members
   2. Direct member votes

vi. Nonprofit Corporation (Board Members)

vii. Unemployed and Retired.

b. Employee number
   i. Micro (1-10)
   ii. Small (10-200)
   iii. Medium (200-10,000)
   iv. Large (10,000+)
   v. indiscriminant

c. Specified within
   1. Specific branch
   2. Specific tier

v.) Domicile
   a. Resident Alien
   b. Citizen
   c. Non resident Alien

vi.) Emergency Professionals (all federal and civil police, militia, fire, and EMT (civil engineering corps).
   x. tier specific (certain military branches are only eligible for certain tiers of government)
      c. municipal
      cc. regional
      ccc. national
   xx. indiscriminant (any Emergency branch and any political branch)

vii. Judicial (only Judges and lawyers)
   a. Lawyers
      x. public sector lawyers
      xx. any licensed lawyer
   b. judges
   c. judges and lawyers

viii. Education
      c. Associates

cc. Undergraduate
x. Differentiated
xx. Undifferentiated
ccc. Graduate
x. Differentiated
xx. Undifferentiated

ix. Jurisdiction (per unit, index equivalent to population, taxes, or GDP - subroutine)
i. cities
a. Above median index
b. Below median index
c. Straight
ii. counties
a. Above median index
b. Below median index
c. Straight
iv. states
a. Above median index
b. Below median index
c. Straight
iii. regions
iv. nations
v. corporations
a. Above median index
b. Below median index
c. Straight

b.) Action
i. to vote
ii. to hold office
c.) domain
i. exclusive
ii. non exclusive

9.) Appointed by
a.) municipal
x. legislature
xx. executive
xxx. judicial
xxxx. reserve
b.) regional
x. legislature
xx. executive
xxx. judicial

xxxx. reserve

c.) national

x. legislative

xx. executive

xxx. judicial

xxxx. reserve

10.) Voting

a.) compulsory

b.) voluntary

11.) Political Parties

a.) Primaries

i.) closed

ii.) Open

b.) Endorsements

i.) Two party system

ii.) Multiple party endorsements

iii.) Endorsement parties

12. Jurisdiction;

a. Jurisdiction wide (Senators)

b. Districts (Representatives)

c. Sectors (Private or Public)

13. Number of Representatives

a. Population

i. Jurisdiction

ii. Employees

iii. Enlisted

b. GDP

i. Straight

ii. Per Capita

c. Taxes

i. Gross

ii. Net

x. Surrendered

xx. Minimum

d. Political Units

i. cities

ii. counties

iii. states

iv. regions

v.. nations

vi. corporations

- e. Feudal
    - i. Military Units supported
    - ii. Military Units volunteered
- f. Executive Representation
- g. Combinational (Scale)
- h. Legislative Brokers
- i. Asset (ratio of land, stock, or bond)

14. Macro Political Votes
    - a. alpha (primary executive, speaker)
    - b. agency director (committee chairs)
    - c. Proportional (Governors and Mayors, check to Federal Legislatures)

Tax Based
Systems of Representation

Chapter 3

Taxes are a dominant theme in most economies and most democracies. Historically, they have been the cause of countless rebellions and revolts. They are a cornerstone in conservative political ideologies. There are few issues that are more emotionally provocative than taxes. Taxes are an incredibly useful and durable index to base political representation on. Taxes are a measure of direct support for a government. It provides the city, state, or nation with the capital resources necessary to build infrastructure, regulate commerce, stimulate and model economy, maintain police and other emergency services, and to deploy military personnel and military equipment. Taxes are mandatory. Withholding that support is treated as an overtly criminal behavior and used only an action of last resort for protest. Taxes are a necessary component of government and therefore the best way to moderate representation and influence within the state.

Tax based representation can be expressed through individual tax liabilities or government tax liabilities. Cities and States are aggregators of tax information with the regions able to declare the volume of taxes paid by their residents and deduct all moneys received in rebate or subsidy. This process permits tax representation to differentiate between gross taxes paid and net taxes paid. This can be incredibly important for installing checks and balances within the system of representation minimizing tax exploitation between states, regions, and parties.

Federalist tax policy is an incredibly important component of government management but any inefficiencies in regards to how representation is apportioned between the legislatures of a nation or state can result in wild imbalances between federal taxes donated within an economic union and those federal rebates and subsidies earned later that year. Federalist tax policy dictates that richer states pay more taxes in an effort to improve the economy of poorer jurisdiction. Federalist tax policy is a very necessary aspect of economic modeling within the union but susceptible to deliberate acts of exploitation. Not only will this result in more political corruption and a slower growth in real economy but abuses found within the tax system can have terribly destabilizing effects including tax holiday, protests, and revolts.

All states capture tax information from citizens and jurisdictions enabling a voting franchise to be based on eligibility criteria or value voting. Performance will be dependent on verified and averaged information dispelling the initial fears and criticisms. Individual tax forms will include income information and asset valuations while state or city balance sheets will demonstrate rebates and gross figures for comparison. The same way a census provides the information necessary to adjust representation based upon population, annual tax information can be used by states to correlate representation based on net or gross taxes remitted within a city, state, or federal system. States and cities are aggregates of population legitimizing wealth representation by making it inclusive of both population and GDP.

More populous regions will generally remit more taxes providing parity with smaller jurisdiction that are wealthier. This is a fairer check on majority rule than contemporary senates provide. Senate structures typically provide a numerical amount of representation determined by state boundaries regardless of population. Senatorial representation disproportionately favors rural populations and less populous states. Senatorial (or Numerical) representation is easily over-represents minorities and in crises can be easily exploited. Indexing representation to tax policies or federalist tax policy accommodates this philosophy but performs a better balances between population and GDP. Tax data captures population metrics preserving majority rule but applies economic terms to moderate it and protect minorities.

Constellations of multi-chambered legislatures accommodate larger varieties in tax based representation. The most basic or fundamental of configurations will enfranchise one chamber with representation based on net taxes while the complementary chamber is based on gross taxes paid within the economic union or federalist system. Powers should be evenly distributed among the two chambers so that checks and balances are provided but where cooperation is still necessary.

The **Gilt Republic** maintains an upper chamber based on net taxes paid and a lower chamber based on gross taxes Paid. The lower chamber has exclusive domain over Taxation while the upper chamber has appointment powers. Both Chambers must agree on budgets by confirming them with independent votes. The budget determines the numerical representation within the upper chamber after federal subsidies by state are subtracted from federal contributions in units of states. This discourages abusive federalist tax policies as any exploitation results in depreciated representation.

Tax policy is a more important and prestigious function than appointment powers and therefore is delegated to the lower house due to its higher correlation to population and majority rule. The sensitivity of tax policy demands that all jurisdictions maintain representation and jurisdictions can be excluded from the upper chamber by virtue of the state receiving more federal subsidies than federal contributions. Tax policy is generally applied in proportions of income rather that flat figures and fees which permits it universal distribution among the participating states or jurisdictions. This will discourage tax policy being the mechanism of exploitation rather than federal rebates but when fails the jurisdictions being prejudiced against or mistreated have access to representation within the same chamber.

Gilt Republic

Primary Traits;

- Unitary Executive
- Upper House Representative of Net Taxes
- Lower House Representative of Gross Taxes
- Appointed Judicial

Advantages;

- All of the typical components of Republican government are present and organized in a conventional manner. This provides all of the same advantages and disadvantages current examples maintain.

- The system positively reinforces more balanced federalist tax policy by apportioning representation based on net tax contributions within the Upper House and Gross tax contributions within the Lower House.

- Federalist tax policy is a moving threshold and jurisdictions not earning adequate representation one year can adjust spending and rebate levels in subsequent years. With a balanced federalist tax policy the system of representation more closely imitates popular representation with its dependence on population and GDP.

- The Upper House is the weaker of the two Houses due to Taxing powers being the exclusive domain of the Lower House. This is intended to keep the balance of power within the chamber more easily accessed by a majority of the jurisdictions. The Upper House has appointment confirmation powers to offset this deficiency.

Disadvantages;

- Sundering the chief executives powers into three is a serious erosion of responsibilities and coordinating actions between the President, Attorney General, and Treasurer General may be strained at times but modern democracies and newer technologies that can accommodate these improved firewalls.

- Policy differences between foreign law enforcement and domestic law enforcement policies can cause tension but new regulations and power sharing strategies should be able to accommodate the differentials.

Specifications;

Executive;

- 2.i (Unitary Executive), 5.a (National) 6.a ii (4 year terms), b.iii (3 maximum concurrent terms), c.i (lifetime maximum), d.i (sum of both elected and appointed) 7.a.i (publicly funded), b.i.x (Presidential), ii.xxxx (One citizen = One vote), c.x (direct elections), 8.a.v.b. (Citizen), b.i.ii (to hold office and to vote), c.i (exclusive), 10.b (voluntary voting)

Legislature;

- 1.i.xx.z (Bicameral legislature, 1st house), ii.x (Representative), iii.1.2.3.5.7 (Laws, Oversight, Ratification, Appropriations, and Appointments), 5.a. (National), 6.a.iii (6 year terms), b.ii (2 terms maximum), c.ii (Intermittent), c.ii (sum of elected only), 7.a.i (publicly funded), b.ii.xxxx (One citizen = One vote), c.x (direct elections), 8.a.v.b (Citizen), b.i.ii (to vote and to hold office), c.i (exclusive), 10.b (voluntary voting), 12.a (Jurisdiction), **13.c.ii (Representative of Net Taxes)**

- 1.i.xx.zz (Bicameral legislature, 2nd house), ii.x (Representative), iii.1.2.3.5.10 (Laws, Oversight, Ratification, Appropriations, Taxing), 5.a. (National), 6.a.ii (4 year terms), b.iv (Unlimited), c.ii (Intermittent), c.ii (sum of elected only), 7.a.ii.x.xx.a, (privately funded, citizen and domestic corporations), b.ii.xxxx (One citizen = One vote), c.x (direct elections), 8.a.v.b (Citizen), b.i.ii (to vote and to hold office), c.i (exclusive), 10.b (voluntary), 12.b (Districts), **13.c.i (Representative of Gross Taxes)**

Judicial;

- 3.A.i. (Judicial, Circuits), B.i.a (Judicial powers only, general), C.ii.x.1 (Appointed by Unitary President), 5.a. (National), 6.a.iii (6 year term), b.iii (3 terms maximum), c.i (lifetime maximum), 8.v.b, b.ii (citizen to hold office)

The Gilt Republic has the a standard distribution of powers and branches. It imitates most contemporary democracies in form and figure with only the legislature adjusted for tax representation. An example of a system where the executive powers are subject to different tax representation entitlements is the **Tax Complex.** It is a multi-legislature that maintains a tri-cameral executive legislature in addition to a judicial legislature. The Tax Complex employs Legislative broker powers and Executive Representation attributes as a mechanism to balance some of the in congruencies created by tax representation.

The executive legislature with Presidential powers is subject to net tax representation which subtracts federal subsidies from federal contributions to calculate the ratio of representation. This results in the likelihood that several states or counties will not be represented within the legislature. This can be reconciled with the fact that they don't make any net contributions into the federalist system and should not be afforded access. It should be noted that all of the Tricameral Presidential executive powers deal with external events and nations. The amount of representation earned is subject to change within a period which means all states have an opportunity to participate but most show restraint within the general legislature when apportioning military contracts, corporate subsidies, and welfare.

The Presidential legislature operates under a system of executive representation which exacts a proportional number of legislative votes from the value indexed but which concentrates the influence within a single individual. This ensures that the Presidential executive branch has fewer members and imitates more conventional or contemporary executive branches with unitary organization. It should be noted that because many states are likely to be excluded after federalist tax rebates the numbers of executive representatives are decreased even further.

The military and state departments are primarily used in foreign relations, negotiations, and interventions. Excluded states can rest assured that they maintain complete access to federal positions relating to regulation and administration within the union. The Attorney General executive legislature is representative of population which means all citizens from every state are permitted to vote and exercise democratic control. As a means to improve the power of this executive legislature the members are legislature brokers allowing them the opportunity to collect a large number of federal and state positions depending on other eligibility constraints. This is an incredible advantage in a Complex of three executive, two general, and one judicial legislatures.

The third executive legislature is indexed to gross taxes paid into the federal system which does favor those states remitting the most money into the union but which does not exclude any jurisdictions due to high federal subsidies. The branch is primary charged with regulation and administration and access should not be restricted to any citizen in any of the jurisdictions. Offices are purposefully correlated to districts to maximize the number of seats made accessible to the Attorney General Legislature with the legislative power. The combined representation should offset the restricted access caused by net tax representation in the Presidential executive legislature and the 1st House of the General Legislature.

The Upper House participates in a bicameral process for legislature and maintains taxing powers. It is representative of population to ensure that the entire citizenry can participate in elections. Taxing powers are more important in a system of representation based on taxes as it ultimately controls the proportion of votes allotted within the various branches and chambers. Larger tax revenues can dilute the number of votes provided to smaller and less productive states while specific tax sources can dictate the volume of tax contributions made by each jurisdiction. This chamber is also empowered with legislative brokers so that they can concentrate representation within the other chambers including the second general legislature.

Although there are two formal chambers in the general legislature the legislative broker mechanism can take advantage of the executive representation feature of the lower chamber. The executive representation attribute concentrates a number of votes based upon gross tax representation within only one representative who can be a member of either the Attorney General executive legislature, the Upper legislative chamber, or both. The Lower chamber is primarily concerned with oversight over the executive legislatures, treaty recognition, and appointment powers. This conforms well with an Attorney General officer looking to consolidate powers over the other executive legislature.

The least dynamic chamber deals with judicial aspects of governance. It is a congress and segregates itself into judicial circuits every year in a process similar to how committees are formed in the other chambers. Elections are publicly funded and terms are unlimited to eliminate most of the corrupting forces found in other chambers while maximizing the amount of experience each candidate or professional politician can amass. It is subject to the legislative broker powers of the other legislators but the lawyer and judge (state or local circuit) eligibility criteria will limit the number of candidates campaigning for the open seat.

Tax Complex

Primary Attributes

- No Executive branch
- No Judicial Branch
- Bicameral General Legislature
- Tricameral Executive Legislature
- Unicameral Judicial Legislature

Advantages

- Each Executive Legislature focuses on one aspect with specialization within the Executive domains of Presidency, Attorney General, and Treasurer General. This allows each executive agency is governed by a committee staffed by most of the viable political parties. This is a more sophisticated way of distributing power and embedding oversight within the executive functions of the state.

- The activities of the executive agencies are no longer coordinated by a single executive but there should be no doubt that a majority party cant exercise its will effectively across a wide variety of otherwise disparate organizations. Partisan politics is typically excluded from the more intense applications of intelligence and military as nationalistic sentiments override most objections while the actions are regressed to obvious interests.

- The Treasury Ex-Legislature branch has its numerical representation indexed by gross taxes remitted to the federal government meaning that all jurisdictions are represented unequally but proportionally. Tax remits are typically correlated to GDP which means that the jurisdictions or states with the highest product earn the largest number of representatives. Financial or commercial expertise is function of higher economic output be it an aggregate of population or specialization in industry. It's also more likely that the jurisdiction have a larger number of more highly qualified experts.

- The Presidential Executive Legislature has the number of representative indexed to Net Tax Representation to reward those states making the largest contributions with access to the most leadership positions. It also provides them with access to the military to protect their franchise but this is check specifically by the location of bases which typically correlates with the amount of tax subsidy and the likelihood less representation.

- The Attorney General Ex-Legislature is correlated to Representation of population. to balance out the Net Tax Representation embedded within the Presidential Ex-Legislature. Those jurisdictions benefiting from the Net Tax Representation will have significantly more representation in a Gross Tax Representative system per capita but can otherwise be balanced by a larger number of smaller jurisdictions. Still the combination of Net and Gross Representation should accommodate a wide variety of states with different populations and different sizes. Representation by population is the most basic index for representation which typically correlates to GDP and Taxes. It is the most common denominator and most populations will feel relieved that the Ex-legislature charged with domestic law enforcement is formatted to traditional democratic standards. For this reason they are entitled to act as Legislative Brokers within all of the other chambers of the legislative complex.

- The legislative branch assuming jurisdiction over the judicial aspect of government can be organized exactly like conventional court system hierarchies already are with trial, appellate, superior, and supreme courts with members elected from a general pool of licensed lawyers and judges where the congress then coordinates itself through internal votes for appointment to the different tiers, jurisdictions, circuits, and roles. Self governance must be tempered by strict term limits, term lengths, and avoiding private campaign finance systems.

- Only those elected to the Upper Chamber of the Legislature can pursue Legislative Broker status; this allows the politician to seek election in all offices he is eligible for according to tier and jurisdiction. They can consolidate power within the Ex-legislatures and the other legislatures. Immediately after losing their seat in the Upper chamber they must relinquish all other legislative seats in the other chambers or branches as soon as new elections are scheduled. When only one remains the individual may petition for re-election in any jurisdiction for any seat they remain eligible.

- The Lower chamber of the Legislature has its numerical representation indexed to Net taxes paid into the Union which effectively correlates tax responsibilities with representation. Populations are normally incentivized to reduce their own tax liabilities which intrinsically reduce their representation and ability to advocate for their own reduction in tax payments.

- Net Tax Representation reinforces sounder fiscal policies by mechanically discouraging tax avoidance. This encourages patriotic acts of tax donation with commensurate increases in representation and power; no doubt that the larger the tax contributions the stronger a state or nation will become as the greater capitalization improves defense/intelligence and performs economic stimulus.

- By correlating the representation to Net taxes paid it effectively removes political franchise from those jurisdictions that receive more tax rebates than they donate. This is necessary to discourage larger states from abusing their power to reduce their tax liabilities by making representation dependent on the net value transferred. Those states which donate more taxes naturally deserve more representation as they make more contributions to the Union or Nation. By limiting this restriction to one chamber of legislature it ensures that those states receiving greater tax rebates still earn adequate representation in other chambers.

Disadvantages

- Excluding segments of the population from a certain branch of government will invoke jealousy and distrust even if exclusive representation in another branch is granted. Only those paying median taxes or above are empowered to vote in the Presidential-Judicial Branch while those paying median taxes or less have domain over the Attorney General Executive Legislature. This is done purposefully to remove access to regulators for business owners and grant the lower classes power over enforcement of the criminal code but recourse is provides by permitting exclusivity over the military and judicial appointments.

Specifications;

Executive:

- 2.iii (Abolished Executive); 5.a.b.c (National)

Legislative:

- 1.i.xx.z (Multi-cameral legislature, 1st house), ii.xx (Representative),.iii.4.a.b.c (Presidential Executive Powers); 5.a (National), 6.a.iii (6 year terms), b.iii (3 terms maximum), c.ii (Intermittent); c.ii (sum of elected and appointed); 7.a.ii.xxx (Privately funded by governments); 8.a.v.b (citizen), b.i.ii (to vote and hold office), 10.a (compulsory), 12.a (Jurisdictions), 13.c.i **13.c.ii (Representative of Net Taxes), 13.f (Executive Representation)**

- 1.i.xx.zz (Multi-cameral legislature, 2nd house), ii.xx (Representative),.iii.4.b.c (Attorney General Executive Powers); 5.a (National), 6.a.iii (6 year terms), b.iii (3 term maximum), c.ii (Intermittent); c.ii (sum of elected and appointed); 7.a.i (publicly funded), b..ii.xxxx (One citizen = One vote), c.x (direct elections); 8.a.v.b (citizen), b.i.ii (to vote and hold office), c.i (exclusive), 10.a (compulsory), 12.b (Districts), 13.a.i (Representative of Population, by jurisdiction), 13.h **(Legislative Broker)**

- 1.i.xx.zzz (Multi-cameral legislature, 3rd house), ii.xx (Representative),.iii.4.c (Treasurer General Executive Powers); 5.a (National), 6.a.iii (6 year terms), b.iv (Unlimited), c.ii (Intermittent); c.ii (sum of elected and appointed); 7.a .ii.x.xx (Privately Funded by citizens and corporations), 8.a.v.b (citizen), b.i.ii (to vote and hold office), c.i (exclusive), 10.a (compulsory), 12.b (Districts), **13.c.i (Representative of Gross Taxes)**

- 1.i.xx.zzzz (Multi-cameral legislature, 4th house).ii.xx (Representative), 5.a (National), iii.1.5.10 (Laws, Appropriations, and Taxation), 6.a.ii (4 year terms), b.iii (Unlimited), c.i (Lifetime); c.ii (sum of elected and appointed); 7.a.i (publicly funded), b.ii.xxxx (One citizen = One vote), c.x (direct elections); 8.a.v.b (citizen), b.i.ii (to vote and hold office), c.i (exclusive), 10.a (compulsory), 12.a (Jurisdictions), 13.a.i (Representative of Population, by jurisdiction), **13.h (Legislative Broker)**

- 1.i.xx.zzzzz (Multi-cameral legislature, 5th house).ii.xx (Representative), 5.a (National), iii.1.2.3.5.7 (Laws, Oversight, Treaty Ratification, Appropriations, and Appointments,), 6.a.ii (4 year terms), b.iii (Unlimited), c.i (Lifetime); c.ii (sum of elected and appointed); 7.a.i (publicly funded), b.ii.xxxx (One citizen = One vote), c.x (direct elections); 8.a.v.b (citizen), b.i.ii (to vote and hold office), c.i (exclusive), 10.a (compulsory), 12.b (Districts), **13.c.ii (Net Tax Representation), 13.f (Executive Representation)**

- 1.i.xx.zzzzzz (Multi-cameral legislature, 6th house), ii.xx (Representative), iii.6 (Judicial) .5.a (National), 6.a.iii (6 year terms), b.iv (Unlimited), c.i (Lifetime); 7.a.i (publicly funded), b.ii.xxxx (One citizen = One vote), c.x (direct elections); 8.a.vii.x.xx (Judge or Lawyer), v.b (Citizen), b.ii (to hold office), c.i (exclusive), 10.a (compulsory), 12.a (Jurisdictions), 13.a.i (Representative of Population, by jurisdiction)

Judicial

- 3.a iv. Abolished (Congress or Executive assumes responsibilities)

There should be no doubt that introducing Net Tax based representation excludes a significant number of citizens from elections within the institution and will be resisted regardless of its implicit legitimacy. A remedy to this inherently flaw in tax based representation is empowering an institution with triangulation powers while maintaining popular elections within a standard bicameral legislature process. This enfranchises those states making positive contributions into the federalist system with a measure of extra power but otherwise preserves the premise of a popularly elected legislature. The **Tax Reserve Republic** marries an elected legislature based on gross taxes with a Reserve legislature to complete a bicameral process. It then employs a third legislature with triangulation powers based on net tax representation.

The Reserve component is comprised of retired legislators from both branches but the intent is to provide the popularly elected legislature more representation in the chamber. This can be accomplished by applying the same ratio of representation between the two non reserve legislatures. The volume of tax revenue captures both gross revenues and net revenues with gross revenues being much larger. If the same ratio for representation is applied it ensures that chamber indexed to gross taxes has many more representatives and candidates within the Reserve Chamber. This regresses the distribution of Reserve legislators towards popular representation by favoring gross taxes over net taxes. Gross tax representation is highly correlated to population which provides the bicameral process more legitimacy as a popularly elected institution.

Tax Reserve Republic

Primary Traits;

- Unitary Executive Branch

- Bicameral Legislature

- Tax Representation in the 1st House
- Elected Judicial Branch
- Unicameral Reserve Branch

Advantages;

- Standard Unitary Executive to maximize the coordination of agencies and departments during national emergencies
- Unorthodox Bicameral Legislature with one elected component indexed to gross taxes and one reserve component accepting only retired legislators.
- The elected Legislature specializes in taxation while the Reserve Legislature specializes in appointments and oversight. Both contribute to the budget and appropriations which ultimately determines the federalist tax policy used to filter representation in the second legislature.
- Second Legislature based on net tax representation with Triangulation powers only. It affords those jurisdictions continuing to make positive contributions within a federalist tax system with extra powers to confirm legislation from the other two components of the legislature but checked by an inability to originate new legislation.
- Standard elected judicial branch based on a hierarchy. Allows legislative brokers to assume roles as long as they have legal or judicial experience

Disadvantages;

- Net tax representation tends to exclude citizens with residency in smaller jurisdictions more heavily subsidized by the central or federal government. It tamps down on tax exploitation so that more jurisdictions favor a more fair tax policy.

Specifications;

Executive;

- 2.i.iii (Unitary Executive, Elected), 5.a (National) 6.a ii (4 year terms).b.iii (3 maximum concurrent terms), c.i (lifetime maximum), d.i (sum of both elected and appointed) 7.a.i (publicly funded), b.i.x Presidential) .ii.xxxx (One citizen = One vote), c.x(direct elections); 8.v.b. (Citizen), b.i.ii (to hold office and to vote), c.i (exclusive), 10.a (compulsory voting)

Legislative;

- .i.xx.z (Bicameral legislature, 1st house), ii.xx (Representative), iii.1.2.3.5.7 (Laws, Oversight, Ratification, Appropriations, and Appointments), 5.a. (National), 6.a.iii (6 year terms), b.iv (Unlimited), c.ii (Intermittent); c.ii (sum of elected only); 7.a.i (publicly funded), b..ii.xxxx (One citizen = One vote), c.x (direct elections); 8.a.v.b (citizen), b.i.ii (to vote and to hold office), c.i (exclusive), 10.b (voluntary), 12.a (Jurisdiction), **13.c.i (Representative of Gross Taxes)**

- 1.i.xx.zz (Bicameral legislature, 3rd house), ii.xx (Representative), iii.9.b (Triangulation and Laws, Appropriations) 5.a. (National), 6.a.ii (4 year terms), b.iv (Unlimited), c.ii (Intermittent); c.ii (sum of elected only); 7.a.i (publicly funded), b..ii.xxxx (One citizen = One vote), c.x (direct elections); 8.a.v.b (citizen), b.i.ii (to vote and to hold office), c.i (exclusive), 10.b (voluntary), 12.b (Districts), **13.c.ii (Representative of Net Taxes)**

Judicial

- 3.i. (Judicial, Hierarchal, Elected); 5.a.(National) 6.a.iii (6 year term), b.iii (3 terms maximum), c.ii (intermittent maximum); d.ii (sum of elected) 7.a.i (publicly funded), b..ii.xxxx (One citizen = One vote), c.x (direct elections); 8.v.b, b.ii (citizen to hold office), 8.vii.a.b.x (public attorneys and judicial experience), c.i (exclusive)

Reserve;

- 4.i.a.ii (Reserve Board, admitting all retired members), .ii.b Bicameral legislative sub routine - 1.2.3.5.7 (Laws, Oversight, Ratification, Appropriations, and Appointments), **iv.1.b.2.b (Pool of retired national legislators),** v.d (Total equivalent terms)

The Tax Reserve deviates from contemporary democracy in one other significant measure. It maintains an elected judicial branch with eligibility constrained to those with public lawyer and judicial experience. The established three term maximum should not discourage professional development as it is expected the elected judge develop years of experience prior to earning the office. The threshold is intermittent so after the expiration of one term the justice is eligible for another office. A consequence of intermittent terms is the incentive for judges to relocate and seek open offices at the end of three terms in their current office. This will provide more diversity in the different courts and circuits of a federal justice system which should ultimately provide more experienced and better opinions and judgments.

This chapter does not include a system which imitates a conventional democracy in every respect accept for indexing representation within the legislature to gross taxes. Gross taxes captures most of the relevant demographic data to accept it as popular elections. The tax based representation captures data on economy and political operations as well. Inefficiencies in procedure and imbalances in representation will be more noticeable in respect to federalist tax policy over extended periods which is a product a polarized politics and exploitative fiscal policies. It must be said the contemporary democracies can convert to gross tax based representation by improvement. Most governments incorporate bicameral legislatures which allows one chamber to be adjusted with the other remaining the same accommodating more conservative citizens by preserving population based representation in at least one part of the legislature.

Tax Liability Based Systems of Representation

Chapter 4

State based tax representation is centered on gross taxes and net taxes paid but personal or entity based tax representation is focused exclusively on individual tax returns, chiefly income. There are two primary methods for distributing the voting rights. One method is based on eligibility criteria and tax liability thresholds. The other method is value voting based on variables determined by gross taxes paid. State based tax representation avoids extra scrutiny placed directly on classes and wealth distributions within the national economy while individual tax based representation can highlight the inequities of the current system or act to correct and mitigate them. Most nations will only enfranchise natural persons with tax liability based representation but other federalist systems might provide corporations with representation as a means to form larger economic unions.

With tax liabilities used as eligibility criteria it is possible to segregate the classes with separate entitlements within the various branches of government or chambers of the legislature. Modern statistics provides the foundations for normally distributing the thresholds within the population so that the net ratio of representation is conserved. Representation for below median tax liabilities will be allocated to one chamber and above median tax liabilities will be a complementary chamber of the same legislature. Exactly half the population will gain representation in one half of the Congress and the other half of the population will gain representation within the other. The division will provide diverse constituents for both chambers in that no single segment will be over represented and afforded too much influence. The distribution will follow the statistical mode with numerical superiority of voters falling near the midline of incomes and liabilities.

One of the biggest advantages of a class based system of wealth representation is all segments of the population have an opportunity to better appreciate their economic roles. Economics is too often confused with other elements of politics be they national security tendencies or social issues. When the economic identities of the voting citizens are more accurately defined in terms of incomes and economy they should start voting for their self interests more often. The net result should be an economy regressed to the interests of the median population rather than coupled to the interests of outliers typically defined by the deciles (top 10% of income earners equivocated to the professional class and owners class). The lower class may appreciate their circumstances more if a bill raising the minimum wage passes the lower chamber based on below median tax liabilities is repeatedly quashed by the upper chamber based on above median tax liabilities. It will broadcast the implications of the bill in purer economic terms with clearer distinctions between the classes and institutions.

One of the more interesting and potent qualities of representation based on tax liability is the ability of individuals to move from participating in one institution to participating in another after changes to the tax code are enacted. Individuals can effectively alter their representation or defend their voter franchises through voter eligibility legislation. Many nations suffer under the corrupting force of gerrymandering and similar policies. Realignment of tax based eligibility criteria is an equivalent action that moves the entire electorate rather than manipulating the boundaries of individual districts. Qualifying voter representation on median values ensures that the population is split evenly between the number of institutions if bicameral and if intended.

Tax representation can be split into the same brackets used to determine the rate applied. Depending upon the complexity of the code this can produce a large number of diverse segments. For simplicities sake the attributes matrix only designates a lower, middle, and upper bracket to simulate the most obvious of class distinctions. The larger number of segments does allow more combinations with specific chambers or branches which can simulate more effective checks and balances between the institutions but they are not likely to be successfully engineered into pre-existing tiers of government and may be dependent on the formation of a new government or nation. Tax Brackets are more useful to pre tax eligibility standards while median thresholds are equivalent to post tax eligibility criteria. Brackets would allow for more complex voter gerrymandering to occur when the multiple compartments and moving thresholds.

Unlike the schism between Gross and Net Tax representation no principle value should be attributed to the volume of taxes paid. Incongruence in taxes paid are typically a function of wealth inequality with structural flaws in the economy the cause of the disparities. Lower income voters may pay less overall taxes than the middle class and owners class but this should have absolutely no impact on political influence. With more stable and more equitably modeled economies the below median tax payers would pay a more equal part of the tax burden rather than subrogating that responsibility to the wealthier segments of the population. All citizens enjoy an equal voter franchise except any difference in powers engineered within the specific institutions. That being said Federalist tax policy and progressive fiscal policies will act to inhibit wealth inequality and contribute to a higher functioning economy.

The **Tripartite Tax Republic** maintains two legislative branches with eligibility constraints based on below median and above median tax liabilities criteria. The Upper House is able to leverage appropriation powers as well as appointment powers. The Lower House governs over appropriations and taxing powers. Above median taxpayers participate in the Upper House and below median taxpayers participate in the Lower House. The Lower House has more political power to offset the Upper Houses dominant economic power; it is far more appropriate for the below median tax payers to maintain control over the taxing powers than it would be for the above median taxpayers.

Tripartite Tax Republic

Primary Traits;

- Tripartite Executive
- Upper House Above Median voter/office eligibility
- Lower House Below Median voter/office eligibility
- Appointed Judicial

Advantages;

- Permitting the Lower House to dictate Tax policy may increase the resentment of the wealthiest segment of the population but it is far more appropriate than letting the leisure class command a vast majority economic influence and granted access to the power to protect their franchise through fiscal policy. Lower income populations will naturally seek to preserve the incentives towards wealth creation and retention while higher income populations often lack the inhibitions to avoid overly regressive systems of taxation.

- The class division in the legislature will produce a more competitive environment for economic reforms and fiscal policy. The differences will be more pronounced when negotiations breakdown between class dependent chambers. Fortunately the numerical superiority will continue to be maintained within lower income rather than higher income voters providing the regression to the center and the votes necessary to manage the bureaucracy.

- Only personal taxes are considered and there is no corporate entitlement.

- The legislators must come from the same class as their constituents which should improve representation on economic issues. The legislators will have many of the same economic stressors as their constituents be it the cost of healthcare, transportation, food, shelter, and education. More of the most important economic issues will be addressed earlier prior to crisis. This will naturally create a divide between the pay rates of legislators from the two institutions but it is necessary to reinforce identity through similar economic stressors. Sharing Incomes and liabilities will create sympathy and impart focus or urgency on issues of more concern.

- The Judicial Branch is appointed by the President as a check against the Attorney General while the Legislature maintains confirmation powers to hedge both of them.

Disadvantages;

- Sundering the chief executives powers into three independent offices is a serious erosion of responsibilities and coordinating actions between the President, Attorney General, and Treasurer General may be strained at times but newer communication technologies can accommodate these obstacles.

- Both of the chambers will have representation from all parts of the nation but unless a living standard adjustment is considered certain regions will be overrepresented in one chamber at the expense of the other and create an imbalance that conjoins tax liabilities with state and regional boundaries. Disdain or contempt between the electorate and officials can accumulate and contribute negatively to a crisis.

Specifications;

Executive;

- 2.ii.x.c (Tripartite Executive Presidential), 5.a (National), 6.a.iii (6 year terms), b.i (1 terms maximum), c.i (lifetime maximum), d.ii (sum of elected), 7.a.i (publicly funded), b.i.x (Presidential) ii.xxxx (One citizen = One vote), c.x (direct elections), 8.a.v.b (Citizen), b.i.ii (eligibility for voting and holding office), c.i (exclusive), 10.b (voluntary voting)

- 2.ii.x.cc (Tripartite Executive Treasury), 5.a (National); 6.a.ii (4 year terms), b.iii (3 terms maximum), c.ii (intermittent maximum), d.ii (sum of elected), 7.a.ii.x.xx.a (privately funded by citizen and domestic corporations), b.i.x (Presidential), ii.xxxx (One citizen = One vote), c.x (direct elections), 8.a.v.b (citizen), b.i.ii (for voting and holding office), c.i (exclusive), 10.b (voluntary voting)

- 2.ii.x.ccc (Tripartite Executive Attorney General), 5.a. (National), 6.a.iii (6 year terms), b.ii (2 terms maximum), c.i (lifetime maximum), d.i (sum of elected and appointed), 7.a.ii.x.xxx (privately funded by citizen and government), b.i.x (Presidential), ii.xxxx (One citizen = One vote), c.x (direct elections), 8.a.v.b. (citizen), b.i.ii (for voting and holding office), c.i (exclusive), 10.b (voluntary voting)

Legislature;

- 1.i.xx.z (Bicameral legislature, 1st house), ii.x (Representative), iii.1.2.3.5.7 (Laws, Oversight, Ratification, Appropriations, and Appointments), 5.a. (National), 6.a.iii (6 year terms), b.ii (2 terms maximum), c.ii (Intermittent), c.ii (sum of elected only), 7.a.i (publicly funded), b.ii.xxxx (One citizen = One vote), c.x (direct elections), 8.a.v.b (citizen), **8.a.iv.c.i.a.xxxx (Tax Liabilities, above median), ii.e (total liabilities), iii.a (Personal Taxes only),** b.i.ii (to vote and to hold office), c.i (exclusive), 10.b (voluntary), 12.a (Jurisdiction), 13.a.i (Representative of Population)

- 1.i.xx.zz (Bicameral legislature, 2nd house), ii.x (Representative), iii.1.2.3.5.10 (Laws, Oversight, Ratification, Appropriations, Taxing), 5.a. (National), 6.a.ii (4 year terms), b.iv (Unlimited), c.ii (Intermittent), c.ii (sum of elected only), 7.a.i (Public Funding), c.x (direct elections), 8.a.v.b (citizen), **8.a.iv.c.i.b.xxxx (Tax Liabilities, below median), ii.e (total liabilities), iii.a (Personal Taxes only),** b.i.ii (to vote and to hold office), c.i (exclusive), 10.b (voluntary), 12.b (Districts), 13.a.i (Representative of Population)

Judicial;

- 3.a.i. (Judicial, Circuit), b.i (Judicial powers only), c.ii.x.2 (Appointed by President), 5.a. (National), 6.a.iii (6 year term), b.iii (3 terms maximum), c.i (lifetime maximum), 8.v.b, b.ii (citizen to hold office), c.i (exclusive)

Powers cant be divided perfectly between the chambers but efficiencies can be gained based upon their primary characteristics. A larger number of professionals and experts should maintain higher tax liabilities making it more applicable that they have greater input on how the economy is regulated and modeled while the poor segments can protect themselves with taxing powers over the wealthier constituencies. It is for this reason that the Upper House has appointment powers, the Lower House determines Fiscal policy, and both contribute to the budget and appropriations. The numerical superiority of the median tax payers within both divisions of class provide the necessary legitimacy of majority rule.

Dividing the legislation by class may predispose the nation to excessive political dysfunction as negotiations breakdown along interests and obligations. An alternative solution would be to divide the voter franchise between executive branches while maintaining universal access to the legislature. The **Bipartite Classed Democracy** bestows exclusive access to the Presidential Executive branch for below median taxpayers and exclusive access to the Attorney General and Treasurer Executive branch for above median taxpayers. The wealth representation is focused on the executive branches to specifically insulate the laws of the nation from direct class related political warfare.

Bipartite Classed Democracy

Primary Traits;

- Bipartite Executive; One Presidential-Judicial Executive and One Treasurer General and Attorney General

- Appointed Judicial

- Filtered True Democratic Lower Chamber

- Republican Legislature with Representational Coefficients based on Gross Taxes

Advantages;

- Only below median taxpayers may vote in the elections for the Presidential executive branch. The vast majority of the soldiers will come from the below median taxpayer population providing an interesting alignment on its deployment. Denying the above median voters access may check colonial sentiments in the owners class as the Presidential executive branch will almost be exclusively used overseas.

- Only above median taxpayers vote for the Attorney General and Treasury branch. A huge portion of this constituency will be professionals and government employees making its interests more aligned with the tax voter franchise. The numerical advantage of professionals over the leisure class should protect the integrity of the regulatory apparatus with the general population still manufacturing the majority of laws through the legislature.

- The tax liability based representation only takes into account personal taxes and corporate entities are not entitled to votes.

- The Legislature maintains direct elections with only citizenship as an eligibility criteria. This helps validates a system with bifurcated representation in the executive branch. The number of representatives afforded to each state are determined by the gross amount of taxes paid by each jurisdiction in proportion to one another. This form of wealth representation should take into account both economic and demographic figures as well as reward more federalist tax contributions with more representation in the tier of government.

- The Upper House is engineered with Executive Representation to capture some of the efficiencies typically earned by unitary executive organization. This makes the Upper Legislature more uniform with the two Executive branches. The general population compensates by exerting itself through the True Democratic legislative chamber

- The second chamber in the bicameral legislature is a True Democracy which draws support from the entire population. The institution has sole appointment powers and is a check on any politicizing forces within the political system. Appointees are subject to exposure to raw sentiments of the population at large with a straight up and down vote. Both executive branches are subject to these appointments and the constancy of voting should keep the population engaged within the political process.

- The Judicial Branch is appointed by the President as a check against the Attorney General with the Legislature maintaining confirmation powers. The economic component of distributing contracts within the domestic economy is the only other check provided against the above median taxpayers controlling the vast majority of other government operations in healthcare, finance, administration, and law enforcement.

Disadvantages;

- Dividing Presidential responsibilities from Attorney General and Treasurer responsibilities and apportioning them between below median and above median tax payers can potentiate a clash between the classes. Regardless of which class maintains which powers there will certainly be problems.

Specifications;

Executive;

- 2.ii.x.c (Executive Presidential), 5.a (National), 6.a.ii (6 year terms), b.iii (3 terms maximum), c.i (lifetime maximum), d.ii (sum of elected), 7.a.i (publicly funded), b.i.x Presidential) ii.xxxx (One citizen = One vote), c.x (direct elections), **8.a.iv.c.i.b.xxxx (tax liability criteria, below median), ii.e (total taxes), iii.a (Personal taxes only),** v.b (Citizen), b.i.ii (eligibility for voting and holding office), c.i (exclusive), 10.b (voluntary voting)

- 2.ii.x.cc.ccc (Executive Treasury and Attorney General), 5.a (National), 6.a.ii (4 year), b.iiv (Unlimited), c.ii (intermittent maximum), d.ii (sum of elected), 7.a.ii.x.xx.a.xxx (privately funded by citizen, domestic corporations, government), b.i.x (Presidential), ii.xxxx (One citizen = One vote), c.x (direct elections), 8.a.v.b (citizen), **8.a.iv.c.i.a.xxxx (tax liability criteria, above median), ii.e (total taxes), iii.a (Personal taxes only),** b.i.ii (for voting and holding office), c.i (exclusive), 10.b (voluntary voting)

Legislature;

- 1.i.xx.z (Bicameral legislature, 1st house), ii.x (Representative), iii.1.2.3.5.10 (Laws, Oversight, Ratification, Appropriations, and Taxes), 5.a (National), 6.a.iii (6 year terms), b.ii (2 terms maximum), c.ii (Intermittent), c.ii (sum of elected only), 7.a.i (publicly funded), b.ii.xxxx (One citizen = One vote), c.x (direct elections), 8.a.v.b (Citizen), b.i.ii (to vote and to hold office), c.i (exclusive), 10.b (voluntary), 12.a (Jurisdiction), **13.a.i (Representative of Gross Tax Liabilities), 13.f (Executive Representative)**

- 1.i.xx.zz (Bicameral Legislature, 2nd House), ii.xxxx (True Democratic), 1.a.i (Mono-chamber, Straight vote), 2.a.ii (Biweekly), 3.b.ii (confirms legislation, bicameral), d. (confirms appointments), e.ii (confirms treaties, bicameral), 8.v.b (Citizen), b.i (to vote)

Judicial;

- 3.a.i (Judicial, Circuits), b.i (Judicial powers only), c.ii.x.2 (Appointed by the Presidential), 5.a. (National), 6.a.iii (6 year term), b.iii (3 terms maximum), c.i (lifetime maximum), 8.v.b, b.ii (citizen to hold office), c.i (exclusive)

Trends of stratification are evident in non diversified political systems resulting from inefficient economic modeling and fiscal policies. The trend is entropic and heavily favors the wealth – which is one of the motivating forces for bifurcating the Executive braches with class based exclusive access. Dividing the powers of executive government and apportioning them between the two classes ensures that one class does not gain an insurmountable advantage over the other. Excessive influence by the owners class and wealth typically results in fascist systems while unchecked proletariat can succumb to communist sentiments. Neither is acceptable and both are made less likely by the power sharing engineered into the system.

Tax class based representation can be an effective implement to balance power between different demographic and economic segments within a population. The first two examples split representation within the legislature and the executive branch. The next example balances exclusive representation within the judicial branch with more conventional representation within the executive legislature and general legislature. The equation is incomplete as over-representation in the legislature is more powerful than exclusive access to the judiciary due to input in law and the exercise of oversight and budgets. For this reason the system employs a Reserve branch taking candidates from all four of the specialized legislatures and using them as a foil in a bicameral legislature process.

The **Complex Tax Reserve** is a complicated system that relies on a large and diverse number of legislatures to balance the various powers and responsibilities of government. It maintains an executive legislature with an electorate based exclusively on citizenship. It maintains a general legislature with a below median tax payer franchise and marries it to a reserve board in a bicameral legislature process. A semi-independent 3rd legislature maintains triangulation powers and is only accessible to states making net contributions to the federalist tax system. The judicial legislature has an above median tax payer eligibility criteria to balance out the below median tax payer entitlement in the upper house of the multi-part legislature.

Complex-Tax Reserve

Primary Traits;

- Executive Legislature
- Upper House includes Below Median voter/office eligibility
- Upper House Representative of Gross Taxes
- Lower House Representative of Net Taxes with popular access

- Judicial Legislature based on Above Median voter/office eligibility

- Unicameral Reserve Branch

Advantages;

- The system is a complex of legislatures with executive, judicial, legislative, and reserve components.

- Below median taxpayers may appear to be vested with more political power due to their possession of the upper chamber but it is really one component of a three part general legislature. There is a Reserve Chamber and a Triangulation Chamber that share power.

- The Lower chamber is accessible to all citizens only with representation between the states dependent on net Federalist tax policy. The Lower chamber commands triangulation powers over laws, appropriations, and taxes.

- Above median taxpayers are granted exclusive domain over the elected judicial legislature. Above median taxpayers should not be equivocated with only the wealthiest of citizens as a significant number of middle class, professional class, and working class members will be included in the enfranchised population. Numerical superiority still favors the lower spectrum of the above median tax payers as the entire distribution regresses to the center.

- Only persons are granted the tax based representation. All corporate and government entities are excluded from the entitlement.

- A Reserve Board composed of retired national politicians from the legislative with term lengths of total equivalency. It is otherwise a co-equal and complimentary branch to the Unicameral Legislature in regards to passing legislation and ratifying treaties.

- Permitting the Reserve branch to act as the second chamber in a bicameral legislature grants access to a large and diverse number of politicians from all of the legislatures providing more expertise and perspectives.

- The total length of service earned during the active portion of the politician's career equals the number of years earned within the Reserve Chamber.

Disadvantages;

- The fact that previously elected politicians are automatically accepted into the ranks of the Reserve Board ensures that the population marinating the franchise continues to grow diluting each individual members influence. This guarantees more human resources for oversight and distributes the power across a larger number of political parties and generations. It provides an interesting balance by immediately empowering the party losing the non reserve commission with access to more reserve presence.

Specifications;

Executive:

- 2.iii (Abolished Executive); 5.a.b.c (National)

Legislative:

- 1.i.xx.z (Multi-cameral legislature, 1st house), ii.x (Representative), iii.4.a. (Unitary Executive Powers), 5.a (National), 6.a.ii (4 year terms), b.iii (Unlimited), c.i (Lifetime), c.ii (sum of elected and appointed), 7.ii.a.x.xxx (Privately funded by citizens and governments), ii.xxxx (One citizen = One vote), c.x (direct elections), 8.a.v.b (Citizen), b.ii (criteria to hold office), 10.b. (voluntary), 12.b (Jurisdictions), 13.a.i (Representative of Population, by jurisdiction)

- 1.i.xx.zz (Bicameral legislature, 2nd house), ii.x (Representative), iii.1.2.3.5.7 (Laws, Oversight, Ratification, Appropriations, and Appointments), 5.a. (National), 6.a.iii (6 year terms), b.ii (2 terms maximum), c.ii (Intermittent), c.ii (sum of elected only); 7.a.i (publicly funded), b.ii.xxxx

(One citizen = One vote), c.x (direct elections); **8.a.iv.c.i.a.xxxx (Tax Liabilities, below median), ii.e (total taxes), iii.a (Personal taxes only),** 8.a.v.b (citizen), b.i.ii (to vote and to hold office), c.i (exclusive), 10.b (voluntary), 12.a (Jurisdiction), **13.c.i (Representative of Gross Taxes)**

- 1.i.xx.zzz (Bicameral legislature, 3rd house), ii.x (Representative), iii.9.a.1.5.10 (Triangulation on Laws, Appropriations, Taxing), 5.a. (National), 6.a.ii (4 year terms), b.iv (Unlimited), c.ii (Intermittent), c.ii (sum of elected only), 7.a.ii.xxxx, c.x (privately funded and open, direct elections), 8.a.v.b (citizen), b.i.ii (to vote and to hold office), 10.b (voluntary), c.i (exclusive), 12.b (Districts), **13.c.ii (Representative of Net Taxes)**

- 1.i.xx.zzzz (Multi-cameral legislature, 4th house,), ii.x (Representative), iii.6 (Judicial), 5.a (National), 6.a.iii (6 year terms), b.iii (Unlimited), c.i (Lifetime), c.i (sum of elected and appointed positions), 7.a.i (Public Funding); **8.a.iv.c.i.a.xxxx (Tax Liabilities, above median), ii.e (total taxes), iii.a (Personal taxes only),** 8.a.v.b (citizen), b.i (to vote), 8.a.vii.x.xx (Lawyers and judges), a.v.b (citizen), b.ii (to hold office), 10.a (compulsory), 12.b (Districts), 13.a.i (Representative of Population, by jurisdiction)

Judicial:

- 3.a.iv (Abolished Judicial); 5.a (National)

Reserve:

- 4.i.a (Reserve Board, admitting all retired members, permanent), ii (legislative sub routine - b.1.2.3.5.10 (Laws, Oversight, Treaties, Appropriations, and Taxes), iii.b (Unicameral), iv.1.a.2.b (Pool of retired national legislators), v.d (total equivalent terms)

The Upper legislature is more dynamic with domain over laws, oversight, treaties, and budgets but the Judicial legislature has the final word in most legislative disputes. This may appear to favor lower income citizens more but the fact is the legislative franchise is shared with a large number of other institutions and voters. In order to avoid all speculation of class favoritism a system can employ class entitlements in more higher differentiated systems. Highly reduced systems such as binary legislatures offer an incredible opportunity to distribute class entitlements in a highly organized and fair way. **Binary Tax legislatures** split all government powers and responsibilities into two institutions which complements an electorate divided into only two tax based classes. Each electorate will be apportioned exactly half of the available powers with the appropriate checks provided over each other.

Binary Tax Legislature

Primary Attributes

- No Executive branch
- No Judicial Branch
- Below Median Tax voter/office eligibility to Upper House
- Above Median Tax voter/office eligibility to Lower House

Advantages

- The two bicameral legislatures split executive and judicial duties but share legislative, appropriations, and taxation duties.
- The upper house assumes the Attorney General and Treasury General Executive Legislature duties while the lower house assumes the Presidential Ex-legislature. The tension during budget administration should precipitate a more equitable distribution of tax dollars between domestic and military adventures as the two chambers will demand their specialization receive the dedicated funding that will empower and enable them to better perform their functions.

- The Upper House is relegated to below median tax payer voter franchise and the Lower House is relegated to an above median tax payer voter franchise. The entire electorate is split between a normally distributed tax liability schedule; this ensures that the wealthiest segments of the population are balanced by median and middle class segments in the same proportions as the poorest segments as balanced by low income and median income segments.

- The voter franchises are as equal in numbers as possible with units formed from families with non tax payers or government dependents contributing to the below median tax payer voter franchise. It should be noted that the voter franchise is paid forward with the last years tax return to justify any changes in status; it is possible for one family or an individual to change participation from one year or the next due to personal performance or from the realignment of tax values around the median figure. Many government beneficiaries in retirement continue to maintain taxable income be they real estate or capital gains which mean the retirement population will carry a moderate amount of diversity in participation.

- The voter franchise is only extended to natural persons to the exclusion of corporations and government entities.

- Both chambers maintain oversight committees regulating the agencies and departments of their counterpart in the Bicameral Congress. Political party membership should be distributed among all of the committees within both chambers ensuring that power doesn't consolidate among a single majority leader or party for an excessive period of time.

- Both chambers are permitted contra- appointment powers over the opposing chamber ensuring that the individual legislators or parties don't over-reach their authority as a result of insulation and independence.

- Only the Lower chamber may enact Tax legislation although it still requires to be confirmed by the opposing chamber to be passed into law. This is meant to be a check against the imposing power of the judiciary in the Upper House where there is no Veto power or triangulation powers.

Disadvantages

- The 6 year term with 3 year intermittent maximum will strain the experience of agency leadership but it is expected that the majority of civil servants remain unelected and unconstrained by the term limits. It does engender competition for majority leadership positions with the 18 year limit moderating more permanent roles.

Specifications;

Executive:

- 2.iii (Abolished Executive), 5.a.b.c (National)

Legislative:

- 1.i.xx.z (Bicameral legislature), ii.x (Representative), iii.1.2.d.e.3.4.a 6.7.10 (Laws, Oversight on A,G, Treasury, Ratification, Executive-Presidential, Judicial, Contra Appointments, appropriations, Taxes), 5.a (National), 6.a.iii (6 year terms), b.iii (3 terms maximum), c.ii (Intermittent); c.i (sum of elected), 7.a.i (publicly funded), b.ii.xxxx (One citizen = One vote), c.x (direct elections), 8.a.v.b (Citizen), **8.a.iv.c.i.a.xxxx (tax liability criteria, above median), ii.e (total taxes), iii.a (Personal taxes only),** b.i.ii (to vote and hold office), c.i (exclusive), 10.b (voluntary), 12.b (Districts), **13.c.i (Representative of Tax Liabilities, Gross)**

- 1.i.xx.zz (Bicameral legislature), ii.xx (Representative), iii.1.2.b.c.3.4.b.c.5.7.10 (Laws, Oversight on Presidential and Judicial, Treatise, Executive- domestic and treasury, Appropriations, Contra Appointments, Taxing), 5.a (National), 6.a.iii (6 year terms), b.iii (3 terms maximum), c.i (Lifelong), c.i (sum of elected), 7.a.i (publicly funded), b.ii.xxxx (One citizen = One vote), c.x (direct elections);

8.a.v.b (Citizen), **8.a.iv.c.i.b.xxxx (tax liability criteria, below median), ii.e (total taxes), iii.a (Personal taxes only),** b.i.ii (to vote and hold office), c.i (exclusive), 10.b (voluntary), 12.b (Districts), 13.a.i (Representative of Population, by jurisdiction)

Judicial:

- 3.a.iv (Abolished Judicial), 5.a (National)

The powers are distributed more arbitrarily than any engineer would care to admit but there are merits in both constellations of advantages. They would have to be for any system to be divided into two classes with only two governmental institutions and then assert their equality and parity. The alignment of interests will still favor the median income earners with a large middle class maintaining significant advantages in balancing out those disparate classes in penury in abject luxury. Both chambers are publicly funded which will reinforce the numerical superiority of the median and middle classes. They may not command all of the nation's wealth but they will certainly suffer the most diversified liabilities and economic stressors while living within the same vicinity and share the same environment as the poorer classes.

Tax Liability based wealth representation is a much more complex topic than can be accurately explained or examined with a few example systems. Simplicity has its merits but specialization and has more. The domain of taxes includes property, sales, vat, income, death, payroll, and many other individual aspects which can be correlated to a specific power or branch. Brackets of tax liability are aspects that can be used to segregate representation into more accurate sections than below median and above median permit. Coupling tax liabilities to the voter franchise opens up philosophical debate on the subject of empowering corporations and other tax paying entities with representation. They can be a powerful tool in forming external cartels, coalitions, and economic unions which permeate traditional national boundaries. Tax Unions are devices that the State can use to bolster their revenues and grant access to business intelligence assets. The relationship would provide voting entitlements to the companies and their employees. They are an improvement on the Tax Union premise introduced earlier in the series.

Voting Tax Unions

In many nations there is typically one epicenter for a specific industry with a majority of the largest competitors located within the same city or states. That region has access to more specialized knowledge for producing regulation and oversight over the industry which translates into significant economic efficiencies for employees, employers, and residents. More predictable environments make companies more competitive and profitable. When political engineers gain direct access to apportioning wealth based representation to specific corporations it will provide a means to economically model the country for specialization in sector headquarters and commercial infrastructure. The corporations would gain votes in exchange for their profit sharing and the tax union.

The states gain access to huge amounts of excess revenues the companies pay in exchange for the payroll benefits and the voting franchise. The differential benefits both parties as payroll efficiencies can save a company 10-20% of labor overhead and payroll revenues can offset a significant portion of state taxes. The voting franchise also imparts identity within the corporate residents who will and support the state and its residents on a wider cross section of national issues. It is a means for one state to express influence within another states jurisdiction. Not only will it have active voters located within the competitors boundaries but the extra revenue gained can be used to lower taxes or improve spending and economy within the host state.

State governments can elect to engineer their own representation to promote industrial relocation within the jurisdiction to foster this concentration and specialization. Politicians can model their tax laws to attract specific companies and sectors or enter into commercial relationships to provide access to benefits like health insurance and retirement which typically gain incredible cost efficiencies in scales that the largest companies and states have access to. In exchange for employee dues and management fees assessed to management and stockholders which produce the revenues for the governments all of the employees can gain a voter suffrage dependent on continued employment with a company engaged in a voting tax union with the jurisdiction. The corporate residency can imitate a work visa system with aligned corporate sponsors needed for eligibility. The fees for the perpetual work visas and corporate residency can simulate either a payroll tax or Union dues.

Even a marginal fee (tax) applied for suffrage could produce incredible returns for the city or state in terms of tax revenue while enfranchising the company with a proxy for governmental powers (representation on multiple tiers of economic-political unions, access to regulation, law enforcement, and the security assets). Both the corporation and the employees will be charged for the benefits based tax union. The extra taxes accrued by the company are to be considered management fees for human resources and categorized as labor costs. Labor costs can account for one half of all overhead with benefits accounting for 35% of all compensation. The benefits tax union will result in large overhead savings from economies of scale and the reduction in personnel not required to handle the paperwork and administration of the benefits. If a government can provide the company with savings on benefits the company might be willing to pay half back in fees which translates to significant revenues.

This revenues could be used to offset taxes by huge margins or enhance expenditures on government programs. The extra taxes accrued by employees can be compared to union dues paid so that no employees are excluded and the terms are negotiated at the onset of employment. This relegates all of the decisions to enter into tax union with a state to the discretion of management and also permits the company to assume multiple relationships in the Market Democracy (*or Capital Democracy*). If proportional rates for Union dues offend too many employees the Union dues could be fixed upon each position and department to better resemble contemporary labor union dues. It should not be neglected that although the employees are granted voting rights they don't have accrue normal liabilities in regards to government outlays for services. For the most part the nonresident voters will be serviced by other governments in regards to police and emergency services, covering the cost of education, social services and the entire host of contemporary public sector services.

Tax Unions based on demographic voting franchises continue to maintain a differential favoring the state over a coalition of corporate residents. A state with a population of 20 million could enfranchise an entire financial sector's workforce amounting to 8 million employees without fearing too much of the liability of losing the majority of a vote to foreign entities. Most states or cities wont engage entire sectors of economy. Even if specific companies were allied with the city and state and granted direct access to general elections the numbers would still likely favor the citizens by an overwhelming margin.

Before any criticisms are levied on a voting tax union system current voter entitlements and circumstances should be scrutinized. Under-regulated political markets subjected to private campaign finance with general elections based on popular votes is the least effective way to introduce the industrial and commercial efficiencies that technocrats need to administer to the demands of the state. Money is confused between special interest groups with favor being distributed more in accord to national trends rather than local or state trends. Private campaign finance invites incredible amounts of corruption and will ultimately have a worse impact on society and economy than any depreciation caused by providing the voter franchise to corporations or unions.

If one recognizes the legitimacy of deregulating campaign finance they must inherently recognize the advantages of enfranchising one sector of the economy with special voting rights for the state legislatures or executive offices. In fact, corporate residency with a voting franchise is a reform from unregulated private campaign finance that establishes clearer distinctions between government and industry with established rules for interaction. The number or proportion of votes gained by the company are more measurable than the soft influence and corruption sustained from private campaign finance and other bribes which makes corporate residency preferable to deregulated political markets. The votes provided in exchange for tax subsidy are not the only advantages bestowed on the state. The entwining of interests permits the state to assemble a large network of professional and business contacts allowing it to export soft influence through trade and aligned interests.

Each sovereign jurisdiction will select the companies they want to partner with for strategic reasons; energy companies provide access to natural resources in addition to extra revenues, technology companies provide communication and data infrastructures, and financial companies provide expertise and access to capital. This relationship will benefit companies with headquarters or large offices within certain regions or states as they can leverage those employees current residing in other jurisdictions for voting within the allied jurisdiction. Most populations are affected by a normal distribution of political preference and ideology which means even small efficiencies earned by aligning employment with voter franchise would be significant.

This alliance can be extended to multiple sectors or multinational and foreign companies as a means for the state to develop a local institution similar to a state department. This would be a major incentive for cities or states developing franchise relationships with certain companies or industries and would certainly complement the increased government revenues or access to more emergency revenues during crises. The states can leverage themselves this way without compromising the federal government or other state governments making Market Democracy compatible with most contemporary forms of republican governments (i.e. democracy). Despite the Federal government insulating itself from this commercial enfranchisement it will gain superficial access to the soft influence and extra capital gained by the states. Not only do higher state revenues equate to lower federal subsidies but a large number of state alliances will increase the number of business assets the federal government earns by proxy. Most systems of democratic representation are predicated on citizenship but more interesting systems with more potential for integration can empower certain resident aliens and non-resident aliens to vote, especially when alien corporations are allied with.

This index is more useful when used in conjunction with other representational indices, especially governmental castes and wealth criteria, so that larger economic unions and empires can be manufactured with a more flexible, partially democratic and partially corporatic political systems. Small business can coordinate to form Cartels for representation while their employees and labor can assimilate within large multinational Unions where both receive adequate representation in multiple competing economic unions. Market Democracy could eliminate national boundaries through enfranchise employees and employers with representation within competing economic unions with wealth representation in a larger super-structure of democratic governance.

The most complex application of wealth representation occurs with value voting for personal taxes. The general inequalities that exist in wealth ownership and income distributions can be accommodated by more specialized reforms to value voting but they all require much more sophisticated computer systems for tracking taxes and then correlating them to voter franchises. This would take considerable effort and will likely discourage most nescient nations from attempting to draw support from the premise. The world is moving towards more integration but it will still be several decades until the trust and expertise is developed to permit the system of wealth based representation to operate with few interruptions and less distractions.

Despite the obvious obstacles at least one tax based system with value voting must be considered to demonstrate the advantages or merits of the possibility. The **Cossack Republic** captures many of the sentiments prevalent in cultures that would overwhelmingly support a tax based voter franchised. It is more authoritarian than other democratic systems relying on only three executive branches and one judicial legislature. All of the legislative duties of the federal government are discharged through the agencies within the dynamic tripartite executive branches. The system experiments with different versions of tax representation applied to the different executive elections. Each attempts to extract advantages embedded deep within fiscal policies and gross tax payments. The system never fully abandons the principle of majority rule by relegating the tax based representation to a value voting system based on brackets with vote multipliers or coefficients.

Cossack Republic

Primary Traits;

- Tripartite Executive
- Abolished General Legislature
- Elected Judicial Legislature
- Abolished Judicial Branch

Advantages;

- There is no General Legislature rendering administrative law from the executive branches the only source of legal canon. Each Executive branch is entitled to a macro-political vote which is used to confirm passage of agency and department laws authored by the other branches simulating the legislatures function of deliberation. Passage requires a majority consensus between the executive branches constituted by the macro political vote requiring 2 of 3 branches to affirm the laws. The repeal of administrative laws must also undergo executive review by the other branches for confirmation.

- Corporations are enfranchised with voting privileges earned from income and property taxes paid. Each entity will send one representative to vote on its behalf Business owners will be over-represented but most will be normally distributed in political affiliations. The fact that they must report their income and assets separately will greatly diminish their numbers (c type corporations, not S type or partnerships).

- These value voting tax based system use a value voting method with a bracket with voting coefficient. The coefficient adjusts the vote cast in a popular election to double or triple an individuals ballot. The bracket system is intended to focus a majority of representation on the middle class to capture their increased exposure to the diversified interests most important to the nation or state. Most brackets are either 2 or 3 with the coefficient determined by above median or below median values or more complex systems with a lower bracket, a middling bracket, and a higher bracket each with a different voting multiplier. Without a bracket based value voting system progressive tax systems will reward wealthier citizens with more representation while regressive tax systems will reward the lower and middle classes with more representation.

- Property Taxes are used to elect the Attorney General. Although non home owners are excluded from voting in this branch, corporations are provided the franchise. Property taxes are generally regressive in that a single rate is applied to all properties regardless of values. Wealthier residents still pay more individual amounts but in proportion of the population the majority of the taxes are paid by the bottom eighty percent of the income or wealth distribution. This produces a much fairer voter distribution in that the more numerous segments of the population maintain superiority and majority rulers still pertains. Fortunately the bracket styled value voting reinforces the numerical superiority of the lower 80% of the wealth distribution in regards to property taxes which are already regressed.

- Total Tax Liabilities are used to elect the President. Gross collections of property taxes should bolster the gross amount of taxes paid by the below median classes and middle classes to an amount closer greater than the wealthiest classes. The bracket system will ensure that the majority of votes are still cast by the middle and median or lower classes even after the coefficient is applied.

- Income Taxes are used to elect the Treasurer. Its meant to provide upper income and wealthier voters who typically have a greater understanding of financial principles and mechanisms a moderate advantage in representation. The bracket system ensures that the middle class gains much more emphasis in the voter distribution even when the wealthiest provided a small advantage. It should be noted that most bracket systems will still surrender the majority of votes to the median and lower classes due to their increased numbers but an empowered middle class should improve public sector administration and finance.

- The Judicial branch is abolished and in its stead stands a judicial legislature elected as a check on the absence of the General Legislature and installment of Executive law. Judges will have an increased role in interpreting the application of laws and policies as three canons will be present rather than just one with more opportunity for contradictory or divergent laws to be argued. Each elected Justice can hold multiple seats within its jurisdiction and earn several different circuits.

Disadvantages;

- The likelihood of creating a cult of personality within one of the three executive branches is increased as they enjoy significantly improved powers over legislation and administration. The threat is mitigated by the fact they are sundered into three distinct branches with lower tiers of government in similar permutations or conventional combinations.

- The Treasury Branch maintains the fulcrum of oversight as it manages the budgets and has access to the proprietary information of the other two branches; funding can be withheld or negotiated for improved function or accepted culpability. Otherwise a more mature system of oversight must be manufactured through committees staffed with appointments from the Executive branches not directly involved in the operation of the critical agency. Access to information will provide an opportunity to cure or remedy disagreement through the court system or media. A court system can accommodate lawsuits and challenges from the other Executive branches or political parties with the Media leveraging public opinion. The distribution of information between independent branches will be necessary during crises and the committee based oversight system would have a dual function for coordinating responses prior to and during events.

- Direct Representation is minimal. There are no jurisdiction dependent legislators to rely on when advocating for regional or personal interests. This might have a beneficial effect of eliminating corruption but it will certainly increase tensions when economic or martial security is strained or compromised.

Specifications;

Executive;

- 2.ii.x.c (Tripartite Executive Presidential), iv.1.9 (Sub routine, Laws, Triangulation), 5.a (National), 6.a.iii (6 year terms), b.i (1 terms maximum), c.i (lifetime maximum);

d.i (sum of elected and appointed), 7.a.i (publicly funded), b.i.x (Presidential), **ii.xx.ccc (Value Voting, bracket),** c.x (direct elections), **8.a.iv.c.ii.e.iii.a.b (tax liability, total, persons and corporate entities),** v.b (Citizen), b.i.ii (eligibility for voting and holding office), c.i (exclusive), 10.b (voluntary voting), 14.a (Macro-political Vote, Alpha)

- 2.ii.x.cc (Tripartite Executive Treasury), iv.1.5.9.10 (Sub routine, Laws, Appropriations, Triangulation, Taxation), 5.a (National), 6.a.ii (4 year terms), b.iii (3 terms maximum), c.ii (intermittent maximum), d.ii (sum of elected), 7.a.i (publicly funded), b.i.x (Presidential), **ii.xx.ccc (Value voting, bracket),** c.x (direct elections), **8.a.iv.c.ii.c.iii.a.b (tax liability, income, personal and corporate entities),** v.b (Citizen), b.i.ii (eligibility for voting and holding office), c.i (exclusive); 10.b (voluntary voting), 14.a (Macro-political Vote, Alpha)

- 2.ii.x.ccc (Tripartite Executive Attorney General), iv.1.2.9 (Sub Routine; Laws Oversight, Triangulation), 5.a. (National), 6.a.ii (4 year terms), b.ii (2 terms maximum), c.i (lifetime maximum), d.i (sum of elected and appointed), 7.a.i (publicly funded), b.i.x Presidential), **ii.xx.ccc (Value voting, bracket),** c.x (direct elections), **8.a.iv.c.ii.b.iii.a (tax liability, property, natural persons only),** v.b (Citizen), b.i.ii (eligibility for voting and holding office), c.i (exclusive), 10.b (voluntary voting), 14.a (Macro-political Vote, Alpha)

Legislative;

- 1.i.x.z (Unicameral legislature, 1st house,), ii.x (Representative), iii.6 (Judicial), 5.a (National), 6.a.iii (6 year terms), b.iii (Unlimited), c.i (Lifetime), c.i (sum of elected and appointed positions), 7.a.i (publicly funded), b.ii.xxxx (One citizen = One vote), c.x (direct elections), 8.a.vii.x. (Lawyers), 8.a.v.b (Citizen), b.ii (to hold office), c.i (exclusive), 10.b (voluntary), 12.b (Districts), 13.a.i (Representative of Population, by jurisdiction), **13.h (Legislative Brokers)**

Judicial:

- 3.a.iv (Abolished Judicial), 5.a (National)

Although its unlikely that a conventional democracy will be converted to a tax based system and maintain its implicit legitimacy there may be evolutions where a single chamber or branch is converted to a value voting method for voter franchise. This way a population making the concession can be accommodated with improved representation within a different chamber or branch. The methodology requires patience and effort with improvements in computer sciences and voting infrastructure. It may be more resource intensive but perfection of value voting will pay dividends in its application bond and other forms of wealth representation.

Value voting combined with bracket based coefficients can be a remarkable improvement in establishing republican empires. This is especially true when the voter franchise is attached to taxes as implicit financial support can be rewarded with political empowerment. A central power and satellite system can be manufactured through the use of a coefficient for citizens of the central state and a standard value based vote for residents in the satellite states. A modest amount of power sharing between the different states will be achieved with roles clearly established. The attribute of citizenship can then be exported to the residents of secondary states to coerce stronger allegiances. These relationships will clearly be more complicated than this passage suggests but value voting coefficients provide the foundations for exporting empire a wide variety of wealth representation.

Although not demonstrated in history yet it is near certain that conquered democracies are eventually incorporated within larger political systems. The previously independent nation will maintain its democratic entitlements but subrogate itself to the new federal system. Most include supremacy clauses able to export regulatory systems and criminal laws to subordinated jurisdictions. Incentives will continue to favor the conquering nation as long as it maintains a large advantage in population. This will guarantee that its majority will continue to exert itself politically with predictable divisions in the assumed population perpetuating the state: federal system relationship. The new states will maintain self determination on a significant portion of legal framework and elections allowing the acquisition to settle over time.

It should be stressed that empire and economic union should be used interchangeably. Both have the opportunity to become fully integrated political unions although economic blocs premised on mutual benefit and cooperation are likely to be more durable and more successful. Attaching political enfranchisement to personal tax liabilities and then reciprocating with financial entitlements such as healthcare and retirement benefits is the best way to cement an economic relationship between citizens of previously independent states or nations. It is then more likely that laws and regulations are exported between the jurisdictions of the economic union. There will always be wealth inequalities but metering out standard entitlements will provide the good will necessary to establish a shared history that will transition from economic to cultural over a number of years.

GDP Based
Systems of Representation

Chapter 5

The intent of using an alternate index for voter representation is not to capture a perfectly correlated data. Locating substitutes for demographic representation will never produce an index more perfect than apportioning political power by a standard based on population. It is to create relationships within different aspects of representation that can triangulate between different attribute by attaching more relevancy or importance to one facet and not another. GDP is an aggregate statistic that can be used as an adequate substitute for Popular representation. Components of GDP include demographics as the product is generally a function of the number of people making contributions into the regional economy. Obviously, it isn't the main component as more sophisticated economies may have a low correlation between production and population but as a general thumb when comparing similar economies those with larger populations typically generate larger values than those with smaller populations capturing both productivity and population in the metric.

GDP is just one measure of economic activity which can be used for representation and any other reasonable measure can be substituted as long as it attempts to capture aggregate information. This cant be understated as the premise behind wealth representation is basing political power on a measure of economic activity or wealth. Different nations, regions, or cultures will evaluate a variety of statistics differently and most are acceptable if they can be reasonably correlated to demographics. It is important to make sure that the measure used is an accurate function of population specifically due to the high probability that population will be used as a foil and that the two should have complimentary relationships (producing alignment). Unrelated modes of representation will produce less congruent or equal forms of influence which might invite more criticism, obstruction, inhibition, instability, or exploitation.

There is one overriding reason to index representation to an economic indicator such as GDP. It is so that the more productive and wealthier jurisdictions within a federalist system or economic union have the opportunity to export their more successful economic policies through a positive gradient in representation. The increased number of representatives will permit the jurisdictions with higher economic output to better ensure passage of economic policies, regulation, fiscal policy, and administration that imitates the policies that produced the differential in wealth and economic product.

Most nations employ a federalist tax policy which redistributes tax revenues from wealthier jurisdictions to poorer jurisdictions. Jurisdictions making net contributions should be rewarded for their effort and if raw tax liabilities aren't factored into representation then other economic data such as GDP should be used. The GDP figure wont take in variance within the rebates involved with Federalist tax policy as raw values outside of the wealth redistribution will be used. This contributes to a more practical strategy of power sharing as poor jurisdictions shouldn't necessarily be penalized while still rewarding wealthier jurisdictions.

In political systems with representation GDP, in terms of population (per capita), will be an indicator of wealth with the differential permitting money to be redistributed to lower GDP (per capita) jurisdictions regardless of political party affiliation. Representation according to GDP would provide efficiencies to jurisdictions with more GDP per capita than the average GDP per capita as the differential between the actual figure and the average figure will be used to dictate the number of representation afforded to the jurisdiction.

Systems of representation based on GDP can be calculated with two divergent methods. The first is using a raw figure and comparing values regardless of population. The second method divides the GDP value by population to arrive at a per capita value. The adjusted value acts as a coaxial representational coefficient with the factor determining the difference in the number of representatives apportioned to the jurisdiction. This is almost always premised on popular representation. The two coefficients are used in tandem. For example, if the number of representatives is determined by population and the jurisdiction with a population of 1.2 million earns 6 officers with a per capita

GDP based coaxial coefficient of 1.7 then the final amount of proportional representation will be increased to 10. A similar state with 1.2 million residents and only a 1.0 per capita GDP would only earn the original 6 officers producing a favorable gradient for the wealthier population.

The per capita value is a higher order as it more accurately captures both economic data and demographic data. Otherwise, a high GDP state with a low population would have the same number of representatives as a high GDP state with a high population netting the smaller population more proportional votes than the larger population state. The distribution of economic representation in proportion of population will provide a more accurate numerical figure to measure the actual deviation from the average which is the value to be rewarded or penalized. The two modes of determining numerical representation can then be offset by each other in binary legislature systems or work in antagonism in even more complex governments. It cant be understated that representation based on economic components are meant to incorporate demographic data within the numerical product in the same respect demographic representation is typically correlated to economy. GDP based representation works best as a foil to standard demographic based representation and will complement other branches or chambers within the political system.

The **Producer Republic** combines a GDP per capita model of representation within a unicameral legislature with three demographic based elections for executive branches. GDP is primarily an economic indicator but the fact that it is per capita does produce a regression back to demographics so that the different regions or states will have comparable representation centered around the population of each jurisdiction. The Presidential branch's election remains dedicated to non economic demographics and continues to appoint federal judiciary. The concentration of power should be an adequate check on the legislature now coupled to wealth representation.

Producer Republic

Primary Traits;

- Tripartite Executive

- Unicameral Legislature based on GDP Representation
- Appointed Judicial

Advantages;

- In most respects the Producer Republic is identical to a standard tripartite government which has equivalency with contemporary democracies.
- Correlating representation to GDP (per capita) is an effective way to capture demographic variables as well as economic variables in the measure of the proportion of representation the jurisdiction. GDP is definitely a function of population in properly function economies as larger populations generally capture larger relative GDP's.
- Higher GDP is often a reflection of more mature and efficient economic policies, which are cultural as well as institutional. Indexing representation to GDP allows more populous and wealthier jurisdictions to export their economic ideologies. This way they propagate across more jurisdictions more quickly and improve economy in the larger region or nation.
- A Tripartite Executive ensures that no single individual assumes too much power within the political system especially after the Presidential branch retains appointment powers over the judicial branch.
- A unicameral legislature is used to streamline efficiency in legislation production and to maximize response times. There is no historical data demonstrating the unicameral legislatures are more fickle or more reactionary than bicameral legislatures. If anything they have demonstrated more agility.

Disadvantages;

- Significant divergence between regional GDP's can invalidate the mandate for democratic representation as wealth is rewarded more than demography. In certain circumstances, cultures of auto-colonialism will permeate one region and seek to exploit the other less represented jurisdictions. Liberal policies typically accompany larger populations which should negate the tendency to seek profits at the expense of community but instances of economic unions including multiple independent nations. Using a per capita value mitigates many of these deficits but the differential can still be abused by corrupt or inept politicians.

Specifications;

Executive;

- 2.ii.x.c (Tripartite Executive Presidential), 5.a (National), 6.a.iii (6 year terms), b.i (1 terms maximum), c.i (lifetime maximum), d.ii (sum of elected), 7.a.i (publicly funded), b.i.x (Presidential), ii.xxxx (One citizen = One vote), c.x (direct elections), 8.a.v.b (Citizen), b.i.ii (eligibility for voting and holding office), c.i (exclusive), 10.b (voluntary voting)

- 2.ii.x.cc (Tripartite Executive Treasury), 5.a (National), 6.a.ii (4 year terms), b.iii (3 terms maximum), c.ii (intermittent maximum), d.ii (sum of elected), 7.a.ii.x.xx.a.xxx (privately funded by citizen, domestic corporations, and government), b.i.x (Presidential), b.ii.xxxx (One citizen = One vote), c.x (direct elections), 8.a.v.b (citizen), b.i.ii (for voting and holding office), c.i (exclusive), 10.b (voluntary voting).

- 2.ii.x.ccc (Tripartite Executive Attorney General), 5.a. (National), 6.a.ii (4 year terms), b.ii (2 terms maximum), c.i (lifetime maximum), d.i (sum of elected and appointed), 7.a.ii.x (privately funded by citizens), b.i.x (Presidential), ii.xxxx (One citizen = One vote), c.x (direct elections), 8.a.v.b. (citizen), b.i.ii (for voting and holding office), c.i (exclusive), 10.b (voluntary voting).

Legislature;

- 1.i.x.z (Unicameral legislature, 1st house), ii.x (Representative), iii.1.2.3.5.7.10 (Laws, Oversight, Ratification, Appropriations, Appointments, Taxation), 5.a. (National), 6.a.iii (6 year terms), b.ii (2 terms maximum), c.ii (Intermittent), c.ii (sum of elected only), 7.a.i (publicly funded), b.ii.xxxx (One citizen = One vote), c.x (direct elections), 8.a.v.b (citizen), b.i.ii (to vote and to hold office), c.i (exclusive), 10.b (voluntary), 12.a (Jurisdiction), **13.b.ii (Representative of GDP, per capita)**

Judicial;

- 3.a.i. (Judicial, circuits), b.i (Judicial powers only), c.ii.x.2 (appointed by the President), 5.a. (National), 6.a.iii (6 year term), b.iii (3 terms maximum), c.i (lifetime maximum), 8.v.b, b.ii (citizen to hold office)

The single chamber legislature is indexed to per capita GDP which presents the opportunity to maximize growth and foster more competitive legislation and regulation. By utilizing per capita values for GDP the nation guarantees itself that representation will still be proportional to population although its in terms of relative productivity. Economy is the most important function of the state with all citizens interacting constantly with conditions dependent on taxes, incomes, and employment status. The military and national security are also critical but most of the citizen don't typically enlist without coercion or incentive and many don't necessarily follow current events and international fairs with the same level of interest as they do the economy. In many respect government is the way a nation organizes and manages its economy which lends credibility and argument to devising its representation to include a component of economy along with demographics.

In this respect it can be concluded that the Producer Republic will be more able to capitalize on hidden advantages and increase productivity, job creation, reduce tax burdens while maximizing revenues, and managing budgets more efficiently when the most productive states gain more representation within the system. The **Echo-Republic** attempts to bound farther into productivity by capturing both per capita and straight GDP values for legislative representation and merging it with the most conventional of Presidential democratic formats. To make it more formidable the politicians within both chambers can be Legislative brokers with all of offices organized by jurisdictions granting each politician access to the most possible seats.

Echo-Republic

Primary Traits;

- Unitary Executive
- Upper chamber indexed to Straight GDP with Legislative Brokers.
- Lower chamber indexed to Per Capita GDP with Legislative Brokers
- Appointed Judicial

Advantages;

- Both legislative branches permit Legislative Brokers to assume multiple seats within the same chamber and the opposing chamber. Both are apportioned by jurisdiction, which means a single residency makes the individual eligible for all of the available seats determined by the index of representation and coefficient.
- One legislative chamber is representative of straight GDP while the other is representative of per capital GDP which fosters an purposeful imbalance to imitate conventional tensions between Senates and Representative chambers. Senates are typically not representative of population or proportional in any respect. This creates a differential between states with different populations typically favoring smaller population regions. It was intended to mitigate the advantages larger population states have in representational congresses. The same measure of inequality is captured but in relation to productivity and GDP rather than population. It generally moderates a political system by disrupting majority rule,

- There is a third rail in wealth representation. Legislative Brokers from richer and more populous states can consolidate tremendously more power than individuals from smaller and poorer states. They will have the advantage in contributions and resources. It is even possible that one Senator maintain more access to the government than an entire state or province as their number of seats can be greater than those apportioned to the territory. Senators from the smaller or poorer states are insulated by virtue of the jurisdiction eligibility component with all competitors equivalent in resources. The advantage is in scales with the larger wealthier states providing more momentum for seat consolidation than the smaller poorer states. It's a matter of probabilities and possibilities.

- The Reserve Branch maintains all appointment confirmation powers. Both legislatures contribute members making the institution a more appropriate venue for influencing the executive branch. Members have oversight powers as well allowing it to follow up on the appointments and review performance. All members are afforded permanent access but the increased number of politicians will dilute each individual contribution.

- The intermittent restriction on legislature tenures means members will leave one chamber, enter another, and possibly return at a later date. Intermittent terms actually increases the chances for returning politicians as a larger number of seats within the jurisdiction will open up more frequently. This presents an opportunity for more sophisticated strategies to be employed by parties when attempting to manage majorities in all or some of the institutions.

Disadvantages;

- Both legislative chambers reflect economy in their representation which will permanently alter the culture and sociology of the nation and its people. There is an argument for preserving demographic based representation in that it recognizes only the individual and their identity but economy is our most prevalent environment. It is expected that once political representation is a derivative of economy or wealth more of the population will think in terms of economy. The extra focus will be a derivative of the improved incentives and alignment of interests. This should prompt the median populations to more accurately interpret the more important economic issues in terms of personal consequence and identity.

Specifications;

Executive;

- 2.i.iii (Unitary Executive, Elected), 5.a (National), 6.a ii (4 year terms), b.iii (3 maximum concurrent terms), c.i (lifetime maximum), d.i (sum of both elected and appointed) 7.a.i (publicly funded), b.i.x (Presidential), ii.xxxx (One citizen = One vote), c.x (direct elections), 8.v.b. (Citizen), b.i.ii (to hold office and to vote), c.i (exclusive), 10.b (voluntary voting)

Legislature;

- 1.i.xx.z (Bicameral legislature, 1st house), ii.x (Representative), iii.1.2.3.5 (Laws, Oversight, Ratification, Appropriations), 5.a. (National), 6.a.iii (6 year terms), b.ii (2 terms maximum), c.ii (Intermittent), c.ii (sum of elected only), 7.a.i (publicly funded), b.ii.xxxx (One citizen = One vote), c.x (direct elections), 8.a.v.b (citizen), b.i.ii (to vote and to hold office), c.i (exclusive), 10.b (voluntary), **12.a (Jurisdictions), 13.b.ii (Representative of GDP, Per Capita), 13.h (Legislative Brokers)**

- 1.i.xx.zz (Bicameral legislature, 2nd house), ii.xx (Representative), iii.1.3.5.10 (Laws, Ratification, Appropriations, Taxing), 5.a. (National), 6.a.ii (4 year terms), b.iii (3 terms maximum), c.ii (Intermittent); c.ii (sum of elected only), 7.a.i (publicly funded), b.ii.xxxx (One citizen = One vote), c.x (direct elections); 8.a.v.b (citizen), b.i.ii (to vote and to hold office), c.i (exclusive), 10.b (voluntary), **12.a (Jurisdictions), 13.b.i (Representative of GDP, Straight), 13.h (Legislative Brokers)**

Judicial;

- 3.a.i. (Judicial, Circuit), b.i (Judicial powers only), c.ii.x.1 (appointed by the Unitary), 5.a. (National), 6.a.iii (6 year term), b.iii (3 terms maximum), c.i (lifetime maximum), 8.v.b, b.ii (citizen to hold office).

Reserve:

- 4.i.a (Reserve Board, admitting all retired members), ii.b.5.7 (legislative sub routine oversight, and appointment), ii.d.x.xx.ii (repealing legislature, excising legislators and judges, and excommunication), iii.b (unicameral), iv.1.a.2.b.c (pool of retired national legislators and judges), v.e (permanent)

The Reserve Board is an important facet for control within the Echo-Republic with retired politicians gaining permanent membership. When groups of politicians from one party are dismissed after losing elections they can defend their previous positions within the Reserve board. This helps moderate the extreme swings a population can experience due to changing economic conditions and progressive movements. The permanence of membership is a double edged sword in that the roll call continues to grow year after year and much faster with excess turnover in the two legislative chambers.

The Reserve Board has sole power over Appointment confirmations and an equal voice in Oversight which makes it a potent component of the government. The General Legislature maintains impeachment powers but the excommunication and exorcism powers are found within the Reserves and. Theses powers can extend the Reserve Board's reach into all other facets of the government. It can be a powerful deterrent to anti-democratic measures being employed within the elections process and a means to coerce bipartisan or centrist efforts.

Reserve board members are not excluded from running for office again which makes the institution a perfect segue for politicians seeking to reposition themselves within new chambers or new branches. The constant interaction will keep them political active, more relevant, and more competitive but limits might be necessary to discourage repetitive and unproductive attempts at office if rejected party members run and lose too often. The powers of the Reserve Board are meant to be attractive enough to entice losing members to simply accept defeat and retirement.

The **Garm Republic** employs a legislature split by per capita and straight GDP based representation but it abandons the conventional form of democracy for an executive legislature based on Net Federalist Tax representation, with legislative broker powers, and an elected judicial system with executive representation. These deviations are significant enough for its classification as a separate class of political system.

Garm Republic

Primary Attributes

- No Executive branch
- No Judicial Branch
- Unicameral Executive Legislature
- Bicameral General Legislature
- Unicameral Judicial Legislature

Advantages

- The Unitary Executive Legislature is representative of Net Federalist Taxes which rewards those jurisdictions making more contributions than withdrawals. This might seem unfair but the states can lobby with their general legislatures to redistribute taxes more fairly providing them more influence within the executive branch. Other states will elect to maintain their federalist tax advantages rather than gain executive legislators and focus on the state level governments.

- Federalist tax policy can change from year to year and if a state transitions from net contributor to net recipient then the representative seat is immediately rescinded. The reverse is true which immediately authorizes a new election for a new representative.

- Those elected within the Executive legislature are entitled to Legislative broker powers allowing them to accumulate a diverse cross section of seats within either of the Legislatures. The standard exclusions apply that limit the selections of oversight committees the Legislative Brokers can petition for but it would grant more access to taxing and budgetary committees. Often an Executive Legislative Broker will consolidate representation on oversight committees to guard against the consolidation of power by other brokers on other executive committees. Due to the fickle nature of executive representation a state could lose access to its representative in subsequent years but those individuals will remain in the government as general legislators.

- Indexing representation to straight GDP in the Upper Chamber and per capita GDP in the Lower Chamber attempts to offset the deficiencies of both by using one another to triangulate a more moderate position.

- By incentivizing higher taxes through representation and discouraging corrupt rebating strategies, it better guarantees that federal dollars are distributed more evenly across all of the participating regions and ensure a stronger more vibrant public sector. Not only `will economic policies be exported based on successful economic engineering but those jurisdictions that contribute more tax dollars to the economic union will have more representation within in.

- The elected judicial branch operates under a congressional structure with Executive Representation. This concentrates more judicial power in a smaller number or individuals by letting each one occupy several different positions within multiple circuits. Each Executive Representative will capture a number of varied circuits and seats in proportion to the population represented but where the location of the circuits is not coupled to the origin of the elected judge.

- Each Executive Representative will employ a moderate number of judges and lawyers to staff the larger number of committees they are responsible for during their terms. The appointments they make can be regulated by the legislature to limit the amount of corruption or interference the Executive Representative can cause by the re-arrangement and re-ordering of their staff between cases or during cases.

Disadvantages

- The electorate will have to be careful about the accumulation of political experience as longer terms with unlimited numbers invites the abuse of institutional powers during campaigns. Often in the guise of deregulating political markets offering more competition for donations but really an attempt to enfranchise those already seated in the legislature and those segments of the population with much greater disposable incomes and permanent wealth.

Specifications;

Executive:

- 2.iii (Abolished Executive); 5.a.b.c (National)

Legislature:

- 1.i.xx.z (Multi-cameral legislature, 1st house), ii.xx (Representative), iii.4.a. (Unitary Executive Powers), 5.a (National), 6.a.ii (4 year terms), b.iii (Unlimited), c.i (Lifetime), c.ii (sum of elected and appointed), 7.a.ii.x.xx (privately funded by citizen, corporations), b.ii.xxxx (One citizen = One vote), c.x (direct elections), 8.a.v.b (Citizen), b.ii (criteria to hold office), c.i (exclusive), 10.a (compulsory), 12.b (Jurisdictions), **13.c.ii (Representative of Net Taxes), 13.h (Legislative Broker)**

- 1.i.xx.zz (Multi-cameral legislature, 2nd house), ii.x (Representative), iii.1.2.3.5.7.10 (Laws, Oversight, Treaty Ratification, Appropriations, Appointments, Taxes), 5.a (National), 6.a.iii (6 year terms), b.ii (Unlimited), c.ii (Intermittent), c.ii (sum of elected only), 7.a.ii.x.xxx (privately funded by citizen, and government), b.ii.xxxx (One citizen = One vote), c.x (direct elections), 8.a.v.b (Citizen), b.i.ii (to vote and to hold office), c.i (exclusive), 10.b (voluntary), 12.b (Districts), 13.b.i **(Representative of GDP, Straight)**

- 1.i.xx.zz (Multi-cameral legislature, 2nd house).ii.x (Representative), iii.1.2.3.5.7.10 (Laws, Oversight, Treaty Ratification, Appropriations, Appointments, Taxes), 5.(National), 6.a.iii (6 year terms), b.ii (Unlimited), c.ii (Intermittent), c.ii (sum of elected only), 7.a.ii.x.xx.a.xxx (Privately funded by citizens, domestic corporations, and governments), 8.a.v.b (Citizen), b.i.ii (to vote and to hold office), c.i (exclusive), 10.b (voluntary), 12.b (Districts), 13.b.ii **(Representative of GDP, Per Capita)**

- 1.i.xx.zzz (Multi-cameral legislature, 3rd house,), ii.x (Representative), iii.6 (Judicial), 5.a (National), 6.a.iii (6 year terms), b.iii (Unlimited), c.i (Lifetime), c.i (sum of elected and appointed positions), 7.a.i (publicly funded), b.ii.xxxx (One citizen = One vote), c.x (direct elections), 8.a.vii.x. (Lawyers), 8.a.v.b (Citizen), b.ii (to hold office), c.i (exclusive), 10.b (voluntary), 12.b (Districts), 13.a.i **(Representative of Population, by jurisdiction), 13.f (Executive Representation)**

Judicial:

- 3.iv (Abolished Judicial), 5.a (National)

The Judicial Legislative system requires the most scrutiny considering its atypical structure. Each state elects one Supreme Justice who is apportioned a number of votes within the judicial legislature in proportion to the size of the population of the jurisdiction. This figure is used when determining the outcomes of supreme court verdicts and when dictating the number of circuit appointments the justice may make. The Justices divide themselves between the various courts and circuits by dedicating a numerical amount of appointments. Each Justice is permitted to appoint a proportional amount of judges (according to population and open positions) within the circuits whose committee the

Justice sits on. The appointed judges are not subject to confirmation by the General Legislature.

The second most important component is the fact that representation within the executive legislature is dependent on net federalist tax contributions. Knowing that even in evenly distributed system half of the jurisdictions must lose access it will create momentum for jurisdictions to dedicate funds to other jurisdictions or to raise national taxes in order to create more efficient gradients for representation within the executive legislature. This system provides an opportunity for states excluded one year to petition for changes in tax policy which will permit them to vote in subsequent years. Fairer allocations of federalist tax moneys will also result in more equal representation which could imitate a format equivalent to popular representation.

GDP based representation can be an incredibly potent form of wealth representation which benefits all participants in an economic system or political union. It shouldn't be constrained only to the forms provided as examples in this chapter or book and there are certainly more aggregate statistics that can be used for more precise representation. The arguments for establishing economic based representation are older than democracy itself and found in corporate systems of governance. There should be no doubt that the premise will spur on a revolution in representation which can open a myriad of different instruments and mechanisms for political control which will be advocated for by both benign and malevolent parties. Economy isn't base but in its present state it bears the burden of excessive exploitation. Its possible that by conjoining political representation and economic representation that more of the population applies more scrutiny and participates more in the political process.

Bond Based
Systems of Representation

Chapter 6

Bond Representation can be one of the most useful tools for political representation as their schedule is typically fixed and finite permitting systems and institutions to be conjoined on temporary bases with clearly stipulated terms. They can be tremendously important to forming new institutions by enfranchising specific populations with voting powers and providing implicit financial support. Bond representation can extend beyond one jurisdiction or federal system to a larger economic union between many nations. The representation can be measured and metered by all participants at an initial stage and then moderated on an ongoing basis for future influence. Bonds are the perfect public sector instrument for empire building and union formation.

Basing a voter franchise on bond consumption can empower conventional states maintaining only taxing powers with the advantages in capitalization typically reserved for public stock companies. The premise is remarkable in its application for insurrections and rebellions as the emergent government has a greater chance of success due to the improved funding capabilities. Financing war efforts is critical to both fledgling states and established nations and any government which can expand its base of support and revenues by offering bonds with common stock properties at fair market values will have a greater likelihood of success. In one stroke of finance, it could form allegiances with internal populations and alliances with external states, nations, or corporations. The government maximizes its own access to the resources necessary for waging war or rebellion. The temporary suffrage provided by the bond based representation can be adjusted after the event to reign in foreign involvement or prevent any corporate concentration of political representation.

Maintaining one chamber of legislature for bond representation captures the positive aspects of market capitalization without compromising the rest of the democratic government. A number of different methods can be employed to ensure that majority rule continues to apply while the wealth representation serves as a critical source of war time funding. The intersection of districts and the installation of residency requirements, corporate and personal, will preclude one citizen or one company from consolidating too much influence. Permitting local municipalities to compete for representation will offset some of the advantages the upper classes and corporations maintain in the wealth based system especially when large numbers of the middle and median class make moderate contributions. Wealthier citizens will compete with other wealthy citizens in their communities and districts while poorer citizens will generally compete with other poor communities and districts.

Not only is the bond representation chamber critical during war for financing it does introduce business efficiencies and interests into the legislature without corrupting the branches or chambers of government and avoids the pitfalls of deregulated campaign finance and an unrestricted private sector lobby. A chamber of congress devoted exclusively to bond based representation is a concession that can be used to negotiate political reforms that include public financing of elections and regulating lobbyism with higher ethical standards. More importantly, it limits the access to one facet of government freeing the other components from the tendency of politicians to accept deregulation within the political markets. Obviously, the two should not be used in tandem.

Coupling voter entitlements to treasury bonds is probably the most effective way to establish international institutions as it attracts investment, rewards contributions, and most important it is adjustable year after year and can accommodate different political conditions. Bond based representation is correlated to commitment but operates exclusive of economy and population despite the alignment; with greater motivation a participant can overcome shortfalls in population and GDP. Economic Unions can be predicated on the mutualization of debts with bond based voter franchises attached as incentive. If carefully coordinated institutions can be vested with political influence proportional to population or some other index and then reciprocate representation within the member nations legislatures by persistently investing in bonds. Other strategies might involve manipulating social security or retirement programs as a means to moderate the political franchise provided to wealthier individuals or corporations through bond based representation; this would be useful in offsetting an improved franchise for institutional investors by permitting government treasurers to leverage public pensions and public programs.

Bond representation can be used in reparations or empire formation when the conquering nation sets repayment conditions and demands political representation through those conditions. Under these conditions democracies could be subjugated to a dominant power where the population maintains many of its former privileges but where another nation makes substantial contributions to how it regulates and governs itself. This mechanism will operate at higher efficiencies when more than a single conquering nation is granted voter franchise; with two or three nations gaining a majority of representation in the legislature it permits the conquered populations to triangulate between the occupiers to gain political advantage and more successfully navigate the dire consequences of the failed war effort. Obviously if the conquering nations are all democracies themselves the net impact of this form of reparation or occupation will be more favorable than if the offending nations are autocratic or colonial. In fact over time and if the representation is reciprocated it presents an opportunity to forge a union or federal system rather than an empire.

The most effective way to ensure integrity in a bond based institution is to prohibit it from issuing its own bonds. This would prevent the institution from controlling its own representation and minimizing the likelihood a monopoly forms. Bond based representation used for war chambers limits the influence foreign entities can gain during events. The voting franchise can be extended for temporary periods and then retracted. The bond issuing powers can be assigned to the another executive branch, another legislative branch, or even state governments. Without this separation of powers a chamber or branch could determine the majority bond holders voting in its own election. It could damn the state or nation to perpetual class warfare or foreign interloping.

Bond based systems of representation are also likely to be the first form of wealth representation acquired as government financiers in the private sector are more likely to earn this concession due to the high incidence of public finance crises. This is important for established governments as it will likely be the only opportunity to reform its democratic system. Most nations suffer from a sclerosis and actively resist even the most practical of reforms. Most of the other wealth based systems of representation require the incorporation of a new state or new institution. Both are far less frequent than the number or wars and financial disasters that occur every few decades.

Bond representation is the first opportunity for resident corporations to gain a voter franchise. Many democratic nations already grant access through under-regulated campaign finance systems and unduly emphasize their role as job creators which can be a terribly corrupting force within politics. This is not to be excused by a corporate voter franchise based on bond consumption but rather replaced by it. The corporations will make contributions to the state above those moneys already conceded through taxes and should be rewarded with the equivalent of one vote. If a maximum of one vote can be gained the extra consumption provided by small and medium sized corporations will aid in the states ability to earn a negative borrowing rate.

Bond representation need not maintain parity with one vote for every person. It need not be a substitute for popular representation and in fact can be a supplement with all residents or citizens enfranchised with one voter per person but where each bond purchased might equal 1/200 of a vote for every part of interest paid. A $10,000 dollar bond paying 2% would provide 100/100ths of a vote or equal 1 additional personal vote. The bond would carry a term of 5 years requiring it to be replaced in order to perpetuate the voter franchise. The 2% rate on a 10 year note would almost certainly provide a negative borrowing rate which is pivotal in securing emergency funds and stable economic stimulus. If necessary a boundary of $10,000 can be established so that at a maximum a citizen or resident entity could gain only one vote regardless of whether it is an extra vote or initial franchise.

A concept related to but not equivalent to the voter franchise based on interest ratios is a bracket multiplier system. Bond consumers can be divided into two or three brackets with a multiplier in voter franchise. With a two bracket system the threshold can divide consumers into below median and above median groups with one achieving a multiplier of 2x and the other 3x after some minimal threshold in bond investment is exceeded. A three tiered bracket system would produce multipliers of 1x, 2x, and 3x with the differential premised on different volumes of bonds consumed. This mode of wealth representation is intended to favor the middle class with small and medium sized businesses where they will represent the largest segment of the population with the greatest vote multiplier. The wealthiest segment of the population is typically the smallest which means even the largest of the three multipliers wont provide them an excessive advantage over the lower and median classes or the middle classes.

In democracies with one person one vote systems the volume of median or lower class voters, the bottom 80% of the income bracket, will still assume a majority of the votes. If the wealthiest are comprised by the top 2% of income earners, and provided a 3x vote multiplier they will still only represent a miniscule fraction of the adjusted total vote. The middle class voters typically make up the top 20%, less the 2% afforded to the leisure class, of the income distribution and would capture nearly half of the adjusted vote with a 2x vote multiplier. The lower class loses a portion of its franchise when compared to the volume of eligible voters but it shares many of the same interests as the middle class and can expect that the over-representation of the middle class will work out to their advantage in more instances than not.

The middle class suffers under many of the same economic stressors the lower class does with higher education rates making them the best class to focus an advantage in voter representation. They typically assume a more diverse demographic disposition and encompass the largest amount of professional or technical occupations. Providing the middle class with the most proportional representation within a democratic system should predispose the nation to better decision making at the polls. They can be counted on to digest the most news content and maintain the most dynamic perspective within a corporate hierarchy. The middle class also includes small and medium sized business owners allowing them to accommodate more than the professional or employee perspective. This segment of the population will be better protected from financial and economic stressors permitting them to make less emotional and more rational decisions regarding fiscal policy, public administration, national security, and regulation.

Straight value voting with bond assets has merits in systems where both public sectors and private sectors are enfranchised. A significant portion of treasury bonds are already held within public pension funds providing governors more influence in national elections. Empowering governments as electors in federal elections takes into account constituents like other aggregators of representation. It is similar to basing a representational coefficient on GDP or tax liabilities. The economies of scale in public sector investment are heavily favored over private investment especially when they deploy retirement programs to supplement public pensions. The return constraints on federal bonds where negative borrowing rates are earned will discourage finance companies and other institutional investors from purchasing too many bonds – they can earn much higher returns with shorter terms from other sources while return on federal bonds actually produce losses compared with inflation for interim or short term investments.

Institutions can be excluded – in particular public pensions, social security programs, federal reserves (central banks), state treasuries, and most corporate entities so that only personal and corporate consumption is rewarded with improved voter franchise. It is also possible to exclude assets based on nationality and residence. This will protect the integrity of an election system but exporting a voter franchise to satellite jurisdictions can lay the fundamentals to a sounder and stronger empire. The federal government could slowly integrate consumers from other states or smaller nations that would not imbalance the current demographic or economic disposition of the nation.

The intellectual or business class would be targeted first creating a durable economic relations and a positive gradient towards improved integration in both nations. Later it may be more feasible to permit government institutions to join in the voter franchise with full reciprocity expected. It would then be only a matter of time until contract laws, regulations, civil liberties and rights are exported/imported manufacturing a more complete and more permanent economic bloc and political union. An interesting reform to bond based representation would be exclusivity for governments so that corporations and individuals were excluded. The exclusivity is premised on universal suffrage continuing to apply to all residents equally regardless of wealth. All citizens continue to vote and are complemented by the governors leveraging the bond based representation.

Bond based representation is slightly easier to manage than tax liability based representation despite the similarities. The single asset can be tracked more easily with the vote calculated much more easily. Effort is still required especially with secondary markets permitting consumers to trade and sell federal bonds freely on an open market. The solutions are mostly internet technology based with automated systems able to capture brokerage information during an eligibility period to dictate the exact proportion of value voting earned or the vote coefficient applied. Gaming the system with period specific consumption can be regulated or outlawed with reasonable ease. The work is well worth the return especially when attaching representation to international institutions. Institutions like the World Bank and IMF already operate on similar principles lending legitimacy to developing a universally accepted system for distributing wealth representation by bonds or other durable assets.

A competitive bond based systems would have the lower governments raise money with bonds and use the proceeds to purchase bonds from a higher government providing representation. This will force the government consumers to pay a premium for the representation. The higher government would achieve much lower borrowing rates for capital intensive projects, economic stimulus, and leverage through borrowing. Most of the money borrowed from the residents and lower governments will be returned through federalist tax policy determined by the legislature an unaffected by the bond based representation. The wealthier states can earn more representation in executive elections but smaller and poorer jurisdictions will be the recipients of larger contributions from federalist tax policy.

Even in open market bond based representation systems the inclusion of governments produces a regression back to the mean. Individuals typically don't have access to the leverage corporations and governments do meaning they are more disadvantaged. However, government generally pay lower rates on their bonds than do corporations granting them more access to the system of representation. The combination of personal and governmental representation will be weighted more than corporate representation adding credibility and integrity to the program. Its not a system of equal entitlement but there should be enough competitive interests to make it a formidable form of representation and public finance

Implementing a straight value voting method for one half of a bipartite executive branch while maintaining a standard numerical voting method based on popular representation for the unicameral legislature and other half of the bipartite executive is a measured way to introduce a bond based representation. The **Bonded Bipartite** does not distribute executive responsibilities evenly between the two halves; all of the domestic law enforcement and treasury responsibilities are apportioned to the popularly elected executive while the bond based representation applies to the military and judicial responsibilities. The majority of government operations are not tethered to financial instruments or wealth providing plausibility and legitimacy.

The Presidential executive is decoupled from popular representation to make it more compatible with other nations or states in political union or empire. This way relationships can be forged with financial contributions and bond purchases. Its expected that the vast majority of the representation will still be afforded to state treasuries and public pension managers but the promise of even limited political entitlement can go a long way when forming economic unions. The Presidential executive will remain heavily indebted to the legislature for continued funding through the budget as most militaries cant be funded perpetually through annual bond purchases. Obviously, if there comes a time when foreign allies are represented too much within the Presidential bipartite it can forsake its judicial powers and become an independent and internally institution. The states can bolster their individual armies and the justices can be emancipated with popular elections rather than appointments.

Bonded Bipartite

Primary Traits;

- Bipartite Executive
- Unicameral Legislature
- Appointed Judicial

Advantages;

- Federal Bond consumption provides voting rights to elect the President-Judicial Executive.

- Popular elections still govern the unicameral legislature which is indexed to GDP representation for the number of representatives per jurisdiction.

- Popular elections still govern the elections of the Attorney General Executive.

- Federal institutions are excluded from the elections process so that they cant help guarantee that the current administration remains in power.

- State and city treasuries and public pensions will accumulate significant amounts of bonds for use in elections. It is expected that the public sector maintain larger proportions of treasuries in order to balance out institutional private investors and the wealthiest citizens. One mechanism to better guarantee this would be state or city level retirement systems for residents which leverage payroll taxes to accumulate federal treasuries for more predictable revenues at longer terms.

- Representation based on Federal or State bond assets encourages more of the population to purchase bonds, which alleviates pressure on tax policy to provide the majority of funding for the tier of government. Increased personal consumption of bonds is expected after attaching the voter franchise. The largest bond consumers are generally pension funds and investment banks but may soon be permanent funds which would be a major component of empowering state or city governments within a democratic economic union.

- Although corporations or unions manage private pensions, the laws regarding fiduciary duty should pertain to demand performance in the domain of vote allocation. Voting publics may retaliate against a company that leverages their pension funds for their shareholder interests when the pension is primarily for the benefit of non management level employees and where their political affiliations are more mixed. These entities might want to hold an internal vote prior to determining how the external vote is apportioned. That or they may opt to refrain from voting in order not to subject themselves to criticism. More sophisticated value voting systems will allow corporate, union, or governmental entities to split their votes in accord with voter distributions within the organization.

- States have access to ample public bond funds and are a fair aggregator of public opinion. Unlike corporations it is expected that a government official vote in accord with their political affiliation despite more mixed distributions within the vested population.

- This structure does not endow foreign individuals and institutions with voting rights within the nation. Representation is conditional on residency or citizenship eligibility criteria, however, bond representation can be the premise or foundation of representation within an economic union when investment capital is exchanged for voting franchises. Terms can be applied to the political entitlements by making bonds available or withholding bonds of various lengths from the bond markets.

- This system can be refined into a bailout process for subordinate governments within an economic or political union (such as the U.S and E.U.). They may be of use in occupations, reconstructions, empire, or coalition building.

Disadvantages;

- Voting demographics can be moderated by withholding access to bonds for public consumption or by overspending and saturating markets with more bonds. Voting dilution and vote concentration can dramatically change jurisdictions election outcomes, especially if consumers relocate to other jurisdictions where they can guarantee themselves more representation. It is expected that these operations will be well regulated and guard against overt manipulation or exploitation. The mechanism would be similar to the corrupting tendency of Gerrymandering with the ability for partisan politics to determine voter eligibility.

Specification;

Executive;

- 2.ii.x.c (Executive Presidential), 5.a (National), 6.a.ii (6 year terms), b.i (3 terms maximum), c.i (lifetime maximum), d.ii (sum of elected), 7.a.i (publicly funded)**, b.i.x (presidential), ii.xx.c (value voting, straight),** c.x (direct elections), 8.a.v.b (citizen), **iv.a.f.2.iii.2 (iv.a.f.2.iii.b (Federal Bonds, Inclusive),** b.i.ii (eligibility for voting and holding office), c.i (exclusive), 10.b (voluntary voting)

- 2.ii.x.cc (Executive Treasury and Attorney General), 5.a (National), 6.a.ii (4 year), b.iiv (Unlimited), c.ii (intermittent maximum), d.ii (sum of elected), 7.a.ii.x.xx.a.xxx (privately funded by citizen, domestic corporations, and government), b.i.x (Presidential), ii.xxxx (One citizen = One vote), c.x (direct elections), 8.a.v.b (citizen), b.i.ii (for voting and holding office), c.i (exclusive), 10.b (voluntary voting).

Legislature

- 1.i.x.z (Unicameral legislature), ii.x (Representative), iii.1.2.3.5.7.10 (Laws, Oversight, Ratification, Appropriations, Appointments, and Taxation), 5.a. (National), 6.a.iii (6 year terms), b.iii (3 terms maximum), c.ii (Intermittent), c.ii (sum of elected only), 7.a.i (publicly funded), b.ii.xxxx (One citizen = One vote), c.x (direct elections), 8.a.v.b (citizen), b.i.ii (to vote and to hold office), c.i (exclusive), 10.b (voluntary), 12.a (Jurisdictions), **13.b.i (Representative of GDP, straight)**

Judicial

- 3.a.i (Judicial, Circuit), b.i (Judicial powers only), c.ii.x 2 (President appoints judges), 5.a. (National), 6.a.iii (6 year term), b.iii (3 terms maximum), c.i (lifetime maximum), 8.v.b, b.ii (citizen to hold office).

Wealth representation based on bonds need not be restricted to a single chamber as is the case of the Bonded Bipartite. Instead it can be applied to both the executive branch and the legislative branch as demonstrated by the **Liability Republic**. In this example bond based representation is premised on both straight value voting and on ratio value voting. The ratio value voting allows the voting franchise to be coupled (exclusive variables) with other voting criteria in order to limit its effect on the election system. The overarching theme of the Liability Republic is representation through financial support and enlistment making it the perfect system for empires and economic unions. In order to gain influence in the government one must either enlist in its military or provide revenues from bond consumption or property taxes. It doesn't distinguish between individual, institutional, or corporate supporters allowing it to attract a large base of support among a diverse cross section of demographic population segments.

Liability Republic

Primary Traits;

- Unitary Executive
- Upper House
- Lower House
- Appointed Judicial

Advantages;

- The system is useful as an export of republican government with most of the political franchise dependent on reciprocal support based on military enlistment, tax liabilities, and bond purchases. By no means is this a form of universal suffrage but it should attract enough support to initiate conversion to a democratic form of government.

- The executive branch is elected by two populations. The first are the enlisted military who gain one vote per person. The second group are those who purchase bonds from the federal government. The voter franchise is dictated by a ratio of interest earned in proportion to the number of current enlisted. This ensures that the total number of votes earned by the bond holders only ever equals that of the current number of enlisted so that both populations have near equal representation. The advantage goes to veteran and retired enlisted who are not tallied in the bond voter franchise but who maintain their voting privileges. It is expected that most of the bond representation will be apportioned to the state treasuries and the governors in charge of them. States can increase their proportion of enlisted by demanding mandatory enlistment at maturity in exchange for education and retirement benefits. In this respect they would be supporting the federal government financially and with recruits which is compensated for with increased representation.

- The upper house of the legislature allocates representation based on net taxes paid into the system. It is the perfect compromise to ensure that neither the central states nor the satellite states are exploited in terms of federalist tax policy. Thos states making fewer contributions than withdrawals will lose representation in the chamber. Those jurisdictions making significantly larger contributions will gain proportional increases in the number of representatives earned.

- The tax used is property values (real estate) which typically use a flat rate applied to the value of the improvement; this will produce a natural regression line that protects majority rule in all participating jurisdictions when complemented by the bracket value voting. Property tax is used rather than incomes to create a more permanent and more obvious attachment between the land associated with the economic union and the financial support providing representation in the union.

- The bond representation offers an interesting opportunity for institutional investors like pension funds and permanent funds to gain access to the government in bulk numbers. It also offers instant compatibility with foreign investors, supporters, with possible implications of immediate economic union.

- Private sector corporate entities and individuals can gain substantial representation in exchange for significant monetary support which can be an inducement attracting the elite classes of emerging economies or satellite states into the economic union. They will earn representation through the property taxes paid on land and homes owned within the jurisdictions and they have the option of purchasing bonds that transmit the voter franchise.

- The citizenship requirement for voting in the executive branch can be lifted in order to incentivize recruitment in the insurrection or revolt stage from foreign legions. This increases the likelihood of forming a viable government with sovereignty and is a predicate for a feudal structure in representation with foreign detachments gaining representation within one branch of a new partner within an economic union.

- The bond based representation in both the executive and second legislative is handled by the Upper House so that neither chamber can determine for itself the proportion of bonds available for use in their elections. Separate bonds for both institutions are issued requiring citizens and states to decide when purchasing the products.

Disadvantages;

- The elites will maintain huge advantages in bond based voter franchises with access to both the executive and the lower house. State governments can try and compete with the corporations and wealthiest of citizens but will be at a major disadvantage with regard to capital resources.

- The inequality in voter representation is partially eliminated by the military enlistment criteria for the Executive branch with the bulk of participation coming from the lower and middle classes.

- The chamber dedicated to tax liabilities offsets the bond based access but disregards those citizens not owning property. It has by far the fairest disposition in voters with median value home owners and lower value both capturing 70% of the total votes while still empowering the top 25% of tax payers with an improved margin of representation.

- The participating states must have strong independent public sectors with their own secure finance system and military industrial complex. The wealth based entitlements are meant to be more dynamic and less reliable – perfect for initializing prototypical unions or for establishing empires based on mutual economy. The central government is designed to imitate an international institution rather than an exclusive federal tier.

- This mode of republic can have democratic sponsors as well as autocratic sponsors with the foreign monetary support making this form of representation compatible with a wider variety of government systems and economic systems. State Capitalist system can interface through financial support or feudal support just as easily as democratic nations. Monetary Democracies are extremely compatible with most corporate governance systems which introduces a third track of compatibility.

Specifications;

Executive;

- 2.i.iii (Unitary Executive, Elected), 5.a (National), 6.a ii (4 year terms), b.iii (3 maximum concurrent terms), c.i (lifetime maximum), d.i (sum of both elected and appointed), 7.a.i (publicly funded), b.i.x (Presidential), b.ii.xxxx (One citizen = One vote), b.ii.xx.cc **(value voting, ratio)** c.x (direct elections); 8.v.b. (Citizen), **8.a.i.xxviii (military enlistment), iv.a.f.2.iii.2 (Federal Bonds, Inclusive**), b.i.ii (to hold office and to vote), c.i (exclusive), 10.a (compulsory voting)

Legislature;

- 1.i.xx.z (Bicameral legislature, 1st house), ii.x (Representative), iii.1.2.3.5.7 (Laws, Oversight, Ratification, Appropriations, and Appointments), 5.a. (National), 6.a.iii (6 year terms), b.ii (2 terms maximum), c.ii (Intermittent), c.ii (sum of elected only), 7.a.i (publicly funded), **ii.xx.c (Value Voting, straight),** c.x (direct elections), 8.a.v.b (Citizen), **iv.c.i.c.ii.b (Tax liabilities, straight property tax),** b.i.ii (to vote and to hold office), c.i (exclusive), 10.b (voluntary), 12.a (Jurisdiction), **13.c.ii (Representative of Net Taxes)**

- 1.i.xx.zz (Bicameral legislature, 2nd house), ii.x (Representative), iii.1.2.3.4.5.10 (Laws, Oversight, Ratification, Appropriations, Taxing), 5.a. (National), 6.a.ii (4 year terms), b.iv (Unlimited), c.ii (Intermittent), c.ii (sum of elected only), 7.a.ii.xxxx (privately funded), **ii.xx.c (value voting, straight),** c.x (and open, direct elections), 8.a.v.a.b (resident and citizen), **iv.a.f.2.iii.2 (Federal Bonds, Inclusive)**, 8.a.v.b (Citizen), b.i.ii (to vote and to hold office), c.i (exclusive), 10.b (voluntary), 12.b (Districts), **13.b.i (Representative of GDP, straight)**

Judicial;

- 3.a.i. (Judicial, Circuit), b.i (Judicial powers only), c.ii.x.1 (Appointed by the Presidential), 5.a. (National), 6.a.iii (6 year term), b.iii (3 terms maximum), c.i (lifetime maximum), 8.v.b, b.ii (citizen to hold office).

If this system fails to be realized on a federal or international level it might still have appeal as an inter-regional tier within an already established federal system. States could independently agree to support a tier with financial support in order to staff the law enforcement and military agencies that typically constitute a fully funded and authorized federal government. This reorganization can be accompanied with a voter union consolidating representation in the federal tier from the participating states; the number of representative apportioned to the individual states remain the same but all surrender their votes to the consensus of the group after an internal debate is concluded. In effect this could official conjoin previously independent states into a larger political entity that enjoys combined representation and the economies of scale normally afforded to larger states. Modern technology will permit the states to be non-proximate and imitate old world colonial systems or empires with participating states in distant and foreign locations.

Bond based representation can be apportioned through three different methods. The first is the straight method which attaches a voter franchise based on the numerical value or dollar value of the bonds purchased. The second is the ratio method which produces a proportion of votes gained by purchase which is typically based on some other population or value. The third method is the bracket method producing a vote multiplier which augments a conventional numerical voter franchise. Numerical values are each assigned to a set with a vote multiplier. The value of the bonds owned determined the vote multiplier earned by the consuming voter.

The **Bonded Binary** is an example of the bracket based method for value voting. It concentrates all government functions into just two legislative chambers with one dependent on military enlistment and emergency service providers for voting eligibility and the other dependent on popular elections with vote coefficients earned by bond consumption. The system heavily favors the service chamber by allowing members in the upper house to gain representation in the lower house with legislative broker powers. The Upper House also employs executive representation maximizing the considerable influence of office holders prior to gaining extra votes in other chambers. Nations can easily translate the military enlistment into a popular form of representation by installing some mandatory service or enlistment. All persons would then have access to voting in both chambers.

Bonded Binary

Primary Attributes

- No Executive branch
- No Judicial Branch
- Legislative Complex

Advantages

- The Upper House of the Executive legislatures has the military eligibility criteria attached to all voting and representation. This should attract and reward significant popular support during the installation phase of the conversion to democracy. All emergency and law enforcement professionals from all tiers are likewise enfranchised. That should bring the total entitlement to 6% of the population or more. Its still a fairly small cross section but these are the citizens that make the effort and sacrifice necessary to maintain a state. Mandatory enlistment and municipal service could distribute the voting franchise to a larger portion of the population and should be considered during peace time and periods of emergency.

- The Lower House has the voting franchise for voting and holding office attached to Asset based value voting for federal bond income. It is based on the volume of dividends paid with minimum thresholds for earning the vote multiplier benefit. The intent is providing itself a negative borrowing rate to maximize the benefits of economic stimulus and defense spending.

- It should be noted that all citizens are entitled to vote with the asset based representation only providing a coefficient for voting determined by the ownership bracket. The ownership bracket segregates bond consumers into two or three segments similar to how income taxes are typically applied in tiers. Each bracket each receives a vote multiplier for all eligible participants. Those not purchasing any bonds or a minimal amount receive a multiplier of 1 so that there is a normal ratio of 1 vote per person. The other brackets will attach a vote multipliers of 2, 3, or 4 so that when those individuals vote they gain the equivalency of two, three, or four individual voters.

- The premise is to reward the median bond holders with a significant margin over non bond holders or corporate bond holders. It is expected that a majority of the population will fall into the median or middle class segment with mild to moderate bond consumption and whose vote multiplier will have superiority in number to both the non bond purchasing population and the leisure class who can afford to purchase excessive amounts of bonds. The corporate and wealthy bond consumers will be in the minority with only 1% qualifying through the bond purchases. Even a vote multiplier of x4 will only increase their total influence from 1% to 4% of votes. The lowest class with 25% of the population will preserve a 12.5% minority in votes. The median class with a vote multiplier of 2x and 50% of the population will continue to maintain a majority 50% interest while the middle class (top 25% less 1%) will acquire a 35% minority with a vote multiplier of 3x. The richest 1% will only gain 2% of the vote with a vote multiplier of 4x. The median and middle classes preserve their dominant role in elections – which correlates to voter participation rates in many circumstances.

- The minimum threshold to earn the first bracket of vote multipliers should be high enough to encourage reasonable investment into the federal government but not discourage the lowest income earners. The differential must be meaningful but not exclusionary – especially when 2nd or 3rd brackets can be used to accommodate more advantaged consumers while still maintaining a favorable disposition for the bottom 75% of the income distribution in terms of aggregate representation earned or maintained in the wealth representation system. The government could actively reinforce bond consumption by rewarding it through sponsored personal retirement programs. (401k plans, not pensions, and not social security).

- Government institutions like pension funds and retirement programs don't earn an entitlement to vote but corporate entities gain a voter franchise equal to that of the multiplier earned. Small and medium business owners stand to gain the most from this entitlement as they occur in the largest numbers and the bracket system produces a regression line that is more sympathetic to majority rule.

- The Upper House maintains legislative broker entitlements which permits its members to assume multiple Lower House seats through election. This subordinates the bond supported chamber to the military supported chamber to check the corrupting force of bond based representation.

- The Upper House is also structured as Executive Representation to capture the efficiencies of a more unitary form of executive government despite its status as a legislature. This means one Representative is elected from each jurisdiction and maintains a staff to coordinate the various oversight and executive committees apportioned to the branch. This also permits the Executive Representative to accumulate Lower House seats with access to a larger administrative staff allowing the significant consolidation and coordination of new powers.

Disadvantages

- Introducing military experience and the Legislative Broker and Executive Representation attributes within a monetized system of representation will make it more susceptible to autocratic overtures within the constituencies or corporate supporters. This can result in greater viability in harsher climates but also result in early devolutions into less ordered or democratic states. There are risks associated with most systems of government and although this system is intuitively more ephemeral this may contribute to more propagation and faster proliferation within the undemocratic environment.

- State level governments can compensate for the lack of access in the Upper House due to military and emergency professional eligibility by making enlistment mandatory and then attaching education and retirement benefits. Those states that do so will gain tremendous representation in the federal tier by virtue of being able to consolidate power in both the upper house and lower house of the legislative complex.

- If the Service component for representation in the Upper House is too constrictive the entitlement can be restructured so that enlistment and service provides a vote multiplier similar to the bond representation. The entire population would gain the right to vote for representatives but government employees would gain an advantage of 2x or 2x the vote. If a 2x vote multiplier was applied and only 6% of the population participated they would earn 12% of the total vote while the remain 88% was distributed to the 94% of the population not enlisting or volunteering.

Specifications;

Executive:

- 2.iii (Abolished Executive), 5.a.b.c (National)

Legislative:

- 1.i.xx.z (Bicameral legislature), ii.x (Representative), iii.1.2.d.e.3.4.b 6.7. (Laws, Oversight on A,G, Treasury, Ratification, Executive-Presidential, Judicial, Appointments), 5.a (National), 6.a.iii (6 year terms), b.iii (3 terms maximum), c.ii (Intermittent), c.i (sum of elected), 7.a.i (publicly funded), b.ii.xxxx (One citizen = One vote), c.x (direct elections), 8.a.v.b (Citizen), **8.a.i.xxviii (military enlistment), vi.x.c.cc.ccc (emergency professionals and law enforcement from the municipal, state, and national tiers), vii.x.a.b (public attorneys and judges),** b.i.ii (to vote and hold office), c.i (exclusive), 10.b (voluntary), 12.b (Districts), **13.a.i (Representative of population, jurisdictions), 13.f (Legislative Broker), 13.h (Executive Representation)**

- 1.i.xx.zz (Bicameral legislature), ii.x (Representative), iii.1.2.b.c.3.4.c.d.5.7.10. (Laws, Oversight on Presidential and Judicial, Executive- domestic and treasury, Appropriations, Appointments, Taxing), 5.a (National), 6.a.iii (6 year terms), b.iii (3 terms maximum), c.i (Lifelong), c.i (sum of elected), 7.a.i (publicly funded), **b.ii.x (Straight), Numerical), ii.xx.ccc (Bracket for Vote Multiplier),** c.x (direct elections), 8.a.v.b (Citizen), **iv.a.f.2.iii.2 (Federal**

Bonds, Inclusive), b.i.ii (to vote and hold office), c.i (exclusive), 10.b (voluntary), **12.a (Jurisdictions), 13.b.ii (Representative of GDP, per capita)**

Judicial:

- 3.iii (Abolished Judicial), 5.a (National)

Bond based representation offers an incredible opportunity for installing democratic reforms within autocratic nations and economies. A value voting entitlement will reward the component of the population most willing to support a rebellion or revolution with immediate influence within the new republican political system. If the banking system remains intact within the jurisdiction it would not be terribly hard to transmit voter franchise through accounting standards and computer science. The monetary support would equal the proportion of political influence as a part:whole ratio. This arrangement would not be adequate in a mature political system but it could attract significant support from both the elites and commoners. It would guarantee support for the fledgling government and guarantee representation for contributors. After a successful campaign more mature democratic reforms and entitlements can be enacted to ensure majority rule and a fairer distribution of votes and representation. It should also be expected that a few of the original enticements to rebellion remain embedded within the system; bond based representation might be as durable as senatorial representation has been with parallels in deficiencies and representational inequalities.

Bond based representation will be one of the most important tools in order to achieve negative borrowing rates for governments. The incentives should increase demand producing a downward trend in obligations owed. Attaching a voter franchise should contribute to a reduced rate paid on the treasuries with the political influence an acceptable substitute. Negative borrowing rates lead to exception returns in defense spending and economic stimulus allowing a nation to emerge as a regional or world power and maintain its status as a world power. Collateralizing the treasuries with private securities or state bonds should aid in the rate suppression by better guaranteeing a return even when threats of default or insolvency plague the nation-state.

Collateralized Treasury Instruments

A negative borrowing rate is one where a fixed liability for borrowing is less than the average inflation rate allowing principal erosion to occur at a rate significant enough to dampen the negative consequences of debt accumulation. With treasury interest rates lower than inflation the nation can expect the difference to accumulate over decades resulting in stable debt reduction. A state could leverage a negative borrowing rate by borrowing twice as much needed and investing the difference in private securities earning a higher rate than the obligation. As long as the collateral earns twice as the obligation originally owed the leverage will be able to pay off the original interest owed and the interest owed on subsequent debt. It would never need to earn a return greater than sum of both obligations if a negative borrowing rate was available: the differential between inflation and obligations will produce principle loss and substantially benefit the state. Any earnings above twice the obligation rate would aid in debt reduction in the same terms as inflation over a given period.

If twenty billion was borrowed at a rate of 2% for a 10 billion project during a 10 year 3% inflationary period when the10 billion remaining is invested in private securities should produce at least a 4% return compensating for the entire obligation with the expected principle erosion reducing 10% of the total cost of the expenditure every 10 years. During the 10 year period the nation could avoid all interest payments with the leverage and at the end of the period the collateral can be sold eliminating one half of the obligation on the bond maturity date. The nation would have to repay the original obligation less the principle erosion and the spread between the return of the 10B leveraged and the 4% obligations. Even if the program only earned 4% returns (twice the original obligation) it would still provide 3x as much principal erosion; an inflation rate of 3% offset with 0% interest equals approximately 34% of principal erosion over a 10 year period (68% in 20 years and 100% in 30 years). Average returns on private securities are typically 7% with an adequately diversified portfolio. Over 10 years a 3.0% surplus in investment returns would contribute to roughly 34% (1.03^10) of the original principle owed. With the entire obligation offset principle erosion attributed to the inflation rate of 3% will equal 34% over the same 10 year period (1.03^10). The combination of the two accounts for a gain roughly equivalent to 68% (34%+34%) the original principle over the same 10 years in exchange for only a modest increase in systemic risk.

This is an oversimplification and the values are off but the process is sound. The real returns on treasuries were understated purposefully to highlight the trend in whole integers rather than smaller but more accurate values. For all intents and purposes the term principle erosion consider the net plus borrowed value rather than the simple inflation adjusted value. If 10 billion is borrowed at 2% after 10 years of 3% inflation the principle would be reduced by 34% but in practice the 2% interest payments are not repaid with tax revenue but rather accumulate in new borrowing. This permits principle erosion to be calculated by inflation less interest to accommodate the difference in value simultaneously as the accumulation of new debt. Unless interest payments are immediately compensated for by increased taxes the mechanism should include both operations so that a more accurate depiction of inflations effect on total debt and debt servicing is earned.

The Federal government can engage in a program that collateralizes its treasuries with state or city bonds in order to create a long term source of revenue for itself or to assist the states in managing their accumulated bond obligations. A collateralization process is an opportunity transfer the advantages of negative borrowing to the states for improved economic stimulus and financial security. Federal Treasuries deal in volumes of debt much larger than the combined deficits of the state governments which means it could easily designate a rate to paid to the state or region far less than the price the market economy will arrive at for consumption of that bond. The same amount money is invested more freely to the federal government at lower rates and can be easily returned to the states through a chartered program for income and liability redistribution. Most state deficits amount to a few billion dollars. Not to underestimate the combined tally of deficit moneys (State = 4T versus Fed =16, for U.S. example) on the state tier but most state bond markets could easily be assumed by the federal government if targeted one state or region at a time within the scope of a bail out, remediation, or economic stimulus program.

Ten Billion borrowed at 2% with five billion invested at 4% frees five billion for use in economic stimulus with no interest payments owed on the amount prior to bond maturity and principal repayment. A return of 4% is a floor with returns averaging 5.5%; one and a half percent is in excess of the total 4% in obligations results in 16% (1.015^10) of principal reduction over a 10 year period. The spread of 1.5% combined with an average inflation rate of 3% for approximately 50% in principal erosion during periods of zero interest payments. Thirty four percent plus sixteen percent equals 50% of the original principle. The remainder equals about 2.5 billion of the 5 billion in unsecured loans. Two and a half billion of the original 5.0 billion will be eliminated for the 10 year bond call after the 5 billion initially invested is liquidated for repayment of the original 10 billion borrowed. This would permit a state to borrow four times as much with no increase in bond liability payments. Conversely, if only twice the normal amount was borrowed it would result in accruing only half the usual amount of debt servicing payments. Systemic risk is increased with borrowing doubling but half will be secured with collateral in state government bond assets and private securities. Nations with negative borrowing rates typically attempt to borrow at the inflation rate to maximize economic stimulus without producing long term drag and this method will double the allowable figure. During periods of emergency the collateral can be leveraged up for access to larger incomes and even greater economic stimulus.

The increased consumption of bond should drive down state and city average rates from 5% to 4% granting them an immediate 25% reduction in obligations and access to a 4% to 7% spread on assets for enhanced principal erosion when using securities as collateral. Private securities average a return of 7% producing the 4% needed to offset the original 4% bond liability with a surplus of 3% depreciating the 4% owed on the second liability. Although enhanced principle erosion isn't earned with returns less than 9% the state level jurisdictions do secure themselves an arrangement replicating negative borrowing rates. The leveraged obligation should equal only 1% or 2% after offsetting earnings. This rate will typically be much lower than inflation during normal economic conditions. State governments would gain principal reductions of 30% or more (per 10 year period) with interest payments at the stipulated 1% rate. Returns beyond 9% on private securities erase all interest payments and contribute a 10% or 20% increase in principal erosion during 10 year periods. The alternative is forcing states to continue borrowing at a rate higher than inflation resulting in principal growth averaging 1-2% a year or 10-20% over a 10 year period.

Most nations with negative borrowing rates attempt to borrow at a rate equal to the inflation rate to maximize GDP growth. The premise being the inflation rate negates many of the long-term consequences of the borrowing. Collateralizing federal bonds with state bonds moves the target from 3% GDP to 6% GDP. The Federal tier can borrow with no interest payments and earn between 50% to 68% in principal erosion over a 10 year period. The states and cities gain access to much lower rates and faster principal erosion: stimulates negative borrowing rate enjoyed by Federal tiers. There is an increase in Systemic Risk and moral hazard with the values ballooning to twice the previous proportion. Despite the state accumulating twice the normal amount of sovereign debt half is collateralized with tax back bonds from state and city governments. The unsecured debt:GDP ratio will remain the same although there will be abridged debt servicing payments. The advent of this program does not alter the calculus of political argument over tax breaks versus increased spending but it can mitigate the long term consequences of the borrowing and economic stimulus.

Land Based
Systems of Representation

Chapter 7

Democratic entitlements based on land ownership were the first significant political reform since the advent of a limited aristocratic parliament after the Magna Carta. The United States had a land requirement to hold office and to vote despite being heralded as the first Democracy since the Greek city-states. Universal Suffrage for adult males wasn't granted until 50 years later after a series of violent protests and dangerous rebellions. Women didn't earn the right to vote until much later. The Roman Republic actually maintained a political system with more liberal voting entitlements before they decayed into a totalitarian regime and split into two empires.

Land represents one the oldest forms of ownership with early nations and most societies completely dependent on farming. Land ownership and management was the premise of Feudal governments in Europe and elsewhere which dominated political science for centuries. It must be clearly stated that taxes and voting rights have been intimately attached for equally as long; land is the source of property taxes, which are one of the most significant contributors to capital for state or municipal governments.

It can be well reasoned that land ownership is the principle definition of a nation or state. It certainly is the most durable and long lasting attribute of nation – more durable than the political system, more durable than the economic system, and more durable than the people. Land is a fungible property which cant be absconded with, destroyed, or assumed allowing for nations and states to evolve over incredibly long periods. Land can be purchased, won from conquest, or lost during war making it a precious resource that typically contributes tax dollars, food, and populations for economic and martial efforts. The wealth and power of most nations are highly correlated to the amount of land a nation can grow into or harvest opportunity from and every politician with ambition is keenly aware of this nearly natural law.

Attaching voting rights to land ownership can be a complex operation especially in more modern eras with computing technology and better records. Votes can be apportioned to property owners so that all adults listed on the land title are afforded the right to vote within the stipulated tier. This is the most reasonable entitlement as it requires no deliberation and debate within the family unit or organization. Votes can be apportioned to each family with one vote between all members. This necessitates consensus or agreement between partners which wont occur within most instances. Patriarchal societies (or the reciprocal) still exist and are likely to persist for many more years – they might require this concession prior to authorizing democratic reforms.

Votes can be metered out by property allowing one individual or family more than one vote. In fact this format is similar to a value voting method in that the voter gains a number of votes proportional to the number of properties owned. Obviously, this favors wealthier individuals over middle class or below median citizens who typically only own one property, if any. More contemporary voting systems may attempt to enfranchise organizations like corporations with all of the other property rights owners enjoy including voting. This entitlement would be heavily regulated; common stock corporations with shareholders and corporate boards would qualify as entities able to exercise their rights where smaller and simpler businesses that don't have separate accounting and pay fewer taxes would continue to be prohibited.

The eligibility criteria for participation in a particular chamber can be based on the value of the property. Typically, the division will be above median values versus below median values. All homeowners will be captured within the two different classes ensuring adequate representation within the entire region or demographic. This will create interesting intersections within states and regions with different costs of living standards as a larger portion of the population will be included within one of the chamber and excluded from the other. Stratification can have both beneficial and negative consequences but all will contribute to the unique democratic identity developed by the nation or state.

The value of the properties can also be used as a measure of political influence with a straight value voting method permitting wealthier citizens more proportional votes in the system.

Slightly less disruptive or offensive is a value voting system based on a ratio of value that provides a voting coefficient to a standard one person one vote or one organization one vote system. A value voting system based on brackets will allow numerical voting systems per property or for a large number of properties to gain a moderate amount more influence based on value while maintaining a voting system that still protects the below median and middle class voters with numerical superiority. The most complicated but fairest systems will have a coaxial value voting system applied through brackets with a numerical popular vote providing the franchise to an entire population. Property values will increase the number of votes bestowed on the individual but each adult will still enjoy the minimum of one vote.

The premise of landed requirements for voting can be modulated with qualifiers. The voting franchise can be denominated by either residential properties or commercial properties. Conceptually, residential property voting entitlements are associated with more popular elections while commercial voting entitlements are associated with aristocracy and corporations. More sophisticated systems can include both or restrict access to specific chambers or branches for each individual entitlement. The voting franchise can be dependent on improved properties or owner occupied properties. Improved property, land with structures, ensures that the wealth representation isn't abused by demanding a larger investment be made prior to earning the voter rights. Owner occupied requirements limit the number of properties used for voting and dictate that the homeowner or corporation must be actively vested in the jurisdiction where the voter entitlement is employed.

Denying renters and disposed the right to vote is a dangerous precedent for contemporary democracies. It might drive those populations to protest and violence. It will certainly demonstrate the clear difference in economic interests in terms of political influence. No successful democracy will entertain land based voting rights for all of its branches and chambers and any assertions otherwise have not been demonstrated in history. However, the voter franchise can be associated with one facet of the government to balance out another deficiency or imbalance in representation. Most governments are comprised of several different branches and chambers of government which permit implicit flexibility in distributing specialized voter franchises between different economic components or demographic segments of the population. One entitlement can be compensated for the loss of another and land based wealth representation can be the mechanism that delivers the differential.

Wealth based representation is a great opportunity for union formation or to expand current boundaries into new territories with restrictive voter entitlements. It is a form of compatibility with other nations or states which can result in a faster expansion or combination of economic blocs. Although reprehensible, the colonial period of world history demonstrated the facility of incorporating new territories into current empires or economies. Cooperation will form a much more durable and useful association. With modern democratic entitlements the process could be equally as profitable but more compelling in regards of morality. Prosecuting land transfers can be based on a temporary basis with political reforms or a more permanent basis with sales terms and transfers of equity.

It is safe to say that a democracy is in dire straights if it is making concessions to an economic class with a voter franchise modeled on land ownership if it previously enjoyed a universal suffrage. However, any democratic entitlement is valuable as it sets a precedent, foundation, and trend to more liberal forms of republican governments. The Baron Republic is more legitimate and more viable from the perspective of the recently liberated or enfranchised. The **Baron Republic** is a simple political system premised on both popular elections and land based voting requirements. It may evoke anti-democratic sentiments with the allusion to royalty or monopolists but otherwise satisfies the defining attributes of a moderately democratic nation.

The primary legislature is entirely dependent on land ownership as a qualification for voting and holding office. Only Residential landowners are provided the voting franchise to th exclusion of corporate land owners and renters. Any adult associated with the ownership of the residential property is eligible allowing multiple owners to claim voting privileges. Motivating politicians to improve the facilities and financial infrastructure making home ownership possible by rewarding them with increased numbers of constituencies should produce increased numbers of homeowners in the system. There may also be innovations in how non family groups cooperate towards ownership of improved real estate to earn voting rights.

The elections process incorporates a two value voting components that distributes elective power. The election process presiding over the Attorney General office is in terms of the value of the tax liability associated with the property conveying the voter franchise. All owners are empowered to vote when they are attached to a title and each are accorded a number of votes equal to that of the properties value. The tendency for Property taxes to be applied as a flat tax allows the enfranchised demographic to regress towards a more normal distribution. First impression might be that wealthier homeowners are rewarded with a disproportionate amount of representation but the differential fails to provide a meaningful advantage as the median valued properties will greatly outnumber the higher value properties. There will be efficiencies for the median class which occur in greater frequency at 50% of the income distribution with moderately priced (average priced) properties.

The distribution will have a right skew but only as far as benefiting the middle class (top 25% of the income distribution less the top 1%) as there increased tax liabilities and increased population provide an advantage for the class. The middle class typically represent more demographics and more interests presumably excusing the over-representation. If property taxes were made more progressive with higher value properties paying more then the voting system might have be adjusted to remain fair and equitable for the median and lower voters but they may also agree with lower tax payments in exchange for the diluted vote. Most property taxes are flat simply because most smaller and medium sized municipalities are comprised of like valued properties. There typically isn't a huge divergence in property values from one town to the next unless it satisfies the conditions of a city or larger population base.

The value voting process for federal unicameral legislature used straight value voting premised on current property values. Many of the same tendencies hold true with the larger number of median and middle class homes overwhelming the combined value of wealthy homes. The property of homes retaining similar values within similar and proximate communities has more advantages when electing a representative in that the property values are more likely to be average despite any perception of median class or wealthy class.

The chamber is much more susceptible to market movements in pricing as it uses values 10x or 20x that of the tax liabilities. Boom time economy can improve the elective power of resident land owners especially if there is incentive and competition to acquire properties for voting powers. This can have a direct effect on economic modeling, regulation, and reforms during periods of heightened economy. This introduces an major source of instability in the system with economic corrections resulting in terrific adjustments to political representation within the executive and legislative branches within the federal tier.

Baron Republic

Primary Traits;

- Tripartite Executive
- Unicameral Legislature
- Appointed Judicial

Advantages;

- The Tripartite Executive is primarily driven by popular elections with the Presidential and Attorney General branches both providing access for citizens with universal suffrage.
- The elections for Treasurer General occur with a value voting system based on Property taxes. This makes sense considering the residential property eligibility criteria in the unicameral legislature. The incentive for communities and states to tax at a higher rate benefits the federal government by making their dependence of federal subsidies with stringer public sectors and more evolved safety nets.
- Legislation still requires confirmation. The unicameral legislature must petition one of the executive branches to provide the affirmation. The individual executive branches can write laws but each requires the confirmation of the unicameral legislature. They may not confirm each others

laws. This should accelerate the rate of legislation production compared to a standard bicameral legislature process but still offer more inhibitions than an unassisted unicameral legislature.

- The Unicameral legislature will preside over all confirmations within the executive branch and the budget which can be passed without confirmation by any executive vote. The check will be provided with a macro-political vote in the Tripartite executive branch governing veto powers. Veto's are less likely after requiring a two thirds majority but the system can also eliminate recourse after a veto making the strike permanent until the next election cycle.

- The Executives all maintain oversight powers over the other executive branches. This will ultimately be the best mechanism to ensure cooperation and complementary action. The executives will contribute members to the congressional committee dedicated to the specific agency, department, or charter. The executive members get to vote on matters and legislation within the committee despite not having representation within the larger chamber.

- Correlating a voter franchise on land ownership actively encourages the purchase of real estate rather than renting. This should have a positive impact on homesteading and equity building. Not only are more fixed liabilities assumed but the investment typically increases in value in addition to having the mortgage paid off

Disadvantages;

- When correlating representation to asset ownership huge portions of the population will be rendered ineligible making the system an inadequate example of democracy. That being said the first democracy in the modern era had land requirements to vote and hold office. The US actively inhibited the vast majority of its urban populations from voting or holding office. The consequence was reforms nearly 50 years later after a large number of successive revolts and rebellions.

- The use of value voting when determining election results will improve the influence of wealthier jurisdictions and states. However this phenomena is already accepted and appreciated in most contemporary democracies as senate representation typically over-represents states with lower populations. The consequence should be equivocated with correlating representation to GDP to export economic policies of jurisdictions with more mature economies.

- 2/3rds of the Executive branch remains accessible to land owners, renters, or those dispossessed. This is the only component of universal suffrage but a significant hedge against the landed classes as it controls the largest organization of armed forces and access to the treasury. The executives have limited legislation powers and more potent veto powers helping rebalance the power in favor of the renting or disposed.

Specifications;

Executive;

- 2.ii.x.c (Tripartite Executive Presidential), iv.1.2 (Sub routine, Laws, Oversight), 5.a (National), 6.a.iii (6 year terms), b.i (1 terms maximum), c.i (lifetime maximum); d.i (sum of elected and appointed), 7.a.i (publicly funded), b.i.x Presidential), ii.xxxx (One citizen = One vote), c.x (direct elections), 8.v.b. (Citizen), b.i.ii (to hold office and to vote), 10.b (voluntary voting), c.i (exclusive), 14.a (Macro-political Vote, Alpha)

- 2.ii.x.cc (Tripartite Executive Treasury), iv.1.2 (Sub routine, Laws and Oversight); 5.a (National); 6.a.ii (4 year terms), b.iii (3 terms maximum), c.ii (intermittent maximum), d.ii (sum of elected), 7.a.i (publicly funded), b.i.x (Presidential) **ii.xx.c (Value voting, straight),** c.x (direct elections), **8.a.ix.c.i.c.ii.b (tax liability, property),** v.b (Citizen), b.i.ii (eligibility for voting and holding office), c.i (exclusive), 10.b (voluntary voting), 14.a (Macro-political Vote, Alpha)

- 2.ii.x.ccc (Tripartite Executive Attorney General), iv.1.2 (Sub Routine; Laws and Oversight), 5.a. (National), 6.a.ii (4 year terms), b.ii (2 terms maximum), c.i (lifetime maximum), d.i (sum of elected and appointed), 7.a.i (publicly funded), b.i.x (Presidential), ii.xxxx (One citizen = One vote), c.x(direct elections), 8.v.b. (Citizen), b.i.ii (to hold office and to vote), 10.b (voluntary voting), c.i (exclusive), 14.a (Macro-political Vote, Alpha)

Legislature;

- 1.i.x.z (Unicameral legislature, 1st house), ii.x (Representative), iii.1.2.3.5.7.10 (Laws, Oversight, Ratification, Appropriations, Appointments, Taxation), 5.a. (National), 6.a.iii (6 year terms), b.ii (2 terms maximum), c.ii (Intermittent), c.ii (Sum of elected only), 7.a.i, c.x (Publicly funded, direct elections), **b.ii.xx.c (value voting, straight),** 8.a.v.b (citizen)**, iv.a.f, (Inclusive) 2.ii.2 (Residential Properties),** b.i.ii (to vote and to hold office), c.i (exclusive), 10.b (voluntary), 12.a (Jurisdiction), **13.b (Representative of GDP)**

Judicial;

- 3.a.i. (Judicial, circuits), b.i (Judicial powers only), c.ii.x.2 (appointed by President) 5.a. (National) 6.a.iii (6 year term), b.iii (3 terms maximum), c.i (lifetime maximum), 8.v.b, b.ii (citizen to hold office), c.i (exclusive)

The Presidential executive branch is still popularly elected and it maintains domain over appointments to the judicial branch. This serves as a great check against any severe imbalance in representation resulting from the homeowner eligibility criteria in the Unicameral legislature. It also serves as the premise for universal suffrage in the legislature if gross exploitation occurs or some other deficiency that threatens the nation with instability or insolvency. At least the renters and disposed will have recourse with representation and employment within the federal government with the courts likely supporting any reform efforts.

The majority of government administration is also subject to popular elections making the system more legitimate from a practical perspective. Administrative or Agency law is a substantial portion of all laws and universal suffrage grants access to the citizens. One major improvement to this land based system of representation is the coupling of military enlistment with land ownership so that a more diverse cross section of demographics has access to the same chamber or branch of government. The **Binary Magna Legislature** splits all of the duties and powers of government into only two chambers with one based on land and veteran (civil) status and the other a universal suffrage with legislative broker powers.

Binary Magna Legislature

Primary Attributes

- No Executive branch

- No Judicial Branch

- Upper House representation based on GDP with residential real estate ownership requirement

- Lower House representation based on popular representation with no real estate requirement

Advantages

- The two bicameral legislatures split executive and judicial duties but share legislative, appropriations, and taxation duties.

- This system of representation is not based on value voting but rather one citizen and one vote quantifiers.

- Land ownership is still used as an eligibility criteria for determining who can cast votes or hold office making the system less democratic than those with universal suffrage within both legislative chambers. The second independent axis for eligibility is military enlistment which is staffed overwhelmingly by non land owners and other lower class constituents. This will balance the distribution of classes involved within this chamber.

- All citizens have access to the second chamber satisfying the definition of democracy at a modest standard. Most of the law enforcement, budgetary powers, and taxing authority is located within the second chamber making this format more digestible.

- The lower chamber with universal suffrage employs the legislative broker attribute which will allows seated politicians eligible to hold offices within the upper chamber to do so as a means to extend the influence of their constituents. This might compromise the integrity of the lower chamber by mixing with entitlements to power but it should still provide net benefits to the system in regards to access and integration. The improved influence for constituents in the lower chamber is one reform on the more restricted access within the upper chamber.

Disadvantages

- Not maintaining an executive accessible to universal suffrage is a major deficit but the legislative broker attributes attempts to overcome the disadvantage.

- The entitlements of land ownership are restrictive but ultimately span multiple income and wealth brackets. Those in the lowest income bracket own properties and occur in larger numbers than the middle class or upper classes. This numerical superiority should be a hedge against more exploitative policies being manufactured from the entitled chambers of legislature.

Specifications;

Executive:

- 2.iii (Abolished Executive); 5.a.b.c (National)

Legislative:

- 1.i.xx.z (Bicameral legislature), ii.xx (Representative),.iii.1.2.d.e.3.4.b 6.7. (Laws, Oversight on A,G, Treasury, Ratification, Executive-Presidential, Judicial, Appointments); 5.a (National), 6.a.iii (6 year terms), b.iii (3 terms maximum), c.ii (Intermittent); c.i (sum of elected), 7.a.i (Publicly Funded); **b.ii.x (one citizen = one vote), c.x (Direct vote);** 8.a.v.b (citizen), **iv.a.f, (Inclusive) 2.ii.1 (Residential Real Estate),** 8.a.i.xxviii (military enlistment), vi.x.c.cc.ccc (emergency professionals and law enforcement from the municipal, state, and national tiers), vii.x.a.b (public attorneys and judges), b.i.ii (to vote and hold office), c.ii (non -exclusive), 10.a (compulsory), 12.a (jurisdictions), 13.a.i (Representative of Population, by jurisdiction)

- 1.i.xx.zz (Bicameral legislature), ii.xx (Representative),.iii.1.2.b.c.3.4.c.d.5.7.10. (Laws, Oversight on Presidential and Judicial, Executive- domestic and treasury, Appropriations, Appointments, Taxing); 5.a (National), 6.a.iii (6 year terms), b.iii (3 terms maximum), c.i (Lifelong); c.i (sum of elected), 7.a.i (Publicly Funded); **b.ii.x (one citizen = one vote), c.x (Direct vote);** 8.a.v.b (citizen), b.i.ii (to vote and hold office), c.i (exclusive), 10.a (compulsory), 12.a (jurisdictions), 13.a.i (Representative of Population, by jurisdiction), **13.f (Legislative Broker)**

Judicial:

- 3.iii (Abolished Judicial); 5.a (National)

The Legislative broker powers in the lower house help ensure if power consolidates it does so in the direction of unrestricted suffrage The legislators must still qualify with land ownership or civil enlistment but those are fairly easy criteria to satisfy for most professional politicians.

The **Real Republic** is an example of land based representation distributed by home values and used as qualifying criteria for different legislative chambers. Above median value homeowners are segregated into the upper house while below median value homeowners are segregated into a lower house. Dispossessed, renters, and all non-owners maintain representation in the unitary executive and judicial branches.

Real Republic

Primary Traits;

- Unitary Executive
- Bicameral Legislature with Executive Representation and Real Estate Qualifiers
- Elected Judicial

Advantages;

- The two legislative jurisdictions are split by eligibility requirements based on asset values of residential real estate. The Upper House requires above median values for voting and holding office while the Lower House requires below median value and rental for voting and holding office. All home owning citizens will be covered by the two divergent criteria. As an inclusive eligibility criteria the political system satisfies the minimum definition of democracy.

- The segregation by home value is apportioned on a state by state basis so that exactly half of the state's voting population will be in the lower House and half of the state will be in the upper house. The alternative would be to allow national figures to dictate which populations vote in which chamber but the composition may break down by state or regional lines inviting more partisan politics. The median values should produce a mixed (diverse) income bracket for each chamber with the upper median home owners in from below median income jurisdictions in one state complementing the upper median home owners from upper income jurisdictions in other states. The reciprocal is true in the below median chamber with all intersections crossing both state and economic boundaries.

- The Executive branch remains accessible from universal suffrage in voting so all citizens are eligible. The helps balance the numerical differences between populations enfranchised to either chamber. Obviously the Upper chamber should have much fewer voters in accord with the higher property values which means the renters and below median value property owners suffer from vote dilution.

- The Judicial branch is elected and segregated into jurisdictions within a congressional structure. A universal suffrage applies with all citizens eligible to vote for candidates within their districts. This is the second check to the legislative branch bifurcated by land ownership.

- The voter franchise governing legislative elections does not discriminate between citizen and resident-alien. The partial enfranchisement of resident alien homeowners should attract more immigration of wealthier professionals and reward the purchase of property in the laboring classes. It is expected that the purchase of a home or property provides long term incentivize to earn citizenship and the stability needed for immigrants to integrate within communities. If necessary the financial instruments providing mortgages can be regulated more intensely to encourage or discourage homeownership within non legal immigrant communities.

- The qualifying real estate must be improved and owner occupied. This will ensure that accurate values are used to segregate the population into the two chambers.

- The Executive and Judicial elections do discriminate between citizen and resident alien with only citizens qualifying.

Disadvantages;

- There will be a large dispossessed population of non-owners and renters that will be discouraged by the lack of representation within the federal tier. This might be accommodated on the state level with more participation in local government. The best solution is to introduce a third chamber with triangulation powers and universal access. The institution could easily be engineered and authorized during a period of instability to satisfy resident demands.

Specifications;

Executive;

- 2.i.iii (Unitary Executive, Elected), 5.a (National), 6.a ii (4 year terms), b.iii (3 maximum concurrent terms), c.i (lifetime maximum), d.i (sum of both elected and appointed), 7.a.i (publicly funded), b.i.x (Presidential), .ii.xxxx (One citizen = One vote), c.x (direct elections), 8.v.b. (Citizen), b.i.ii (to hold office and to vote), 10.b (voluntary voting), c.i (exclusive)

Legislature;

- 1.i.xx.z (Bicameral legislature, 1st house), ii.x (Representative), iii.1.2.3.5.7 (Laws, Oversight, Ratification, Appropriations, and Appointments), 5.a. (National), 6.a.iii (6 year terms), b.ii (2 terms maximum), c.ii (Intermittent); c.ii (sum of elected only); 7.a.i (publicly funded), b.ii.xxxx (One citizen = One vote), c.x (direct elections); 8.a.v.ab (resident, citizen), **iv.a.d.2.ii.2. (Residential Real Estate, above median),** b.i.ii (to vote and to hold office), c.i (exclusive), 10.b (voluntary), 12.a **(Jurisdictions),** 13.a.i (Representative of Population), **13.f (Executive Representation)**

- 1.i.xx.zz (Bicameral legislature, 2nd house), ii.x (Representative), iii.1.3.4.5.10 (Laws, Ratification, Appropriations, Taxing), 5.a. (National), 6.a.ii (4 year terms), b.iv (Unlimited), c.ii (Intermittent), c.ii (sum of elected only), 7.a.i (publicly funded), b.ii.xxxx (One citizen = One vote), c.x (direct elections), **iv.A.e.2.ii.2. (Residential Real Estate, below median value),** b.i.ii (to vote and to hold office), c.i (exclusive), 10.b (voluntary), **12.a (Jurisdictions),** 13.a.i (Representative of Population), **13.f (Executive Representation)**

Judicial;

- 3.a.ii. (Judicial, Elected, Congressional), b.ii. (Legislative sub routine, Oversight), c.i.x (Elected, Representative), 5.a. (National), 6.a.iii (6 year term), b.iv (Unlimited), c.i (lifetime maximum), d.ii (sum of elected), 7.a.i (publicly funded), b.ii.xxxx (One citizen = One vote), c.x (direct elections), 8.v.b, b.i.ii (citizen to hold office and vote), c.i (exclusive), 10.b (voluntary), **12.b (districts),** 13.a.i (Representative of Population)

The reliance on Executive Representation focuses all of the legislative power on a single elected official. Their total influence is proportional to the size of the population in the represented jurisdiction. The official maintains a staff to occupy the various committee positions and report back to them. This is reminiscent of a unitary executive structure but interposed on top of a traditional legislative structure. The size of both legislative chambers will contract to one fifth of more conventionally sized legislatures including both senators and representatives.

Granting resident – alien homeowners voting rights will almost certainly result in a boon in importing permanent professional classes and leisure classes. It is a higher order of work visa that promotes naturalization with many of the most important benefits occurring prior to finalizing the process. It's a competitive advantage in recruiting immigrant workers. Wealthy and educated emigrants will seek out employment within the nation or state aiding consumption and productivity in the economy. Laborers and other emigrants will seek work visas for the promise of future home ownership with voter rights. This is especially true of the prospectors currently residing in autocratic and less democratic regions.

Progress towards democratic entitlements with universal suffrage is slow. Presenting concessions on land ownership might accelerate the trend to popular representation. The elites and aristocracy could be convinced, coerced, and cajoled into a system of representation based partially on land ownership. The produces incentive towards democratic reform and possibly rebellion. The history of the United States is a great example of how voting entitlements can be expanded once earned which will retroactively justify any concessions made on the path to universal suffrage or more sophisticated systems of representation.

Equity Based
Systems of Representation

Chapter 8

Corporate governance is typically determined by shareholder elections and votes where each participant is granted a number of votes equal to the number of shares they own. Those individuals and entities that own the most shares control the most votes. Asset based representation imitates this method and delivers to all equity owners a number of votes equal to the number of certificates or shares they own. Equity representation is equivalent to bond representation in all resects except for the more durable voter franchise. Stock ownership is not exhausted after a single term. It is chattel which can be bought, sold, or traded. Equity representation allows meta-investment to distribute voting shares and influence through a huge cross section of entities. Index funds, ETFs, and mutual funds are examples of stock which is representative of other stock. This is the perfect mechanism for a public sector to gain administrative and regulatory control over public and private companies within its jurisdiction.

Stock ownership grants limited rights to financial reports, limited rights over corporate board votes and elections, and rights to profit. This can be equivocated to taxation and regulation with stipulated terms operated on by market forces. Equity representation is much more economical than bond representation in the respect that the state isn't burdened with long term payment obligations. Money is transferred for exclusive access to voting rights and profits. There is no implied threat of bankruptcy if profit expectations are not met or exceeded. This voting method is subject to criticism from over representing the wealth. It also excludes non equity owners from the voting process or elections. However, one must consider public pensions as significant institutional investors where Treasurers can act of a fulcrum for representation for residents of that particular jurisdiction. The modern era will be dominated by permanent funds on the state and local level and sovereign wealth funds on the national level. This will skew security ownership in the favor of city and state representatives which are heavily influenced by voter trends and political parties.

The government can assemble agencies into authorities and organization for the express purpose of translating them into equity for sale to the public. The proceeds of the stock sale is then used to purchase stock in public companies regulated or governed by the constellation of agencies and departments. This form of meta-representation can be an effective fulcrum when applied from the vantage of a state governor or agency director. The asset distribution will make the agencies much more effective at regulating the sector as it can apply executive law and vote in corporate elections. The returns on investment will help pay for the agency or authority to exercise their powers but dependence will be avoided with the governments continued ability to raise revenue by taxes and fees.

In most instanced governments will primarily sell agency equity to other governments be they federal, state, or local. Equity trades between governments is more acceptable than public offerings on market exchanges. Equity based representation is more permanent than bond based representation and can result in more imbalanced and more dangerous concentrations of power. The public sector can always decide to issue more stock diluting current ownership proportions and extending the voter franchise to new governments or parties. In this respect equity representation provides a mechanism for the expansion of reciprocal representation. Corporations can be legitimate recipients or consumers of the public sector equity with the intent on slow assuming the infrastructure within a private-public initiative or system of meta-representation.

It is expected that shareholder activism will result from the political franchise. More investors will view their representation within the corporation as a means to forward their personal political ideologies or agency charters. They will certainly be insulated from the immediate consequences of diminished returns and lower dividends. The state deals in aggregate figures where the losses accrued by one company are likely to be compensated by the gains made by another. Contemporary interpretations of the fiduciary duty is extremely shortsighted in this respect as environmental concerns, regulatory concerns, trade concerns, and other political concerns can impact government overhead in a more profound way than simple budgetary controls and minor investments. In political systems with under-regulated private campaign finance systems corporations already have tremendous influence over elections. By exposing the companies to political pressures resulting from permanent fund investment a public could recapture the headwinds of progress and majority rule. It would at least present an opportunity for state or city treasurers to reform and regulate the companies internally as opposed to external controls imposed by a state or nation.

Where legislatures fail to pass laws and executive agencies fail to regulate permanent funds and sovereign wealth can still advocate for more responsible management policies. This is a form of shareholder activism but there can be not doubt that modern politics does not distinguish well between public sectors and private sectors with the massive amounts of corruption stemming from deregulated campaign financing and an almost insurmountable amount of subsidies and tax incentives. Many business practices dependent almost exclusively on contributions made by governments be they tax breaks for corporate profits or welfare for laborers not adequately compensated.

If shareholder activism is a deterrent then the permanent funds can be structured for the export of investment capital so that there is no domestic interference. The jurisdiction or nation stands to lose tremendous amounts of economic stimulus from the reinvestment but over longer terms the import of rents and incomes from the investment will likely produce proportionally more representation. The stock owned will translate to strategic assets for intelligence efforts and permit the government to integrate with other economies more effectively. An economic bloc need not be officially sanctioned by another participating government but can rely exclusively on investments made into companies with significant market share in the territory. The effort must be permitted by regulators but is otherwise subject to more market forces than government forces.

The exercise of forming permanent funds within states and cities will contribute to the financial security of the jurisdictions. They will rely less on borrowing, they can maintain lower taxes with higher spending, or they can afford more comprehensive social programs without taxing. It is in the best interests of the nation to incentivize the formation of permanent funds and this can be accomplished best by founding a new democratic institution premised on representation through equities but otherwise maintaining the traditional or historic structure of the government. The **Midgard Republic** interjects a third legislative chamber with limited powers which services as the outlet for all equity based representation earned by the incorporation of permanent funds within the state level.

Midgard Republic

Primary Traits;

- Unitary Executive
- Upper House
- Lower House
- Midgard Chamber
- Appointed Judicial

Advantages;

- The structure purposefully imitates one of the most basic and common variations for democratic government. This includes one executive branch, two legislative branches, and an appointed judicial branch. The intent is to focus on how the interjection of permanent fund based representation has on a conventional government.

- The Midgard Chamber maintains triangulation powers that permit it to confirm passage of laws and budgets originating from either of the two other legislative chambers. It is a powerful tool wielded by the a group of politicians that represent both commercial and political constituencies in the permanent fund managers and treasurers from the city and county governments.

- Permanent Fund managers would gain representation in a federal tier institution with triangulation powers and complement them with direct representation within the private sector. It is expected that the treasurers and managers actively promote public policy through shareholder activism. The increased number of managers will ensure there is no consolidation of economic influence in any monopolistic form, especially from the public sector. If necessary the legislators can enact regulations or charters governing how permanent fund assets are deployed for representation within the economy – as a component of the fiduciary duty.

- Permanent funds will be expected to maintain a large variety of assets but only the common stock and convertible stock or bonds actually provide extra-representational powers to the treasurer.

- Only municipal governments are granted access to the Midgard chamber through the assets located within their permanent funds.

- It is expected that municipal governments remain democratic and the entire national electorate is covered by the distribution of representation among the mayors (treasurers) of towns and cities. This form of representation is a check on the accumulated power of the state governments in that the cities have direct access to the federal tier. It will reinforce continued participation within the economic and political union.

- The increased number of permanent fund managers helps to protect free markets by diffusing the government owned stock and assets across a larger cross section of cities and systems.

- The increase number of participating jurisdictions also ensures that a larger cross section of political ideologies are included in the elections process.

Disadvantages;

- Correlating representation on equity based assets in permanent funds is arbitrary and could easily be abused if it were not relegated to municipal tiers. The fact that officials are elected in jurisdictions limits the coercive effect larger more populous cities or states would have on lower population and smaller city or states.

- In order to make the chamber more competitive earlier on in its deployment access could be granted for both permanent fund and retirement fund or treasury based assets. This would immediately provide most municipal jurisdictions with a minimum of assets for use in a representational system. It would incentivize jurisdictions to incorporate permanent funds as well as local social security based programs for residents. Both would be a major improvement to economy within the state or nation.

Specifications;

Executive;

- 2.i.iii (Unitary Executive, Elected), 5.a (National), 6.a ii (4 year terms), b.iii (3 maximum concurrent terms), c.i (lifetime maximum), d.i (sum of both elected and appointed), 7.a.i (publicly funded), b.i.x (Presidential), ii.xxxx (One citizen = One vote), c.x (direct elections), 8.a.v.b. (Citizen), b.i.ii (to hold office and to vote), c.i (exclusive), 10.a (compulsory voting)

Legislature;

- 1.i.xx.z (Bicameral legislature, 1st house), ii.x (Representative), iii.1.2.3.5.7 (Laws, Oversight, Ratification, Appropriations, and Appointments), 5.a. (National), 6.a.iii (6 year terms), b.ii (2 terms maximum), c.ii (Intermittent), c.ii (sum of elected only), 7.a.i (publicly funded), b.ii.xxxx (One citizen = One vote), c.x (direct elections), 8.a.v.b (Citizen), b.i.ii (to vote and to hold office), c.i (exclusive), 10.b (voluntary), 12.a (Jurisdiction), 13.a.i (Representative of Population)

- 1.i.xx.zz (Bicameral legislature, 2nd house), ii.x (Representative), iii.1.2.3.4.5.10 (Laws, Oversight, Ratification, Appropriations, Taxing), 5.a. (National), 6.a.ii (4 year terms), b.iv (Unlimited), c.ii (Intermittent), c.ii (sum of elected only), 7.a.ii.xxxx, (privately funded and open), b.ii.xxxx (One citizen = One vote), c.x (direct elections), 8.a.v.b (Citizen), b.i.ii (to vote and to hold office), c.i (exclusive), 10.b (voluntary), 12.b (Districts), 13.a.i (Representative of Population)

- 1.i.xx.zz (Unicameral legislature, 3rd house), ii.x (Representative), iii.9 (Triangulation), 5.a. (National), 6.a.iii (6 year terms), b.ii (4 terms maximum), c.i (lifelong limit), c.ii (sum of elected only), **7.a.ii.x.xx.c (privately Funded, individuals and domestic corporations), ii.xx (Asset value Voting),** c.x (direct elections); 8.a.v.b (Citizen), **8.a.iv f.2.i.1.2.3 (Equity Asset, Inclusive, Governmental),** c.i (exclusive), 10.b (voluntary), 12.a (Jurisdiction), 13.a.i (Representative of Population), **13.h. (Executive Representation)**

Judicial;

- 3.A.i. (Judicial, Appointed, Hierarchal), B.i (Judicial powers only); 5.a. (National) 6.a.iii (6 year term), b.iii (3 terms maximum), c.i (lifetime maximum); 7.d.x.2.i (Tyrant, appointed by Presidential Executive); 8.v.b, b.ii (citizen to hold office), c.i (exclusive).

The defining quality is not incomes generated but stock maintained transferring the voting franchise in both corporate entities and political entities. As a rule of thumb permanent fund qualifications should include all public pensions under management and other retirement or treasury related assets. All can contribute to the net influence the system can leverage within a private sector permitting shareholder votes with common stock instruments.

Equity based representation for governments is perhaps the most restrictive and imbalanced of wealth representations but there should be no expectations that the larger jurisdictions save more than the smaller jurisdictions. Most of the larger states incur significantly more obligations and as a result borrow much more than smaller jurisdictions. This might balance the fact that larger jurisdictions typically have more GDP for a base to levy tax revenue. As a result equity based representation has a low correlation to population or GDP and will be hard to legitimize. However, it is one of the most potent forms of wealth representation due to its ability to interface with the economy. This makes for easier integration into larger economic unions and the establishment of looser empires.

Manufacturing a synergy between democratic process and economic influence through an equity based system of representation can be criticized as a depreciation of popular or majority rule. However, those same criticisms are translated into benefits when the system of representation is interposed as an economic union between independent nations. The powers prescribed to the new tier in government will be more specialized in terms of fiscal policy, monetary, and regulation with less access to the military and other more intimate mechanisms of control. Take for example the **Mandrake Union,** which elects the executive officer and all of the legislators with assets from all of the retirement programs, public pensions, and permanent funds.

The central tier of the Economic Union is heavily influenced by the equity portfolios of participating lower jurisdictions (states or nations) in that each is entitled to representation in proportion to the value of their equity assets. The State administrators participate in federal executive elections while municipal administrators participate in both executive and representational elections (i.e. the congress). If necessary the state governments can be substituted by federal governments and the municipal descriptor replaced with a state descriptor.

In this respect the political system can be used as either an economic union between many nations or as a political system used for one nation. More complicated systems of representation will permit the state administrator to participate in legislator elections but comparisons to an appointment based system (atomization) will be justified. This is still a legitimate form as democracy as long as the state governor remains elected. The municipalities may still pay an important part but they will generally be relegated to a non performing position.

Mandrake Union

Primary Traits;

- Unitary Executive Branch

- Unicameral Legislature
- Appointed Judicial Branch
- Unicameral Reserve Branch

Advantages;

- Participating states and nations will be incentivized to invest a portion of tax revenue in permanent fund equities or develop more advanced retirement and pension systems. This will provide a democratic reform when representation is indexed to the shares of equity. It will also provide significant economic benefits where the established government reserves decrease dependency on taxes and provide incomes from for jurisdictions. Robust and retirement programs endowed with private securities can provide significant cost savings and induce tax reductions when they replace older less productive retirement programs which were almost exclusively dependent on government expenditures and unsecured tax contributions.

- Significant permanent fund assets insulate a nation from public finance crises by reducing the need to borrow, provide collateral for leverage, increase government revenues, and provide economic stimulus for faster and more stable growth.

- This political system can be relegated to a single public sector institution with oversight over a single domain in economy but it is much more useful when implemented in a political-economy dominated by State Capitalism. Many of the government services will be provided by competitive jurisdictions within the Union and there will be less of a distinction between the private sector and competitive public sectors. When more of an economy is owned through permanent funds and sovereign wealth the representation based on equity investments within the State Capitalist infrastructure will produce a more valid index of population and GDP.

- The Economic Union doesn't discriminate between foreign investments and domestic investments for the express purpose of incentivizing foreign investment to expand its sphere of influence on corporate boards and other wealth based democracies. Restrictions can be easily enacted to make a more refined representation of domestic corporation equity so that it can be more accurately correlated to population or GDO within the Union. In fact, individual institutions can be engineered with different entitlements dependent on their charter and purpose.

- These entitlements can easily be converted into an occupation or reconstruction phase for sovereignty but this would entail more specific restrictions on voter franchise and asset allocations. In these instances only, the Reserve board can be staffed with those officials which were formally democratically elected but deposed due to the renovation in entitlements.

- By substituting private can commercial asset eligibilities a foreign corporation can interface with and integrate its corporate governance with the public sector of the host nation.

- The state governments and participating national government should have elections and representation based on population and demographics which provide more legitimacy to the Union dependent exclusively on wealth representation. In other scenarios, the wealth representation within an economic union permits democratic nations to form political bonds with autocratic nations with a common denominator of economy; although fundamentalist capitalist and communist nations wont be able to successfully integrate it does not preclude capitalist dictatorial systems from integrating with democratic socialist systems through permanent funds and sovereign wealth. Communism should not be confused with state capitalism which involves a more competitive market for private/public finance infrastructure. With more of the state capitalist businesses owned by cities and states rather than nations and only operating within competitive jurisdictions rather than were access to the judicial and regulatory is granted the mode of political-economy can bear the integrity necessary to provide high quality services with less corruption and more diversity.

Disadvantages;

- This version of political representation won't be effective until the state or nation is more vested in securities through permanent funds and sovereign wealth. It is true that the representation is proportional so that early implementation will be accurate but all of the extra-governmental access provided by the investment will be denied due simply to the abridged scale of investment and entanglement. This mode of representation can be phased in so that more access is granted over a protracted and elongated period of time. Most economic unions require slow integration which is accommodate by the accumulation of wealth within permanent funds and sovereign wealth. Even if only one institution is authorized at a time it will set a precedent for other institutions with more expansive powers.

- Wealth representation is an incredible democratic reform that can be forwarded by autocratic nations as a substitute for political reform in regards to free and open elections. Nations with significant state capitalist infrastructure and permanent funds assets can enfranchise populations with democratic process within the economy while a poly-autocratic or autocratic political system remains in place. This is a reform as it does condition a population for eventual democratic political control but it can be a measure where the reforms are installed slowly in a more controlled environment.

- The primary reason poly-autocratic nations will seek to make this democratic reform in the economy is that it makes the state capitalist infrastructure more exportable. It is a less overtly hostile form of empire that distributes the state owned infrastructure over a larger area through peaceful economy rather than violent military force. The democratic reform permits the satellites to administer their own public sector services while the autocratic leadership is able to insulate itself while gaining access to significant returns or profits. Integrating public sectors through a private/public finance initiative similar to state capitalism is nearly as effective as establishing martial control over a jurisdiction. As a a least common denominator, the assets provide a cause for invasion if they are threatened by confiscation and where a significant portion of the population will implicitly support the action for fear of losing their services. In more benign systems of integration, the successful state capitalist infrastructure continues to remit incomes to the originating state or nation which helps to moderate tax rates and provides significant economic stimulus.

Specifications;

Executive:

- 2.i.iii (Unitary Executive, Elected), 5.a (National), 6.a ii (4 year terms), b.iii (3 maximum concurrent terms), c.i (lifetime maximum), d.i (sum of both elected and appointed), **7.a.ii.xxx.cc (privately Funded, domestic governments), b.ix.ii.xx (Presidential, Asset value Voting),** c.x (direct elections), 8.a.v.b (Citizen), **8.a.iv f.2.i.1.2.3 (Equity Asset, Inclusive, Governmental),** b.i.ii (to hold office and to vote), c.i (exclusive), 10.a (compulsory voting)

Legislative:

- 1.i.x.z (Unicameral legislature), ii.x (Representative), iii.1.2.3.5.7.10 (Laws, Oversight, Ratification, Appropriations, Appointments, Taxing), 5.a. (National), 6.a.iii (6 year terms), b.ii (4 terms maximum), c.i (lifelong limit), c.ii (sum of elected only), **7.a.ii.x.xx.c.xxx.cc (privately Funded, domestic governments), ii.xx (Asset value Voting),** c.x (direct elections), 8.a.v.b (Citizen), **8.a.iv f.2.i.1.2.3 (Equity Asset, Inclusive, Governmental),** c.i (exclusive), 10.b (voluntary), 12.a (Jurisdiction), 13.a.i (Representative of Population)

Judicial:

- 3.a.i. (Judicial, Appointed, Hierarchal), b.i (Judicial powers only), c.ii.x.2 (Appointed by the President), 5.a.(National)) 6.a.iii (6 year term), b.iv (unlimited), c.i (lifetime maximum), 8.vii.a.b (legal and judicial experience), v.b (Citizen)

Reserve:

- 4.i.a.ii (Reserve Board, admitting all retired members, permanent), .ii.b (legislative sub routine - 1.2.3.7 (Laws, Oversight, Treaties, Appointments), .iii.b (Unicameral), iv.1.a.2.b.c (Pool of retired national legislators and judges), v.d (total equivalent terms)

Many nations permit corporations to participate in the elections process with campaign contributions and other means of financial support which introduces an interesting component of influence reciprocated across typical political boundaries. This potentiates the equity based representation when shareholder activism can result in the export of political ideology by the mechanism of campaign contributions. The corporate entity will become the vector for a state or municipal government seeking to influence the elections and political officials of another state or nation.

The next step in equity based representation is to expand eligibility to commercial and private assets so that all securities owned with voting powers translate to representation in the political system. This is intended for a more mature commercial government vested more heavily in private common stock securities with the intent to balance out those securities owned by individuals or corporations. A premature conversion would result in a political system overwhelmingly benefiting the wealthiest segments of the population. It would be equivalent to a modern aristocracy with limited representation also distributed to pension fund managers and retirement fund managers. However, this form of wealth representation is a concession that is more likely to entice the elite classes to enter into rebellion and wage war against the entrenched powers be they autocratic, theocratic, communist, or republican and that is can be an advantage for other mature systems.

The **Industrial Republic** balances its asset based representation with a popularly elected bipartite executive and an empowered legislature. The Presidential Executive maintains most regulatory and all military powers and the Upper House manages the vast majority of legislative powers and appointment powers over the Judicial Branch. The two facets of the government coupled to equity representation have restricted powers. The Lower House has focusing exclusively on taxation and budgets and the Treasurer General concentrates on monetary policy. The intent is to match the wealth based representation with the government responsibilities must aligned to business interests or requiring more financial expertise.

Industrial Republic

Primary Traits;

- Bipartite Executive
- Imbalanced Bicameral Legislature
- Appointed Judicial

Advantages;

- The Presidential Executive, the Attorney General Executive, and the Primary Legislature are all popularly elected with public financing of campaigns. Only the General Treasurer and Auxiliary Legislature have specific voter franchise based on Equity and Tax Liabilities. This is to ensure that any economic efficiencies gained by the representation aren't compensated for corrupting forces in the other branches and cameras. The Equity franchise is split between the private and public sectors ensuring more accurate representation correlated to population, GDP, and demographics.
- The Primary Legislature appoints the Judicial branch by virtue of majority rule in accord to the discretion of the

majority leader of the chamber. This should balance the combined power of the Bipartite Presidential-Attorney General and emphasize the importance of the Primary Legislature over the Auxiliary Legislature.

- The Auxiliary Legislature is representative of Net Taxes paid into the economic union incentivizes higher gross tax liabilities with a fairer distribution of tax rebates. The representational coefficient can use a 2-4 year average depending on the length of offices so that adjustments occur at staged and predictable intervals. The intent is to reinforce pro-tax sentiments in the same chamber dedicated to equity based representation with publicly accessible securities.

- The equity providing the representation is made available to the public with no exclusions based on incorporation status other than domestic incorporation. It is expected that the majority of assets continue to be owned by treasuries and permanent funds but private sector retirement programs and corporations will start to accumulate the stock. The government can regulate consumption by requiring the brokerages to document and certify citizenship eligibility prior to authorizing the purchase and transfer of stock.

- The next era in economy will be dominated by permanent funds and sovereign wealth which will already introduce these topics to the public domain by virtue of other governments converting. Correlating representation to security wealth will incentivize both public sectors into accumulating more private sector securities for wealth and income.

- Governments with adequately proportioned permanent funds and pension funds can start influencing regional and multinational corporations through shareholder activism and representation on the corporate boards. This reciprocity in influence helps mitigate the effect of corporate ownership and representation. The result will be an complex network of equity swaps between government and corporate organizations in different states, regions, and nations.

- To balance the encroaching powers of commercial governments private individuals and corporations are vested with the same representation the governments are. Obviously, this can be a stunting or corrupting force if the entitlement is introduced too early as a small margin of private individuals and corporations can accumulate and concentrate equity based representation.

- Permanent Funds and Sovereign Wealth might be a more effective form platform for regulation and oversight over the multi-national corporations especially if they have successfully interfaced with the nation through deregulated private campaign finance laws. Permanent Funds can subject themselves to equity based representation with the proceeds of the public stock sale used to purchase private securities and earn meta-representation in the economy. The population will be able to elect the Permanent Fund Manager who then governs over the asset allocation and implementing their political agenda.

Disadvantages;

- The Equity representation does give the wealthier segments of population a disproportionate amount of influence over the Treasury Executive and the Auxiliary Legislature but the vast majority of power is still located within Offices insulated by popular representation and public finance of campaigns.

Specifications;

Executive;

- 2.ii.x.c.ccc (Bipartite Executive Presidential- Attorney General), 5.a (National), 6.a.ii (6 year terms), b.ii (2 terms maximum), c.i (lifetime maximum), d.ii (sum of elected), 7.a.i, b.x, c.x (publicly funded, presidential, direct elections), 8.a.v.b (Citizen), b.i.ii (eligibility for voting and holding office), 10.a (compulsory voting)

- 2.ii.x.cc (Bipartite Executive Treasury,); 5.a (National); 6.a.ii (4 year terms), b.iii (3 terms maximum), c.i (lifetime), d.ii (sum of elected), **7.a.ii.x.xx.c.xxx.cc (privately Funded, citizens, domestic corporations, domestic governments), b.ix.ii.xx (Presidential, Asset value Voting),** c.x (direct elections), 8.a.v.b (Citizen), **8.a.iv f.2.i.1.2.3 (Equity Asset, Inclusive, Private, Commercial, Governmental),** b.i.ii (eligibility for voting and holding office); c.i (exclusive), 10.b (voluntary voting),

Legislature;

- 1.i.xx.z (Bicameral legislature, 1st house), ii.x (Representative), iii.1.2.3.5.7.10.11 (Laws, Oversight, Ratification, Appropriations, Appointments (Confirm), **Appointments (Direct),** Taxing), 5.a. (National), 6.a.iii (6 year terms), b.ii (4 terms maximum), c.i (lifelong limit), c.ii (sum of elected only), 7.a.i, c.x (publicly funded, direct elections), 8.a.v.b (Citizen), b.i.ii (to vote and to hold office), c.i (exclusive), 10.b (voluntary), 12.a (Jurisdiction), 13.a.i (Representative of Population, by jurisdiction)

- 1.i.xx.zz (Bicameral legislature, 2nd house), ii.x (Representative), iii.2.5.10 (Oversight. Appropriations, and Taxing), 5.a (National), 6.a.iii (6 year terms), b.ii (4 terms maximum), c.i (lifelong limit), c.ii (sum of elected only); **7.a.ii.x.xx.c.xxx.cc (privately Funded, citizens, domestic corporations, domestic governments), b.i.x, ii.xx (Presidential, Asset value Voting),** c.x (direct elections); 8.a.v.b (Citizen), **8.a.iv f.2.i.1.2.3 (Equity Asset, Inclusive, Private, Commercial, Governmental),** b.i.ii (to vote and to hold office), c.i (exclusive), 10.b (voluntary), 12.a (Jurisdiction), 13.c.ii **(Representative of Tax Liabilities, Net)**

Judicial;

- 3.a.i (Judicial, Appointed, Hierarchal), b.i (Judicial powers only), **c.ii.xx (appointed by primary legislature)**, 5.a. (National) 6.a.ii (4 year term), b.iii (3 terms maximum), c.i (lifetime maximum); d.ii (sum of elected)

The most significant defect in this system is the empowerment of individuals for equity based representation. A major improvement is to restrict the voting entitlement to corporate and government entities. The **Commercial Complex** accomplishes this reform while compressing all of the government's responsibilities into six legislatures. There are three executive legislatures, two general legislatures, and one judicial legislature. The Attorney General Executive and the Lower House are subjected to a bond based form of wealth representation while the Presidential, Treasurer General, and Upper House are all elected through equity based votes. Only the Judicial congress maintains popular elections.

Commercial Complex

Primary Attributes

- No Executive branch
- No Judicial Branch
- Bicameral General Legislature
- Tricameral Executive Legislature
- Unicameral Judicial Legislature
- Legislative Broker
- Executive Representation

Advantages

- The equity based representation is bestowed on only corporations and governments. The premise is that public corporations distribute their leadership to common stock share holders which can include commercial governments and retirement fund managers. Individuals are not subjected to any extra-influence and the fact that wealth generally consolidates into a relatively small population makes them less eligible for this voter entitlement.

- Elections dependent on equity values are held in an inferior position to those elections based on bond obligations. Bond value voting is indexed less to corporate profits and more to federal support which provides the mandate to make those legislators elected able to earn election to subordinated offices in the other chambers. Legislative Brokers can earn appointments within any of the other chambers which will vastly improve the integration between executive and process legislatures.

- There are four different modes of representation used within this economic union. The first is predicated on equity held exclusively in permanent funds and pension funds and only occurs within the Presidential branch. This is meant to focus indirect representation through the governors of the states involved in the Union with the value or number of shares correlated more to population than to the number of states.

- The second mode of representation based on equity owned by corporations and governments. It permits corporations, permanent fund managers, public pension fund managers, and treasury officials significant representation which is proportional to the number of government common stock their portfolios.

- The third mode of representation is based on bond consumption which is a function of economy and patriotism. Not only do treasuries provide returns on an investment but they are an active form of support for the government. With significantly more demand for government treasuries producing lower returns in an environment of higher inflation it is possible for the government to generate incredible revenues for economic stimulus and military subsidy. Consumers will permit government bonds to pay lower returns with access to the Upper Legislature and Attorney General elections as enough of a reward. This will provide the possibility of a Negative Borrowing rate for participating jurisdictions.

- The fourth mode is popular elections with direct votes based on one vote per citizen. They govern the judicial branch.

- Maintaining popular elections on the city and state tiers will improve the legitimacy for wealth representation within a federal tier. This allows for the governments equity value voting for the Presidential Ex-legislature and other legislatures.

- The Attorney General Ex-Legislature maintains legislative broker properties as a means to consolidate power towards a more unitary government without compromising the initiative with static powers and responsibilities. The fact that the integration of legislative seats from the legislative broker attribute shifts from year to year makes it less likely that institutional inefficiencies and abuses occur as other personalities from other chambers can more easily maneuver and accommodate the deficiencies.

- The fact that the Presidential Executive is consolidated around net tax representation and executive representation means that there will be dramatically fewer executive legislators than the other chambers in the complex legislature. This lends itself to military organization as the leadership is pyramidal and integrated within a tighter hierarchy.

- An important function of the Presidential Ex-legislature is the State department and the value voting incentivizes asset accumulation that can be used to integrate with capitalist or state capitalist systems exclusively through the securitized infrastructure or in coordination with permanent funds assets from other allied jurisdictions and nations. In a new world order including incredibly powerful, highly capitalized, expertly staffed multi-national corporations more influence gained by representation on their corporate governance will benefit the states, nations, and economic unions.

Disadvantages

- The lack of direct popular elections on a federal tier will discourage a large cross section of the lower and middle classes from supporting this mode of representation. There is merit to the position as individual voter representation is extremely diluted in regards to private consumption of bonds and securities. The only way this system remains viable is with popular elections on the city and state level where the natural accumulation of assets in permanent funds and pension funds is in the favor of the middle and lower classes. Stronger fiduciary agency laws that include non monetary rewards in fund management where shareholder activism is expected and necessary to make this system viable especially in regards to private pensions for employees managed by the sponsoring corporations. Stronger Union movements will also help distribute the commercial political representation as their private pension funds can command incredible amounts of political influence especially when coordinated with independent money managers, government permanent fund manager, and other aligned private sector corporations.

- Access to equity based representation can be withheld until the company makes its own stock available on the public stock exchanges. Its an important reform that will incentivize small, medium, and larger business to offer common stock investment opportunities. It will also present the opportunity for reciprocated representation. The permanent fund will have votes on corporate boards and the corporate boards will be able to vote for the executive branches and legislators.

Specifications;

Executive:

- 2.iii (Abolished Executive), 5.a.b.c (National)

Legislative:

- 1.i.xx.z (Multi-cameral legislature, 1st house), ii.xx (Representative), iii.4.a. (Unitary Presidential Executive Powers), 5.a (National), 6.a.iii (6 year terms), b.iii (3 terms maximum), c.ii (Intermittent), c.ii (sum of elected and appointed), **7.a.ii.xxx.cc (privately Funded, domestic governments), ii.x (Asset value, Numerical per stock),** c.x (direct elections), 8.a.v.b (Citizen), **iv f.2.i.3 (Equity Asset, Inclusive, Governmental),** c.i (exclusive), 10.a (compulsory), 12.a (Jurisdictions), **13.c.ii (Representative of Tax Liabilities, Net), 13.h (Executive Representation)**

- 1.i.xx.zz (Multi-cameral legislature, 2nd house), ii.xx (Representative), iii.4.b (Unitary Attorney General Executive Powers), 5.a (National), 6.a.iii (6 year terms), b.iii (3 term maximum), c.ii (Intermittent), c.ii (sum of elected and appointed), **7.a.i (publicly funded), ii.xx (value voting, straight),** c.x (direct elections), **8.a.v.b (Citizen), iv.A.f.2.iii.a (Federal Bonds, Inclusive),** b.i.ii (to vote and hold office), c.i (exclusive), 10.b (voluntary), 12.a **(Jurisdictions), 13.b (Representative of GDP), 13.f (Legislative Broker),**

- 1.i.xx.zzz (Multi-cameral legislature, 3rd house), ii.xx (Representative), iii.4.c (Unitary Treasurer General Executive Powers), 5.a (National), 6.a.iii (6 year terms), b.iv (Unlimited), c.ii (Intermittent), c.ii (sum of elected and appointed), **7.a.ii.x.xx.c.xxx.cc (privately Funded, citizens, domestic corporations, domestic governments), ii.x (Asset value, Numerical per stock),** c.x (direct elections), 8.a.v.b (Citizen), **iv f.2.i.2.3 (Equity Asset, Inclusive, Commercial, Governmental),** c.i (exclusive), 10.a (compulsory), 12.b (Districts), 13.a.i (Representative of Population, by jurisdiction)

- 1.i.xx.zzzz (Multi-cameral legislature, 4th house), ii.xx (Representative), 5.a (National), iii.1.3.4.5.10 (Laws, Treaty Ratification, Appropriations, and Taxation), 6.a.ii (4 year terms), b.iii (Unlimited), c.i (Lifetime), c.ii (sum of elected and appointed), 7.a.i (publicly funded), b.ix.ii.xx (Presidential, value voting), **8.a.v.b (Citizen), iv.A.f.2.iii.a (Federal Bonds, Inclusive),** b.i.ii (to vote and hold office), c.i (exclusive), 10.b (voluntary), 12.a **(Jurisdictions), 13.b (Representative of GDP), 13.f (Legislative Broker)**

- 1.i.xx.zzzzz (Multi-cameral legislature, 5th house).ii.xx (Representative), 5.a (National), iii.1.2.3.4.5.7 (Laws, Oversight, Treaty Ratification, Appropriations, Appointments, and Taxation), 6.a.ii (4 year terms), b.iii (Unlimited), c.i (Lifetime), c.ii (sum of elected and appointed), **7.a.ii.xxx.cc (privately Funded, domestic governments), ii.x (Asset value, Numerical per stock),** c.x (direct elections), 8.a.v.b (Citizen), **iv f.2.i.2.3 (Equity Asset, Inclusive, Commercial, Governmental),** c.i (exclusive), 10.a (compulsory), 12.b (Districts), 13.c.ii **(Representative of Tax Liabilities, Gross)**

- 1.i.xx.zzzzz (Multi-cameral legislature, 6th house,), ii.x (Representative), iii.6 (Judicial), 5.a (National), 6.a.iii (6 year terms), b.iii (Unlimited), c.i (Lifetime); c.i (sum of elected and appointed positions), 7.a.i (Public Funding), c.x (direct elections), 8.a.vii.x. (Lawyers), v.b (Citizens) b.ii (to hold office), c.i (exclusive), 10.b (voluntary voting 12.b (Districts), 13.a.i (Representative of Population, by jurisdiction)

Judicial:

- 3.iii (Abolished Judicial), 5.a (National)

The bond based representation is meant to accommodate private voters with a franchise that balances out the new representational powers afforded to corporations and governments. This is not perfect as the wealthiest citizens have access to tremendously more capital for investment into bonds but at least the return earned is less competitive than securities and goes for the exclusive benefit of the state. State and municipal governments can also seek extra votes when the vest their retirement programs in federal treasuries. Although far from perfect, the combination of different modes of wealth representation can contribute to a well managed economic union or individual political system.

The slow accumulation of permanent fund assets which legitimizes this particular form of wealth representation can be best facilitated by long term budget strategies to earn significant cost savings. Modernizing the public finance system must be a top priority for all political architects and government operators. Agency Capitalization is a strategy that can be employed for the express intent on amassing private securities for a wealth based system of representation while out performing other nations with more expert management of tax revenues, expenses, and borrowing.

There should be no doubt that permanent funds, sovereign wealth funds, and other public sector financial technologies will dominate the next era of economy and public finance and will be pivotal in maintaining economic competitiveness and exerting political hegemony in the next few decades. Rather than installing a single unspecialized permanent fund a state or nation could authorize their composite agencies and departments to initialize their own Agency funds. There are a variety of methods this could be implemented but they all share many of the same advantages. Balanced budgets are more necessary as the primary method for developing the permanent fund diverts deficit financing from the genera budget to the agencies budgets. Deficit spending can persist but they extra liabilities must be added accommodated by mitigating the obligations with leverage. Principle erosion from negative borrowing rates will also contribute to maintaining longer periods of moderate deficit financing.

Agency Capitalization

Agency capitalization provides all of the public finance benefits of sovereign wealth without an of the ideological pitfalls. The assets will be distributed across a large and diverse cross section of agencies and departments mitigating the fears of government monopoly or interference of the private sector. The distribution of assets may actually prove advantageous when the directors actively participate in shareholder votes to forward regulatory schemes outside the apparatus of the government or reciprocate influence those public companies that exploit deregulated campaign finance. There may be some criticisms of susceptibility to corruption but those nations already employing deregulated campaign finance systems are already subject to the same inefficiencies. If anything the distribution of assets may reform campaign finance by interjecting another axis of regulation in term of investment and shareholder representation.

The first method is to dictate leverage limits, borrow against the general fund, and then distribute the moneys amongst the participating agencies. Borrowing figure set at inflation rate in terms of proportion of GDP. For example, at 3% inflation 3% of GDP can be borrowed. The 3% of GDP is distributed to all targeted Agencies which immediately vests the proceeds in securities to offset future costs. These revenues may not be used for operations and must be embedded within permanent funds. As the Permanent Funds grows in size and produces a greater subsidy the budget in terms of dedicated revenues will decrease but the ratio of borrowing will remain the same (albeit at a proportionally smaller amount). Eventually the amount will become negligible as Agencies gain self sufficiency and budget shrinks.

The 3% inflation:GDP rate is more efficient than the economic stimulus that typically accompanies deficit spending. All of the moneys are distributed among private security instruments whose returns are then used to substitute for government spending producing the same result but with no corresponding tax liability. There is a multiplication effect, there is a reduction in capitalization costs for companies, taxes are reduced, and government spending is maintained. The Agencies

Rather than applying borrowed moneys across all agencies equally certain agencies can be targeted and others excluded so that the budget subsidy and asset accumulation occurs within the more strategically important agencies and departments. The amount of net income subsidy will remain the same but it will be applied unequally within the budget. Fee based agencies which rely on the budget less should be permitted to use their income for borrowing with powers to adjust fees up to cover interest on loans. Permit the same agencies to charge fees higher than operational costs to coerce a slow accumulation of assets in their Agency permanent funds.

Assets available for leverage for income subsidy purposes – and regulated by the treasury. The income will justify unsecured borrowing resulting in assets which can be used for more borrowing and up-leveraging the agency to accommodate more demand for public sector services at a lower cost. This is an alternate method for accommodating deficit spending within the general fund without endangering the dedicated finance for Agency capitalization. The agency may depend on funding stemming from the general fund for several years but after a decade or two it should have amassed adequate permanent fund assets to perpetuate its own accumulation and budget subsidy. Although the leverage will be handled by the individual agencies and possibly regulated by the Treasury Department all will continue to be insured by the general fund for the entire amount of the authorized budget.

Debt cant be prematurely retire. Most instruments are on a schedule with set interest and payments. Although debt cant be repaid and could last between 10-30 years past the point of resolution. Investment returns could be applied directly to mitigate the interest associated with the debt for as long as the debt remains valid. Permanent Funds are the perfect mechanism to manage the assets used to neutralize public debt obligations. Leverage and collateral based strategies will be necessary to mitigate significant and detrimental accumulations of debt over moderate and long periods of deficit spending, especially those connected to Agency Capitalization strategies. Permanent Funds will be instrumental in helping states deal with the consequences after years of neglecting balanced budgets.

The federal tier can borrowing 3% of GDP to fund the Agency capitalization and then borrow another 3% to offset the liabilities associated with the program. This is leverage and carries may significant risks but most can be mitigated by raising taxes in the short term until markets recover. All contemporary evidence demonstrates that capital markets are incredibly resilient and will often recover much faster than the general economy making it more appropriate that governments leverage themselves with the expectations that current tax revenues will be supported by future gains in the equity markets.

If a state borrows at 2% with 3% inflation rate and 4% return it can compensate for the 2% interest rate paid on the original debt and the 2% interest rate paid on the leverage debt resulting in 0% obligations and no debt servicing costs. The higher inflation rate will produce principle erosion of nearly 1/3 over a 10 year period and 90% over a 30 year period. With leverage the state or nation can mitigate the debt servicing cost and permit the normal monetary inflation to erode the total costs of borrowing (future value of the original debt).

In scenarios where a 4% target rate is required for mitigation and earned it produces the desired 0% interest while securing additional assets for leverage to be used during emergencies. Missing the 4% target rate by half and only securing a 2% return only results in the original obligation. The expected debt servicing of 2% will occur but the state or nation will gain additional assets for up leverage during emergencies. Most permanent funds should be diversified so at most earnings will only miss their target by half with the default obligation resuming.

Exceeding the 4% target rate will produce extra revenues for the government to balance out and secure more debt, increase spending for economic stimulus, or lower taxes for austerity. Worst case scenario 100% of the assets values are lost and the state doubles its debt servicing costs with interest owed on the original debt and the leveraged debt. This scenario is the least likely and if it occurs there are definitely more pressing problems for the government.

Obviously once the debt associated with the agency capitalization is mitigated more deficit financing for general budget expenditures will be available. Deficit financing should be coupled to the inflation rate to maximize the amount of economic stimulus applied to the economy through borrowing while posing the least risk to the system with the fastest amount of principle erosion. If budget overages don't exceed the inflation threshold the remainder should always be borrowed and distributed through Agency capitalization or preserved for use in a federal Sovereign Wealth Fund. It is actually important to constantly strive for a balanced budget so that critical functions aren't dependent on borrowing and that excess revenues can be distributed into wealth accumulation and more sophisticated economic stimulus programs.

Budget Amortization is discussed every few decades as a solution to high borrowing costs and routine rejected due to the logistics involved in predicting the future costs and the discipline involved in segregating general fund moneys for use in future expenditures. The effort cost more than the return. The calculus can be changed by incorporate a permanent fund and allowing the government to invest in private equities. Not only do the returns earned on investment typically outpace monetary inflation but the improved budget amortization process has uses in integrating political systems based on wealth representation. This includes instances where the nation deploys permanent funds and sovereign wealth with its own economy as well as occasions where the government permits deregulated campaign finance and unrestricted corporate lobbying. The equities purchased through the amortization process imparts direct representation within the corporate boards providing the products or services. This might be critical in an era of economy dominated by state capitalism.

Budgetary Amortization
(Market Acceleration)

Current public finance systems are dependent on imminent and yearly purchases with the difference between tax revenue and government expenditures being accommodated by sovereign debt. There is a better alternative that introduces cost savings through interim and long term investments in private/public securities or obligations. Deficit and Budgets are often related to as mortgage of United States future; it can be structured like a mortgage with financial innovations in permanent fund technologies providing cost savings and efficiencies not previous earned by governments.

Amortizing spreads payments for large products over an extended period making each contribution more manageable. The rate paid can be based on an assumed earned interest rate so that standard obligations and payments can be generated. This rate can be based on future borrowing costs and returns earned on private securities. Like variable rate mortgages the payment can be adjusted upwards on downwards based on historic payments and expected future returns. Instead of variable rate political engineers could entertain variable term with extra revenues allowing produced to be purchased earlier with fixed rate applied to payments.

This is a funding strategy for militaries and policing agencies that demands yearly contributions into SPE instruments (long term investments managed by a 3rd party according to the pre-manufactured contract to perform a specific function or task) or fixed income financial products or index and mutual funds dedicated to specific product purchases (tanks, fighters/bombers, naval vessels, bridges, tunnels, highways, dams, and monuments) with the costs based on the inflation adjusted value at the end of a products expected life time (or utility) where the contributions are vested in diversified portfolios composed of securities and bonds to cut the overall costs in half or thirds. The market will accelerate the initial contributions with compound interest over the designated period which reduces the burden on government revenues and taxpayer liabilities. In essence the Auto-funding system provides companies tax incentives to dedicate funds to their own capitalization with a final return applied to production. The governments gain displaced costs over period with accruing excess amounts of sovereign debt with exceptional market acceleration of taxpayer contributions.

Government can borrow the amount needed at origin and vest with expected return greater than inflation, repay the obligation during instruments duration, and compound the remainder for costs depreciation. Inflation will continually depreciate the original cost of the loan while the repayment schedule will ensure no long term liabilities are assumed, and tax payer subsidies can account for the differential between expected returns and actual returns. If the Government borrowed 1B at 3% for 30 years and vested it in a mutual fund earning 8% for a duration of 30 years it would effectively gain a 5% rate of return on the principal with no significant liabilities accrued and where the predicted costs of a future product inflating at a average rate of 3% can be accommodated with the final value at roughly half final costs producing a savings of 40-50% for taxpayers; a 5% return discounted for 3% inflation leaves an average of 2% net earnings to compound for the term of 30 years. Zero liabilities is a major component with liability shifted from General Fund to Mutual Fund where and the differential between the borrowing rate of 3% and an average inflation rate of 3% produces adequate principal erosion.

There is minimal market risk with diversified portfolios compounded over 20-30 year periods and where only imminent corrections must be accounted for – primarily with more borrowing. Government with much higher borrowing rates will still benefit as long as the return is greater than the liability with cost savings at 10-30% still able to produce amazing long term increases in economic activity and growth. Durable products and infrastructure products with much shorter terms will produce smaller costs savings but even cost savings of 5%-20% are meaningful in regards to tax policy and economic growth. The government's borrowing would be collateralized with the vested securities which might contribute to lower initial rates and greater returns on the differential between liabilities, inflation, and returns.

The cost savings can be translated into accounting force multipliers in public accounting as a reduction in half the costs allows for double the amount of purchases allowing smaller cities, states, and nations to purchase a larger number of more important infrastructure improvements and renovations on the city and state tiers and more sophisticated military grade weapon and surveillance systems for federal or central tiers. A Spread of 20 year difference between a predicted 5% public bond liability and a speculative 11% Private security return (normalized bond liabilities and security returns are expected to be lower over longer periods) and 3% average inflation = 3% annual difference that over 20 years achieves an efficiency of nearly 260% return on contributions.

With a dedicated savings process (through SPE products) a government can effective employ collective bargaining to secure larger discounts of 10-20% on future orders in lots of predicted annual equipment costs 10-20 years in the future and accommodating average inflation rates. Guaranteed revenues on a consistent or predictable basis should persuade manufacturers or retailers of military/police grade equipment to offer large discounts on the future orders, especially if they are contracts are agreed to on consistent yearly basis for 10 – 30 years in the future. These cost savings will effectively double the amount of military or police grade in equivalent dollars spent.

Most significant military purchases have a life expectancy of several years or decades and the amortized contributions enable for immediate replacement after the 20 or 30 years it takes the war machine to become superfluous. Even at low risk fixed liabilities a ROI on a 30 year investment will likely double or treble the initial contribution amount making the final cost equivalent to ½ or 1/3 the cost of the product compared to relative or inflation adjusted costs. Even with tax deductions for interest earned producing the worst ratio of cost savings for governments it still should typically result in 70/30 or 80/20 splits where the jurisdictions saves between 10-30% of final costs.

However, with more favorable tax schedules market acceleration of principal can theoretically permit even 80 or 90% cost savings for predictable long term purchases and expenditures by making the initial contribution tax deductible (or a tax credit) and then compounding the earnings within private sector securities for the prescribed duration until maturity. Nothing suggested is unconventional except for the fact it requires government administrators to start saving and investing revenues for use in long term accounting schedules.

Much more substantial savings are earned on much larger purchases like battleships, aircraft carriers, or installations that naturally have longer periods of usefulness as a 30-40 year period (exampled by a Nimitz styled aircraft carrier, first manufactured in the 1970's) produces a savings efficiency much higher with nearly 500% returns for 20% the cost (or purchasing 5x the number of large assets not accounting for increased maintenance). Normal supplies and weapon systems can be batched for predictive consumption and paid for in lots of future production just as easily as the larger more sophisticated and expensive weapon systems. This pubic finance method introduces economies of scale over extended durations which make larger purchases more affordable on a more regular basis.

Capital Infrastructure projects involving highways, bridges, and tunnels have skewed returns as once built they can maintain their utility for many more decades than even the most versatile and modern military system. A bridge or tunnel can last 60-100 years, with dams and highways persisting for an equally long period. The maintenance costs could be subrogated with a more complex S.P.E. device but the original cost can be reduced to minimal amounts with accurate predictions on replacement rates. Governments are imbued with a longevity that far surpasses most companies and even generations of families and this provides an invaluable advantage in that more sophisticated and patient models of public finance can utilize market acceleration to depreciate the largest expenses over incredibly long periods.

The Contractors' bidding process can be reform by implementing an upfront fee for participation that is translated into a contribution to the vested principal for the project when contract is won a moderate contribution is made as a pledge to execute the contract. A bid process between construction companies can be more open that defense contractors supplying hardware and war machines. This should attract more competition and increases the initial contribution paid into the instrument and lower profit margins once the contract is awarded. A higher initial contribution should account for inflation related costs in predicting a renovation or construction project 10-30 years in the future. By requiring all bidding companies to be Public companies it provides the enhanced Public/Private Finance initiative more regulation on accounting, more accountability for governance, more financing methods/profit sharing methods, government providing contract has more immediate access (legal/corporate/regulatory), Increased scrutiny & cheap capitalization makes it less likely that vested public companies are bankrupted.

Contributions can be vested in diversified instruments earning returns in excess of the inflation rate or they can be vested in the stock (conventional or preferred) of the company earning the contract (compounding the gains). Contributions reinvested within public companies produce free capitalization for company as the proceeds as vested for the duration and continually compound until the maturation date. The contributions towards the future project are guaranteed future revenue for company as the principle is sequestered in a third party managed S.P.E. (incorporated financial device). It is possible to use preferred stock rather than conventional stock so that compounding vehicles gain some bond holder protections during insolvency and have more predictable returns for prediction and modeling.

More sophisticated construction companies can bid for projects, distribute the initial contributions, possibly earn tax deductions on the principal earned, and then guarantee themselves a significant project with a stipulated cost and profit margin (making the job more profitable). In the worst case scenarios where there is heavy government intervention the net cost of the project will remain the same except that it will be distributed over the length of investment. Even if jurisdiction responsible for 100% of the costs of the project – it will be borrowing for zero costs as tax deductions and credits are applied over the 10-30 year period. In conventional rates this can be from 2-7% savings which over a 10 year period could be 20% or 75% over a 30 year period. Not paying obligations is equivalent to earning extra revenues especially when the capital provided originates from the private sector and not up front from the general fund. Avoiding borrowing payments produces just as many cost savings as market acceleration from returns on financial devices.

Contributions in diversified security or fixed income instruments provide a government insurance against decreased local economic activity depreciating returns allowing for a positive gradient in economic stimulus with higher returns earned from regions with more economic activity. If the company does enter bankrupt protections and the S.P.E. was not vested in the company's own stock the infrastructure project can be auctioned off to another company or it could be transmitted like an asset to creditors (in case where the government is not vested within the construction companies stock to earn returns and lower bid costs.

Risk of premature bankruptcy increases with time money sequestered which means 10-20 year durations more appropriate but where 30-60% cost savings are still meaningful. Capital investment can entail shareholder protections in regards to examining the finances – with public companies suffering under more scrutiny to being with. This process can even be a mechanism for bailing out ailing construction companies with upfront access to capitalization for future performance on large infrastructure projects (for reduced costs). Most cities and states will diversify their construction bids for bridges, tunnels, and highways which permits any losses resulting from premature bankruptcy to be ablated by a large portfolio with multiple companies and projects planned.

The S.P.E could be recorded or transferred like a traditional security with a value based on future rewards from tax deductions on earnings. Tax advantages can be provided by the S.P.E. so that the Instruments provide tax deduction/credits on initial contributions, provide tax deduction/credits on interest earned on the dividends it pays itself, or on the capital appreciation after the instrument is liquidated and transferred to the company executing the contrast (simulating capital appreciation). The earnings are treated as losses. If necessary the Initial contributions can be treated exactly like Charity except that dedicated to government for specific projects (advertising for Green improvements, Business improvements) regardless of where or not the financial instrument earns more tax advantages from its capital appreciation or dividends.

Principal corrections can be issued by offering the public tax deductions for contributions into the projects to accommodate for higher than average inflation in year preceding instantiation of the project. Accounting W.O. strategies including the ability to justify 5-15 years of earnings (losses) retroactively allows tax benefits to accumulate over extended periods for use in reconciling larger amounts typically earned by both S type incorporations or C type incorporations. Differentials between State and Federal capital gains or tax benefits can produce favorable terms for the local jurisdictions where larger initial contributions by bidders can be incentivized with more access to deductions/credits but where the cost is shifted to the higher governments.

A successful bid might entail investment within the public company which should induce lower costs/profit margins and lower overall cost for project. In effect public funds vested in the public company provide it a low cost loan for 10-30 years which ultimately results in the production of work for the company. At average capitalization costs for business are an average of at least 7% per annum producing a net savings rate of 84% on the dedicated money during the 10 year period (or 15% cost of job). During a 30 year period the cheap capitalization amounts to approximately 700% of original contributions (or 1.75x cost of job with original contribution of 25%) while providing accumulating access to more capital for business expansion. More sophisticated Construction companies could use the leverage and cheap financing to increase production on other jobs while providing a buy price on the infrastructure project within the jurisdiction. This reduction in capitalization costs should contribute to lower profit margins within bids and more cost savings for jurisdictions especially when an industry average margin of 10% could be reduced to 5% with access to low cost capitalization for leverage on other projects.

A possible reduction in profit margin from 10% to 5%)with 5% cost savings on top of 700% growth of principal accumulates to within 75-80% of total costs as the construction company winning the bid 10-30 years in future benefits from massive amounts of cheap capitalization for significant periods justifying the 5% reduction in project costs. At 5% average differential in returns with a 25% initial contribution will result in a 15% reduction in future costs after 10 years. A Possible additional 5% reduction in infrastructure costs when access to cheaper capitalization is provided (stipulated at time of bid). A 20-80% reduction in Infrastructure costs can produce savings that results in lower borrowing, lower taxes, or greater production (more jobs and economic stimulus). Infrastructure is a predictable cost with timeframes that permit market acceleration in periods of 10 years -

30 years which can accommodate expected decay rates and expansionary needs.

- Perpetual contributions by tax payer incentivized with deductions to maximize principal earning returns from public bonds or private securities. The government will end up paying one third of one half of the total cost after allowing the contributions to compound with earnings over 30 years; The deductions should be distributed across the length of the maturation period to prevent the vested jurisdiction from being overwhelmed.
- The infrastructure project can be vested in a public construction company that pays a dividend (or commit to capital appreciation) which then is the recipient of the compound capital investment - low cost and long term loans at a variable rate pegged to the growth of the company. When the instrument matures it is liquidated (with market expectations of earning the large infrastructure project offsetting any complications from the increase volume of selloff). The proceeds are then transferred back to the company in execution of the construction contract; with the construction company agreeing to lower profit margins (buy rates) or agreeing to make scheduled contributions into the vehicle.
- Even a small infrastructure project set 10 years in the future can reduce its overall cost by 1/3 or a margin of 75% purchase price with market acceleration of 4% over inflation if that 75% can be secured at the onset by tax payer participation (deductions, not tax credits);
- The initial costs can be immediately offset by borrowing, with the private security returns subsidizing the bond liabilities, and where the inflation itself produces the erosion of future costs (original principal) and increase in costs savings when applied to the construction project.
- A Nation or state with lower than inflation borrowing costs will earn significant differentials between its borrowing rate and returns from the private sector especially for long term infrastructure projects requiring 20-30 years for maturity. With a federal tier vested in state and municipal bonds it would be a means to secure modest 2-3% returns and maintain lower borrowing costs for lower tier

governments who can expect the long term investment. A 4% liability and 7% earnings = 3% (includes inflation erosion) over 10 years which is equivalent to 1/3 earnings (30% of principal), 3% over 30 years = 140% of principal - with no liabilities At 5% average differential return on infrastructure projects 30 years in the future will be discounted up to 75% with initial contribution of 10%.

- Cost savings range from 10%-75% for vested governments across a 10 year to 30 year period. Even a 25% reduction in costs over a 10-15 year period justifies the increase in initial expenditures/dedications. The cost savings ratios are still favorable with borrowing initial contributions rather than paying upfront with government tax revenue while sequestering capital for 10-30 year periods also permits larger infrastructure projects to be attempted than current budgets permit - small contributions over 30 years will increase the scale of fixture (Bridge/Tunnel) or energy (Hoover Dam) infrastructure attempted.
- Market Acceleration Initiatives using Public Bonds from associated jurisdictions will improve costs savings derived from the difference in lower capitalization rates paid by jurisdictions (constant and predictable access to infrastructure designated capital) and modest returns of 2-3% above inflation providing the 20-80% cost savings.

Different taxing strategies will produce different incentives and burden shifts. When the interest earned on investment is applied as a tax deduction the upfront costs are 20% for consumer with backend costs of 80% for the taxpayers with the market acceleration capitalized almost exclusively by the taxpayers. In regards to translated costs the product is still a 20% discount with the 80% costs distributed over the discrete period without a dependency on sovereign debt obligations. The liabilities can be accommodated exclusively by government revenues rather than institutional investors. Applying a tax deduction on initial contributions provides the best ratio of return for the government with only moderate benefit for the consumer but in the absence of better alternative should generate adequate interest. After market acceleration of 80% dependent on an initial contribution of 20% the consumer will have paid 80% of initial costs with the government paying only 20% but where that ration equals approximately

15% of total costs for consumer and only 5% final costs for the government. The vast majority of the costs are transferred to the market which compounds the interest earned over the designated period; returns don't have to be exceptional as longer durations will accommodate the difference as public sectors can seek less competitive returns. Depending on the initial contribution and tax incentives applied to a Future Funding initiative (i.e. prototypical sovereign wealth fund) a 10/90 split over 30 years, 30/70 split over 20 years, 50/50 split over 10 years can be achieved.

If tax credits are offered on the initial contribution the up-front costs will be the amount of the initial purchase of 20% (or whatever threshold is established) with market accelerating the principal to 100% of the cost after the period which will not burden taxpayers with any liabilities; the consumer achieves 0% liabilities while the government only assumes 20% liabilities for any scheduled purchases meaning the market carries 80% of the costs while benefiting from lower capitalization costs from guaranteed investments over 10-30 years. Legislating tax credits on the interest earned by the initial contributions provides the worst returns for the government at only a 10-20% rate equal to the original contribution with consumers or investors earning 80% of the final costs over the period (allowing tax accounting advantages over durations between 10-30 years). A 20% discount on final cost should not be underestimated as a means for achieving accounting multipliers for defense, intelligence, and policing budgets. The increased government consumption will provide significant economic stimulus as will the consistent capitalization from long term public/private finance initiative.

These approximations are based on 20% profits tax rates and contribution rates of 20% but any structured private/public finance initiative can be controlled by manipulating the minimum and maximum contribution rates as well as maximum allowance for the tax credits and deductions. A 50% initial contribution threshold would maximize returns for the government with smaller purchases making the tax credit achievable by more taxpayers. Larger initial contributions will contract the maturation periods necessary which means a combination of low contribution long term tax incentives and high contribution shorter term investments will be accessible to coordinate an efficient future fund with allowance for quick adjustments and adaptability. Applying the tax deductions and credits to incomes taxes of 35% or more will invite more aggressive participation from consumer taxpayers rather than corporate taxpayers. Nation's whose tax rates are higher have more natural maneuverability while providing a menu of eligible investments permits the government more exact control over production and capital resources by withdrawing selections or making new additions based upon adjusted demand.

The government can accommodate the differential between the expected amount and the realized amount after Market Acceleration. It may depreciate the effectiveness of the program but in comparison to ordinary budgeting procedures it still maintains 10-20% greater efficiency for exceptional long term cost savings to taxpayers. It must not go unnoticed that Market Acceleration will occasionally produce returns in excess of 20-30% which will negate or soften the net loss accrued and additional tax payer contributions demanded after missed targets. Excess returns can be allocated to other scheduled future fund investments or returned to the general fund for distribution among external departments and agencies with the production being withheld until the due date to preserve integrity within the future fund schedule.

The majority of budgets will continue to be subsidized by general fund supported by annual tax revenue which permits a future funding initiative to accommodate a differential in expected versus realized gains. The risk is only a continued reliance on government revenue which is already the primary mechanism of funding. This poses a problem when future funding increases productivity beyond general fund capacities as the overages will need to be accommodated but almost no risk is accepted for when future funding initiatives are used for reducing long term government costs while maintaining current consumption/production output.

Fiscal Policies incorporating Market Acceleration can be achieved by offering products on an exchange modeled after the stock markets and commodity markets with investments recorded as losses for 5 years or 15 years. Tracking the products like securities also permits the interest, the capital appreciation, and original contribution to be more easily recorded and used in tax accounting by both the taxpayers and by the government. Both individual and corporate taxpayers can accumulate portfolios of the products they helped fund with the value and interest earned advertised for prestige and evidence of charity. Corporations could advertise their sponsorship of products prior to and post manufacture with possible commoditization of the naming conventions for larger naval vessels or for tank and fighter squadrons; during active engagements it would engage a larger segment of the civilian population by permitting more of an emotional reaction and pride in supplying the equipment. All of these attributes and factors should contribute to more participation in the Dedicated Future Funding program (i.e. prototypical permanent fund). Even more complex instruments can be engineered for even greater returns of public finance enhanced by Market Acceleration strategies.

Most defense budget purchases require tremendous capital investments for equipment that can predictably last several decades; these costs can easily be accommodated by a more sophisticated system of public finance dependent on market acceleration enabling much lower taxpayer liabilities. Flexibility can be guaranteed by manipulating the specific product purchase list for tax incentive eligibility targeting an assorted list of individual, corporate, and direct manufacturer consumers. This permits specific orders to be fulfilled on demand even when the largest purchase orders take a full year to reach the initial contribution amount. A menu of dedicated products will attract more consumers as both individuals and corporations will be attracted to making specific investments; commoditizing naming conventions or advertising them prior should attract more interest. Products with different maturity dates will permit investors and taxpayers to schedule tax deductions very similar to returns on returns on bonds and other fixed liabilities. However the greatest advantage in scheduling tax incentives for individual products is the interest it can elicit from the manufacturers of the durable defense products.

Trusts set up for dividend reinvestment (S.P.E) allow the government to compound dividends and capital appreciation into new stock purchases which on the maturity date are sold with the proceeds paid to the manufacturer for the intended product. This provides the listed defense manufacturer access to more predictable and larger volumes of consumption with a predictable and more consistent velocity of consumption resulting in more stable growth and lower cost in capitalization. Companies can estimate borrowing costs better and enter into commercial infrastructure improvements and other capital intensive projects. More exact estimates of future government consumption and expected profits after revenues will provide an environment conducive to increased investments into research and development or mergers and acquisitions. This allows guaranteed production to accommodate static overhead in down cycles where the overages to preserve manufacturing capability. More importantly manufactures can create their own product market share by agreeing to manufacturing discounts on final costs for purchase order placed 10-20 years prior but resulting in revenue from backend maintenance and upgrade orders. Governments can expect Market Acceleration in addition to significant backend reductions in final costs and during crises these trusts can serve as collateral for leverage and increased emergency government expenditures.

If the Dividend Reinvestment Trust process is accepted it could lead to greater variety in S.P.E products with a huge increase in utility and specialization; every Special Purpose Entity can be manufactured with a different function and more practical combinations of financial instruments. They can be governed by contract clauses that produce legally enforceable rules and performance mechanisms. They have the potential to profoundly impact public and corporate finance by providing a large number of long term financial solutions and advantages. Not only will taxes be measurably effected with significant new revenues being extracted through market acceleration rather exacting payment through income, estates, sales, and property taxes. The net benefits are decreased taxes with enhanced government revenues and improved production in the durable manufacturing sector; all of which can be achieved by reorganizing public finance to interface more effectively with contemporary finance sciences and the private sector economy.

When the investments are incorporated separately as S.P.E. the specialization in public bonds may provide more exceptional collateralization and up-leverage benefits as public bonds are implicitly back by tax payers and typically earn more stable revenues. This is in addition to the fact that S.P.E. provides transferable and partial systems of representation and ownership by securitized corporate governance which introduces a myriad of extracurricular governmental uses for merging public sectors or distributing costs across a larger number of jurisdictions. Incorporating the financial devices as S.P.E. also provide the originating jurisdiction protections against disruptions in the revenues extracted and assets embedded as only the corporate entity is subject to bankruptcy laws; any loss in revenue can be accommodated by emergency economic maneuvers (or participating in a Government Revenue Guarantee Corporation). The devices assembled and offered in the secondary markets will benefit the private security sector by making the products more accessible to groups of veteran entrepreneurs (amortizing the costs) as well as more engendering more opportunities or integration between the larger more institutional security service providers or other private sector corporations seeking more advanced security solutions.

It is a near certainty that new highways, bridges, and tunnels will be necessary to accommodate changing demographic and economic conditions and dedicated funding systems enacted generations earlier may be the difference between modern states and old empires. It must not be forgotten that infrastructure projects improve economy but providing jobs and accelerating commerce and consumption – they are often the most effective purchases state and local governments can make to improve economy for their jurisdictions. Defense budgets are one of the most significant contributing factors to government spending and debt accumulation which pose serious threats to the nation's sovereignty. Reducing the costs associated with maintaining a modern military may be a determining factor in the ability of the jurisdiction to navigate public finance with maximum economic growth and financial security. Even at 3% spreads between public bonds and returns on private investments the accrued benefit over 10 years or 30 years is substantial enough for experimentation in a dedicated finance system. Small efficiencies in interest or liabilities distributed over the span of decades or centuries will produce accumulating results.

Emergency Spending and tax revenue must always be depended on to account for the difference between expected costs and actual costs but future funding systems earning returns from the private sector Private sector investments can include reinvestment within the same companies contracted for the 10 year manufacturing cycle. Not only can public moneys be used to leverage better discounts through consistent stock purchases but the vested positions will provide governments with greater long term access to board meetings, elections, votes, and financial briefs. Private sector companies can use the guaranteed income from the contracts as collateral and with the span encompassing 10 year periods or more they can be useful in long term capitalization projects. During imminent emergencies the bond/security instruments can be reformulated for 3 or 5 year maturity dates but the cost efficiencies will be severely depreciated without incredibly fortunate or precise modeling through its investments. Any securities owned by the jurisdiction can be used as collateral for up-leverage which compensates for other economic deficits during crises.

The increased production resulting from Market Acceleration should stimulate economy with more government revenue purchase a larger number of products with the same amount of tax dollars deployed meaning resistance with remain the same with the difference coming from returns after providing extra capitalization to companies whose securities are purchased. The greater production (and future maintenance) and extra capitalization will likely produce more jobs with a larger number of military assets. There is a small reduction in government spending with its transfer to the future consumption by the difference can be accommodate by uncollateralized public debt whose liabilities should cost less than the future production and stimulation.

Lower public sector borrowing costs and better private sector performance will have dramatic impact on the benefits but the effects are accumulative especially over several decades. The compound interest earned by returns on private securities should provide cost efficiencies in regards to total costs as borrowing costs (in terms of typical Central Bank or Federal Treasury instruments) are smaller than private sector returns and the SPE sequestration process accounts for temporary or severe interruptions in public financing the militaries. There are numerous extracurricular benefits for the economy which must also be considered when deliberating a future funding engine.

The Prototypical model of SWF (i.e. Market Acceleration applied within General Funds) permit the gradual accumulation of assets which can be used as collateral and up-leveraged in a similar manner conventional SWF can be during emergencies. This can facilitate increased production with maturity dates accelerated or the new incomes can be appropriated for other programs or costs. There are generally indicators several years prior to a major event which will permit the doubling or trebling of returns which could produce an extra 10-20% savings. Major martial events like regional or world wars disrupt global trade and supply which necessitates more emergency economic maneuvers to maintain income production, price control, and supply. Up-leverage of assets can help alleviate pressures during economic crises where capital markets may seize or stimulate the economy with cheap capitalization available to companies with security and bond purchases.

At the very least the up-leverage increases the number and volume of business intelligence assets available to the jurisdiction or nation to coordinate responses and navigate more treacherous trade gradients. The extra governmental revenues should preserve jobs or create new jobs with increased production of durable products and infrastructure projects which will contribute to stability within the nation. In extreme economic environments a nation typically relies on government borrowing to maximize enlistment in the military which minimizes unemployment and provides a large portion of the population access to predictable incomes (welfare substitute) and benefits; Sovereign Wealth provides governments with more options and more tools to supplement, augment, or enable more borrowing with collateral, up-leverage, and increased governmental revenues - all used in determining the interest rate applied to obligations on sovereign debt.

Prototypical SW's enable jurisdictions and nations otherwise ideological opposed to Sovereign Wealth to experiment with the premise in a more controlled environment gaining access to most of the advantages but without abandoning their principles. Major martial events like regional or world wars disrupt global trade and supply which necessitates more emergency economic maneuvers to maintain income production, price control, and supply. Up-leverage of assets can help alleviate pressures during economic crises where capital markets may seize or stimulate the economy with cheap capitalization available to companies with security and bond purchases. At the very least the up-leverage increases the number and volume of business intelligence assets available to the jurisdiction or nation to coordinate responses and navigate more treacherous trade. The extra governmental revenues should preserve jobs or create new jobs with increased production of durable products and infrastructure projects which will contribute to stability within the nation.

In extreme economic environments a nation typically relies on government borrowing to maximize enlistment in the military which minimizes unemployment and provides a large portion of the population access to predicable incomes (welfare substitute) and benefits; Sovereign Wealth provides governments with more options and more tools to supplement, augment, or enable more borrowing with collateral, up-leverage, and increased governmental revenues - all used in determining the interest rate applied to obligations on sovereign debt. Prototypical SW's enable jurisdictions and nations otherwise ideological opposed to Sovereign Wealth to experiment with the premise in a more controlled environment gaining access to most of the advantages but without abandoning their principals.

Prototypical Funds can be relegated exclusively to public bonds from associated governments. This will constrict returns but the conserving the savings and liabilities within the system should maintain similar efficiencies; it ensures that the leverage of one jurisdiction directly benefits the investment of another while the market economy will preserve the expected differential between obligations, returns, and inflation. The LCD is a more standardized profit margin which as a more stable measure can be used more effectively for prediction in engineering public sector budgets. Differentials between 3 and 5% are still large enough to produce significant cost savings on budgets in periods of 10-30 years. The longer a prototypical fund devoted to public debt is relied on for access to borrowing capital and investment returns.

With more dedicated funds circulating within the system and more governments exacting cost savings the interest rates (returns) on public bonds will be lower but so will the liabilities paid by the governments - the spread should remain equivalent but inflation will erode the effectiveness if new jurisdictions aren't included engendering more diversity and competition within the funding program; foreign jurisdictions can be included as a function of treaty or trade negotiations). The budgetary process will simulate a capacitor in many respects as it can moderate budgetary costs with savings on durable product purchases as well as limiting government debt obligations. Restricting the system to public debt within associated governments provides access to regulating both the consumption and production sides of the financial equation as it is easier to apply regulations between public sectors of different tiers than attempts to impose trading regulations on the private sector.

Pre-Tax Income Based Systems of Representation

Chapter 9

No introduction into wealth representation would be complete without entries premised on income. Income can be derived from business profits, salaries, or investments. Although an effort has been made to discriminate and differentiate between all income sources it is understood that the discourse might be inadequate. The best method to determine if a revenue should be treated as income is whether it is taxed as personal income. Income is a determinant and indicator of future wealth accumulation and economic class and one of the most useful implements for wealth representation.

Incomes generally dictate the class of the citizen and the economic stresses associated can be fairly easily predicted. This is of incredible importance to the individual and the political architects. A wealth based system of representation is intended to emphasize the economic conditions of citizens, advertize them, and then set them in antithesis to improve the problem solving strategies employed. Publicity forces the inequities to be acknowledged and increases the probability they are addressed. It will be of critical importance that the elected representatives suffer under similar economic conditions as those they represent so that they come to the same conclusion and must endure the same solution. Systems of representation where constituents and legislators don't share economic stressors will be far less successful in producing equitable solutions as the consequences wont be felt equally between partners.

Tension between the classes are less important than their ability to correctly identify the stresses most associated with their income bracket. Contemporary democracies attempt to differentiate economic issues based on class but the parties and chambers are not well differentiated making it much more likely that the issues are confused and the correct interests are harder to identify. An electorate specialized into income dependent classes should be far better advocates for their own interests. They will demand more adequate wages, labor rights, union protections, more progressive tax schedules, with more emphasis placed on regulating exploitative and destructive corporate practices. More importantly they will start protecting the public sector and the economies of scale their social and financial programs provide to the median and lower classes.

Income can be separated into pre tax values and post tax values. Specialization in one provides very discrete advantages over the other. Pre-Tax is the gross amount of compensation earned and is irrespective of the actually proceeds earned. Progressive tax brackets could seriously diminish the amount of income enjoyed by the person or family. This has a profound impact on income based wealth representation as the value used will barley resemble the final value earned. Without doubt taxes applied to incomes for use in wealth representation will have direct and profound changes on the system of representation.

The two methods most applicable to income dependent representation is value voting and income eligibility. The two may be used individually or interchangeably and offer different advantages or disadvantages. Value voting equates income with power and provides inducements to acquire incomes of significant sizes. The larger the income the more representation the individual has earned within the chamber, branch, or system. Superiority in numbers or majority rule will still be present as a large volume of moderate incomes will tend to crowd out the outliers in magnitude. This tendency will break down in economies with terrible wealth inequality and might contribute to significantly more political instability when the imbalance in representation makes it less likely the inequality in incomes is corrected.

The deficits of value voting with income is that it is exploitable and imbalanced. The top decile will maintain a disproportionate amount of representation. In nations with low voter turnout the wealthy and middle class already dominate the voting system as they are more likely to participate. The difference is even less appreciable in nations that employ deregulated campaign finance systems. There are methods the remaining portion of the income distribution can improve their representation within the system but it will likely be based on consensus from the segments looking to suppress their access to political power.

Value voting is susceptible to minimum wage increases and retirement fund adjustments. Increasing the minimum wage by 20% or 2 of 10 dollars would impact a huge number of retail employees and set an escalating trend for higher paid employees. Even if only 10% of the workforce earned 20% it would have a incredible effect on the distribution of wages with the median figure moving upward and the cumulative scale of retail wages making tremendous gains on the top decile in terms of the proportion of voter representation afforded to the bottom 80% of the income distribution. The same is true of retirement programs that distribute pensions to the aged, disabled, or entitled.

Wages can be moderated by installing work week regulations. By stalling the work week at 35 hours rather than 40 it would diminish wages by nearly 8%. Employers wouldn't likely maintain the 40 hour work week under the threat accruing sever overtime liabilities – and instead increase the workforce by 8% to accommodate the conserved demand. The 8% reduction in wages is scaled with higher incomes losing a terrific amount of influence especially when aggregated into demographic or regional population segments. This would regress the median threshold downward and improve the voter representation of the wealthy in a value voting system. It would be non-consequential in a below and above median eligibility system as the population would be reorganized and recentered but otherwise both components would have equal influence and access.

Income dependent representation reinforces citizens desire to claim income on tax forms. This should result in more taxable income and higher tax revenues which would be an incredible benefit to the state or nation. Underfunded governments present a terrible risk to the economy and international community as they breed cultures resistant to regulation, resistant to taxation, and ultimately make the nation and world a much less stable environment. Nations with access to more tax revenues can build larger militaries and contribute more to international institutions. Its more likely they have better regulated financial sectors and sounder public finance systems with less debt. Incentivizing

All Income is tracked on tax records and reports can be used retroactive to justify eligibility and value for voting. In order to provide a more stable environment an average of the income over a period of 3 or 5 years can be mandated to smooth out outliers and exclude frequent or substantial changes. An average also eliminates a states dependency on immediate values and records and permits some flexibility for less predictable circumstance. Otherwise, an individual might be forced to frequently switch participation in designated legislatures during arbitrary periods. At the very least it would be an inconvenience for the citizen and worst case scenario it would disrupt the elections process and contribute massive instabilities.

Income eligibility criteria will be used to engineer constellations of chambers or branches working in coordination to provide suffrage to the whole population but with exclusive domains and powers for each segment. Usually, one segment will be used in antithesis to another. Otherwise, a spectrum will be used to allow each spectrum to focus on their own interests but ultimately include all perspectives within the political landscape. Using income as an eligibility criteria has equal potential to be egalitarian or exclusive. Egalitarian systems will grant suffrage to all income distributions but delegate each class to a different chamber. Exclusive systems might enfranchise one class or income bracket and exclude another manufacturing a partisan or apartheid environment. Incomes can be split into above median and below median like the other value based systems of wealth representation. This allows the entire population to be captured within the eligibility criteria with a coequal and proportional counterweight.

Income thresholds not used for value voting will determine eligibility in a segregated system; political influence is distributed evenly through entire population with half of the population is represented in one house and half of the population is represented in the other house. The only relevant criticism is that certain states or regions will be over-represented in one chamber and under-represented in another. Cost of living is a function of average or median wage and more populous and denser states can have much higher figures. This might contribute to partisan divisions within the nation along class and state boundaries but most political systems have fault lines that are as potentially divisive.

Income changes during one's lifetime allowing individuals to seek representation in different chambers or branches of government. This assures a more diverse and experienced demographic among the constituencies represented. Non income for adults can be factored into median calculations in segregated systems of representation along with pensioners and retirement income. This will liberalize both chambers with lower median threshold and larger number of income producing population. The **Lion Republic** is an example of a segregated system of income based wealth representation with its bicameral legislature split into above median income eligibility and lower median income eligibility.

Lion Republic

Primary Traits;

- Tripartite Executive
- Bicameral Legislature
- Appointed Judicial
- Reserve Board

Advantages;

- The General Legislature is split into two identical chambers with one dedicated to representing below median income earners and the other dedicated to representing above median income earners. The Reserve branch has triangulation powers to pass legislation from either of the two legislative branches making the environment incredibly competitive.

- The Reserve Branch has sole control over appointment which is a significant compliment to the triangulation powers. The Reserve remains a important component of the political system despite the criteria being loss of office due to elections or term limits.

- The intermittent term limits on the legislatures ensures that those politicians entering the reserve branch will have other opportunities to regain office. This will permit legislators to perpetually move in and out of the legislatures and reserve branch to maximize competition for elections.

It will permit the parties more stratagem with the revolution of members from chambers and reserves. The tactic is costly as a representative forsaking their whole term in the Reserve for a new term in a chamber is subject to the smaller term allowance during a subsequent reserve position or the loss of election and loss of representation in the Reserve.

- The intermittent term limits on the appointed justices ensures that the benches are rotated every few years. They are empowered with representation within the Reserve branch along with members of both legislative chambers. Judges can be re-appointed after the intermittent break but will require a second confirmation vote prior to earning the appointment. The judges already require re-confirmation after every term served so the procedure will be fairly routine after service in the Reserve is executed.

- The Tripartite executive branch maintains a Veto power over legislation confirmed by triangulation through the Reserve Chamber. The Veto powers don't extend to legislation confirmed by both chambers of the bicameral legislature.

Disadvantages;

- The Reserve Board can dictate national policy for extended periods of time when significant margins by a single party are earned within the institution. This can translate into popular tension between the classes as the two primary legislatures are divided by income. Complaints of class warfare should keep both sides honest in negotiating appropriations and fiscal policy.

Specifications;

Executive;

- 2.ii.x.c (Tripartite Executive Presidential), 5.a (National), 6.a.iii (6 year terms), b.i (1 terms maximum), c.i (lifetime maximum), d.i (sum of elected and appointed), 7.a.i (publicly funded), b.i.x (Presidential), ii.xxxx (One citizen =

One vote), c.x (direct elections), 8.v.b. (Citizen), b.i.ii (to hold office and to vote), c.i (exclusive), 10.b (voluntary voting), 14.a (Alpha Macro-political vote – for Veto)

- 2.ii.x.cc (Tripartite Executive Treasury), 5.a (National), 6.a.ii (4 year terms), b.ii (4 terms maximum), c.ii (intermittent maximum), d.ii (sum of elected), 7.a.i (publicly funded), b.i.x Presidential), ii.xxxx (One citizen = One vote), c.x (direct elections), 8.v.b. (Citizen), b.i.ii (to hold office and to vote), c.i (exclusive), 10.b (voluntary voting), 14.a (Alpha Macro-political vote – for Veto)

- 2.ii.x.ccc (Tripartite Executive Attorney General), 5.a. (National), 6.a.ii (4 year terms), b.ii (2 terms maximum), c.i (lifetime), d.ii (sum of elected), 7.a.i (publicly funded), b.i.x Presidential), .ii.xxxx (One citizen = One vote), c.x (direct elections), 8.v.b. (Citizen), b.i.ii (to hold office and to vote), c.i (exclusive), 10.b (voluntary voting), 14.a (Alpha Macro-political vote – for Veto)

Legislature:

- 1.i.xx.z (Bicameral legislature, 1st house), ii.x (Representative like House), iii.1.2.3.5.10 (Laws, Oversight, Ratification, Appropriations, and Taxes), 5.a. (National), 6.a.ii (4 year terms), b.iii (3 terms maximum), c.ii (Intermittent), c.ii (sum of elected only), 7.a.i, b.ii.x, c.x (publicly funded, one citizen = one vote, direct elections), 8.a.v.b (Citizen), **iv.b.1.i.ii.iii.iv.w.d.g (Income from employer, employee, and self employed, below median, pre-tax),** b.i.ii (to vote and to hold office), c.i (exclusive), 10.b (voluntary), 12.a (Jurisdiction), **13.b (Representative of GDP)**

- 1.i.xx.zz (Bicameral legislature, 2nd house), ii.xx (Representative like House), iii.1.2.3.5.10 (Laws, Oversight, Ratification, Appropriations, and Taxes), 5.a. (National), 6.a.iii (6 year terms), b.ii (2 terms maximum), c.ii (Intermittent), c.ii (sum of elected only), 7.a.i, b.ii.x, c.x (publicly funded, one citizen = one vote direct elections); 8.a.v.b (Citizen), **iv.b.1.i.ii.iii.iv.w.e.g (Income from em-**

ployer, employee, and self employed, above median, pre-tax), b.i.ii (to vote and to hold office), c.i (exclusive), 10.b (voluntary), 12.a (Jurisdiction), **13.c.i (Representative of Gross Taxes)**

Judicial;

- 3.a.i (Judicial, Circuit), b.i (Judicial powers only), **c.ii.x.2 (appointed by President**), 5.a. (National) 6.a.ii (4 year term), b.iii (3 terms maximum), c.i (lifetime maximum); d.ii (sum of elected)

Reserve:

- 4.i.a. (Reserve Board, all retired officials), ii.b.1.5.9.a.7.10 (legislative sub routine, appointments, triangulation over legislation, appropriations, and taxes), ii.d.x.xx.i.ii (Repealing, Excising Legislators and Executives), iii.b (Unicameral), iv.1.a.2.b.c (Pool of retired national legislators and justices), v.c (total equivalent terms)

The Reserve Board is not segregated by income which mediates the hyper partisan tone established with the separate legislatures. It plays an incredibly important function with its undifferentiated demography and triangulation powers over legislation, appropriations and taxes. No doubt that the budget is incredibly important in determining capacity to regulate and maintain its militia and the Reserve board captures tremendous authority over the process. Whenever the Reserve uses triangulation powers to confirm legislation it is subjected to a veto by the tripartite Executive. The branch exerts influence over the appointment process of the executive branch granting it unconventional oversight over the administrators.

Segregated representation in the legislature can be supplemented by value voting in an executive branch or equivalent institution. Value voting has limits but can be amended by wage regulation and other attempts at economic modeling. The **Wealth Complex** is an example where income based value voting is applied to an executive legislature while segregated income based eligibility is applied to the bicameral general legislature. Value voting is much fairer when applied to districts and jurisdictions rather than national elections as the cost of living and relative wealth of residents is conserved within the same area. Otherwise, richer states would have considerable advantages over poorer states in federal elections. The complex employs popular elections for the congress delegated judicial responsibilities in an attempt to insulate it from any of the economic tensions harnessed in the other legislatures.

Wealth Complex

Primary Attributes

- No Executive branch
- No Judicial Branch
- Unicameral Executive Legislature
- Bicameral General Legislature
- Unicameral Judicial Legislature

Advantages

- Both segregated and value voting methods for wealth representation are used in this political system. This ensures that all segments of the population and income distribution are represented albeit not in equal proportion.

- All of the appropriations and tax responsibilities are administered through the lower house with above median income requirements. It is expected that the candidates with higher incomes will have more practice and acuity for handling budget and taxes. There is the tendency for this population to enact regressive tax policies to protect their own interests and incomes. The nation would have to develop some faculty and facility to avoid this consequence otherwise it would devolve into hyperpartisan conflict.

- All of the appointment and oversight responsibilities are administered through the upper house with below median income requirements. This is intended as a counterweight to the above median income chambers ability to manage fiscal policy. The majority of enlisted will participate in the chambers and establish more intimate connections. More of the politicians will earn more experience delegating intelligence and law enforcement details. This is important provided the executive legislatures income dependent value voting – and its preference to ally with above median income earners. Of course, the appointment powers are expected to be an appropriate foil to this incongruent engineering.

- Both chambers delegate the laws through a binary confirmation process.

- All elections are publicly funded to eliminate any extra advantage above median income earners have within a system devoted significantly to different wealth representations.

- The Executive Legislature is indexed to Gross Tax representation but uses value voting indexed to taxable income as the qualifier for eligibility to vote and constituency representation. Retirement stipend incomes, welfare incomes, and pension incomes are used to calculate salaries while all investment related earnings must be translated into taxable wages prior to being used as a qualifying figure. Using Gross Tax Representation within the Executive legislature is a means to check the regressive fiscal policies almost certain to be propagated from the above median income chamber in the general legislature – hopefully more of the politicians will recognize the importance of fair tax systems and contribute to a more progressive and robust system for improved representation.

- The Judicial branch maintains a congressional structure with open and direct elections. It remains representative of the general population and accessible to all citizens

Disadvantages

- During economic crises wealth representation based on above median and below median thresholds will naturally result in class warfare rhetoric despite the fact the middle class maintains the greatest proportion of influence between both chambers of legislation. It is far worse to disguise economy and class differences within a standard population based system of representation. More of the guile and exploitation is removed when cohorts are created around the economic conditions that elicit stress responses from the enfranchised population. Not only are the chambers more insulated but peer pressure and shared circumstances are powerful motivations for reform. A positive gradient is manufactured with the middle class entitlement as they maintain more similarities in economic pressures and social environments.

Specifications;

Executive:

- 2.iii (Abolished Executive), 5.a.b.c (National)

Legislature:

- 1.i.xx.z (Multi-cameral legislature, 1st house), ii.x (Representative), iii.4.a. (Unitary Executive Powers), 5.a (National), 6.a.ii (4 year terms), b.iii (Unlimited), c.i (Lifetime), c.ii (sum of elected and appointed), **7.a.i (publicly funded), b.ii.xx (value voting)**, c.x (direct elections); 8.a.v.b (Citizen), **iv.b.1.i.ii.iii.2.d.g (Income from employer, employee, and self employed, in below median, pre tax),** c.i (exclusive), 10.b (voluntary), 12.b (Jurisdictions), **13.c.i (Representative of Tax Liabilities, Gross)**

- 1.i.xx.zz (Multi-cameral legislature, 2nd house), ii.x (Representative), iii.1.2.3.7 (Laws, Oversight, Treaty Ratification, Appointments), 5.(National), 6.a.iii (6 year terms), b.ii (Unlimited), c.ii (Intermittent), c.ii (sum of elected only), 7.a.i (Public Funding), b.ii.x (one citizen = one vote), c.x (direct elections), 8.a.v.b (Citizen), **iv.b.1.i.ii.iii.2.d.g (Income from employer, employee, and self employed, in below median, pre tax),** b.i.ii (to vote and to hold office), c.i (exclusive), 10.b (voluntary 12.b (Districts), 13.a.i (Representative of Population, by jurisdiction)

- 1.i.xx.zzz (Multi-cameral legislature, 3rd house).ii.x (Representative), iii.1.5.10 (Laws, Appropriations, Taxes), 5.(National), 6.a.iii (6 year terms), b.ii (Unlimited), c.ii (Intermittent), c.ii (sum of elected only), 7.a.i (Public Funding), b.ii.x (one citizen = one vote), c.x (direct elections), 8.a.v.b (Citizen), **iv.b.1.i.ii.iii.2.e.g (Income from employer, employee, and self employed, above median, pre tax),** b.i.ii (to vote and to hold office), c.i (exclusive), 10.b (voluntary), 12.b (Districts), 13.a.i (Representative of Population, by jurisdiction)

- 1.i.xx.zzzz (Multi-cameral legislature, 4th house), ii.x (Representative), iii.6 (Judicial), 5.a (National), 6.a.iii (6 year terms), b.iii (Unlimited), c.i (Lifetime), c.i (sum of elected and appointed positions), 7.a.i (Public Funding), b.ii.x (one citizen = one vote), c.x (direct elections), 8.a.vii.x. (Lawyers), b.ii (to hold office), c.i (exclusive), 10.b (voluntary), 12.b (Districts), 13.a.i (Representative of Population, by jurisdiction)

Judicial:

- 3.iii (Abolished Judicial), 5.a (National)

All Legislature Complexes distribute power more evenly than contemporary political systems but the Wealth Complex compromises this attribute with the value voting within the executive legislature. Wealthier individuals will have considerably more influence on the elections but this is a defect that already plagues many political systems with deregulated campaign finance systems. The concession is diluted by the simple fact that the executive legislators are elected across a large diverse cross section of jurisdictions making it less likely a single voter wields too much influence. At last resort the taxing powers can be transferred to the upper house in exchange for the appointment powers. This would create the tendency for progressive tax policies resulting in more equal wealth distributions and more open economies.

Bipartite systems distribute the executive responsibilities within the two general legislatures which tentatively prevents the accretion of too much power within too few offices. However the coupling of wealth representation to a binary system might provoke greater specialization in the chambers and more political dysfunction than intended. The perfect compromise is a Reserve Branch with triangulation powers that can mediate most disputes with the bicameral legislature. The **Charlemagne Republic** contains all three aspects of government in an attempt a balanced income based representation captured by segregated chambers with above median income eligibility criteria in the upper house and below median income eligibility criteria in the lower house. The single equivalency in terms should smooth out some of the more irregular political swings without protecting failed ideology over too extreme a period.

Charlemagne Republic

Primary Attributes

- No Executive branch
- Upper Legislature has above median Income eligibility
- Lower Legislature has below median Income eligibility
- Unicameral Reserve Board
- Appointed Judicial Branch

Advantages:

- All of the same advantages that apply to the Binary Legislature apply to this system.
- The Upper Chamber has an above median income eligibility criteria and the Lower is based on below median Income eligibility. Retirement stipend incomes, welfare incomes, and pension incomes are used to calculate salaries while all investment related earnings must be translated into taxable wages prior to being used as a qualifying figure.

- The Lower Chamber has Legislative broker properties allowing for some of the more important functions to be consolidated around single individuals for ease in integration and coordination. The increase in income resulting from the accumulation of offices does not exclude them from participating in the lower chamber and instead provides access to the Upper House for dual representation.

- The Reserve Board attempts to negotiate the more partisan economic segregation in the two primary bipartite legislatures. Without a third chamber with mixed economic legacies the nation might be stagnated by the balance of powers in the Upper and Lower House.

- The Reserve Board is empowered with a Legislative Sub Routine with Triangulation powers allowing it to negotiate the legislation and appointment powers of both chambers of the Binary Legislature. This is a potent benefit in the Binary Legislature structure as it can relegate a party or chamber less relevant for a small number of years until a correction in the election cycle occurs.

- The fact that the Reserve Board has triangulation powers with the Lower branch and where the Lower branch will have the numerical advantage in the number of transplants helps correlate the leadership within the government to the larger segments of the population without completely disenfranchising the professional and leisure class. It should be noted that a huge proportion of the public sector will be staffed by above median income earners and professionals which is the ultimate check against both the lower classes and the leisure classes.

- The Reserve Board also maintains the more conventional excising and excommunication powers when super majorities are gained within the institution. Large majorities in the Reserve Chamber bestow incredible powers to the party wielding them but they are checked by the single equivalency on term limits which make it very likely such movements are only temporary.

- The Reserve Board has single equivalent terms rewarding representatives who serve in the upper house with longer reserve tenures. The Upper House maintains 6 year terms while the Lower House only has 4 year terms. The Lower House will contribute more members on an annual basis simply due to the larger number of exhausted term limits. The two perpendicular attributes should balance each other in the number of current Reserve participants.

- A major source of variability will be the difference between the number of representatives correlated to GDP and the number correlated to population. It completely depends on the how the LCD is determined and what figures are used. It is expected that the lower house maintain a slight advantage in member sizes.

- This might introduce an imbalance in representation that completely disrupts and inhibits government function – especially the regulation of minimum wages, tax policy, and welfare infrastructure. If the Lower House maintains durable advantages in numbers it is more likely that there will be the tendency towards more progressive welfare systems, more progressive fiscal policies, and better regulated labor systems. The opposite is true if the Upper House with GDP representation maintains larger numbers. That being said both Houses are intersected by party making all attempts at prediction impossible without more context and circumstance being known.

Disadvantages:

- Politicians might be enticed to leave office prematurely to gain admission to the Reserve Chamber to coordinate majorities and numbers within all three. The Binary Legislatures condition parties for this strategy by placing intermittent term limits on candidates as after they have exhausted their access they can enter the Reserves and gain access to new eligibilities after their term away.

Specifications;

Executive:

- 2.iii (Abolished Executive); 5.a.b.c (National)

Legislative:

- 1.i.xx.z (Bicameral legislature), ii.x (Representative), iii.1.2.d.e.3.4.b.6.7 (Laws, Oversight on A,G, Treasury, Ratification, Executive-Presidential, Judicial, Appointments), 5.a (National), 6.a.iii (6 year terms), b.iii (3 terms maximum), c.ii (Lifelong); c.i (sum of elected), 7.a.i, b.ii.x, c.x (publicly funded, one citizen = one vote, direct elections), 8.a.v.b (Citizen), **8.iv.b.1.i.ii.iii.2.e.g (Income from employer, employee, self employed, above median, pre tax),** b.i.ii (to vote and hold office), c.i (exclusive), 10.b (voluntary), 12.a (Jurisdictions), **13.b (Representative of GDP), 13.f (Executive Representation)**

- 1.i.xx.zz (Bicameral legislature), ii.x (Representative), iii.1.2.b.c.3.4.c.d.5.7.10 (Laws, Oversight on Presidential and Judicial, Executive- domestic and treasury, Appropriations, Appointments, Taxing), 5.a (National), 6.a.ii (4 year terms), b.iii (3 terms maximum), c.i (Lifelong), c.i (sum of elected), **7.a.i, b.ii.x, (publicly funded, one citizen = one vote),** c.x (direct elections), 8.a.v.b (Citizen), **iv.b.1.i.ii.iii.2.d.g (Income from employer, employee, self employed, below median, pre tax),** b.i.ii (to vote and hold office), c.i (exclusive), 10.b (voluntary), 12.a (Jurisdictions), **13.a.i (Representative of Population, by jurisdiction), 13.h (Legislative Broker)**

Judicial;

- 3.a.i (Judicial, Circuit), b.i (Judicial powers only), **c.ii.x.2 (appointed by President)**, 5.a. (National) 6.a.ii (4 year term), b.iii (3 terms maximum), c.i (lifetime maximum); d.ii (sum of elected)

Reserves:

- 4.i.a.ii (Reserve Board, admitting all retired members), .ii.b (legislative sub routine - b.9 (Triangulation for Laws. Appointments), x.xx.ii.xxx (repealing legislation, excising legislators, excommunication), iii.b (Unicameral), iv.1.a.2.b (Pool of retired national legislators), v.a (single equivalent terms).

The Charlemagne Republic designed its upper house with Executive Representation to imitate conventional Executive branches without adopting the unitary structure. This way, representation is focused onto a discrete few decision makers but there is no opportunity for a cult of personality to develop without other political officers to check them. The lower house will ultimately balance out this entitlement with their own access to Legislative broker powers. Lower House members could end up managing several lower house offices and up to one Upper House office. The power structure is flexible allowing for different configurations of matching offices and responsibilities to manifest over generations or longer periods. This will help develop a legacy of different personalities and characters to aid in the nations mythology and history safely without exposing it to potential tyrants and usurpers.

Tax revenue can be equivocated with incomes for states with value voting systems easily deployed as the information has already been aggregated during the tax collection process. Correlating representation by state tax revenues ensures that the participating states do not exploit federalist tax policy. It also ensures that the states are stronger individual components with more developed militaries and regulatory apparatuses. Tax revenues are a function of economic activity with those states enjoying higher GDP naturally capturing more of the representation. This will help the Union by exporting more successful economic policies from the larger states to the smaller and less successful economies. It should be stressed that the **Spartan Union** is structured is not a federalist system with the difference being an absence of direct voter representation within the superstructure.

Spartan Union

Primary Attributes

- Tri-cameral Executive
- Democratic Legislature
- Appointed Judicial

Advantages

- Treasury has oversight over both the Presidential (Judicial) and the Attorney General Ex-legislatures, and maintains exclusive access to taxing powers

- The Presidential relinquishes oversight powers but gains appointment powers over the judicial branch and court systems. The Presidential maintains appointment confirmation powers over the Treasury.

- The Attorney General branch maintains oversight over the Treasury branch and maintains appointment confirmation powers over the Presidential, Judicial, and Treasury.

- All three branches may write laws and use their triangulation powers to confirm another branches legislation to hedge out the third. This simulates the first House of a conventional bicameral legislatures in that consent is required to pass laws and it will take considerable effort to clearly define which constitutes agency laws and which constitutes legislation. It will take even more effort to create a process for collaboration between the executive branches permitting the others to amend the sponsored legislation and submit it for reconciliation.

- Once the legislation passes with 2/3rds consent it is sent to the Democratic chamber for confirmation. Only after both halves of the multipart legislature have confirmed the legislation will it be ratified. The Democratic Legislature is provides the intimate connection between citizens of the participating states or nations. It should be a much stronger bond than Republican governments in that all citizens have a direct impact on the legislation passed.

- Correlating representation to tax revenue already accounts for population and GDP allowing the net representation to trend around the median or aggregate amounts but with each state jurisdiction allowed to moderate their influence by taxing more.

- The Treasurer General Branch is popularly elected which instills some federalist qualities into these overwhelmingly unionist system. The fact that the other two executive branches are elected by state tier executives makes this system more related to a Union rather then a more intimate Federal system.

- The states will attempt to maximize revenues without offsetting growth. The States level executive officers leverage the tax revenue for proportional representation within the federal system. Those states with the highest revenues will gain the most influence when voting for the Presidential Ex-Legislature and the Attorney General Ex legislature.

- By incentivizing increased state revenues the union can successfully manage (or limit) their shared dependency on the federal tier. It will also result in much stronger states with access to more military assets, more infrastructure improvements, and more mature systems of popular and corporate welfare.

- Those states that model for lower taxes and more dependency on the federal tier will have less representation as a check to exploitative tax policies redistributing capital from one state jurisdiction to another through unrepresentative government or inefficient policies.

- One of the largest expenditures of the state is defence and the Spartan Union intentionally rewards military spending by increased representation based on tax revenues. The Union will maintain larger standing armies and spend more on R&D for weaponry and equipment. This will permit it to more successfully negotiate hostile environments and extend its sphere of influence.

- By incentivizing tax payments the state can secure more stable access to larger amounts of funding which should produce significant geo-political gains over modest extensions of time. The government operates in economies of scale, whose services can make business more competitive, and whose militaries and intelligence agencies can work to provide more secure trade routes and access to more markets.

- This mode of representation should invoke patriotic sentiments with individuals guaranteed more political franchise with larger contributions to the state.

Disadvantages

- Obviously, there is a lack of a legislature compressing the responsibilities of government onto only three different offices. This is a self limiting quality as fewer member states will feel comfortable subrogating their interests to such a small number of representatives – especially if they are already a minority population within the economic union.

Specifications;

Executive:

- 2.ii.x.c (Tripartite Executive Presidential), iv.1.9 (Sub routine, Laws, Triangulation), iv.; 5.a (National); 6.a.ii (6 year terms), b.ii (2 terms maximum), c.i (lifetime maximum); d.i (sum of elected and appointed), **7.a.ii.xxx (Privately Funded by Governments), b.ii.xx (value voting), c.xxxx (Coalition of State level executives), 8.a. iv.b.1.vi (Tax Revenue),** 8.a.v.b (Citizen), b.i.ii (eligibility for voting and holding office); c.i (exclusive), 10.a (compulsory voting), 14.a (Macro-political Vote, Alpha),

- 2.ii.x.cc (Tripartite Executive Treasury), iv.1.5.9.10 (Sub routine, Laws, Appropriations, Triangulation, Taxation); 5.a (National); 6.a.ii (4 year terms), b.iii (3 terms maximum), c.ii (intermittent maximum); d.ii (sum of elected), 7.a.i (Publicly Funded);b.ii.x (one citizen = one vote), 8.a.v.b (citizen), b.i.ii (to vote and hold office), c.i (exclusive), 10.a (compulsory voting), 14.a (Macro-political Vote, Alpha)

- 2.ii.x.ccc (Tripartite Executive Attorney General), iv.1.2.9 (Sub Routine; Laws Oversight, Triangulation); 5.a. (National); 6.a.ii (4 year terms), b.iii (3 terms maximum), c.i (lifetime maximum); d.i (sum of elected and appointed), **7.a.ii.xxx (Privately Funded by Governments), b.ii.xx (value voting), c.xxxx (Coalition of State level executives), 8.a.iv.b.1.vi (Tax Revenue),** v.b. (citizen), b.i.ii (for voting and holding office); c.i (exclusive), 10.a (compulsory voting), 14.a (Macro-political Vote, Alpha)

Legislative;

- 1.i.x (Unicameral Legislature), ii.xxxx. (Democratic legislature), 1.a.i (Monochamber, straight vote), 2.a.iii (Referendum, monthly votes), 3.b.ii (Laws by triangulation with the tripartite executives), e.iii (Treaties by unicameral process), v.b (Citizen), b.i (to vote), 10.b (voluntary)

Judicial:

- 3.a.i. (Judicial, Circuit), B.i (Judicial powers only), C.ii.x.2 (appointed by President), 5.a. (National), 6.a.iii (6 year term), b.iii (3 terms maximum), c.i (lifetime maximum), 8.v.b, b.ii (citizen to hold office), c.i (exclusive)

The Democratic Chamber needs professional representatives to research the laws and author them. It is the perfect opportunity for executives to enter the realm of legislation. Not only is the most expert civil servants writing the laws but the consensus is provided directly by the masses. All citizens in the participating states vote and this will serve as the binding force within the Union. Segmentation into republican representatives is avoided and they won't have an opportunity to elicit partisan sentiments

More sophisticated systems can dictate which tax is empowered with the wealth representation on the state level. This will allow the nation or state make a complete conversion to wealth representation within its own borders and make it compatible with the economic union between other nations and states. Its an excellent opportunity to engineer the economy and the political systems seeking maximum correlation between representation and state power. Fiscal policy will provide the more intimate controls a political engineer needs to forge stronger, more responsive, and more practical systems from representation and wealth.

Post-tax Income Based Systems of Representation

Chapter 10

Post Tax Incomes can be moderated by most of the same tools as pre-tax incomes with one major improvement. Fiscal policy can be used to adjust the amounts and correlate them to more rational proportions for use in political entitlements. This will offer post tax income based systems of representation more legitimacy than pre-tax income systems. It will also present a frontier of conflict with different economic classes vying for a superior position through the realignment of eligibility and value voting criteria around movable means, averages, and monuments.

Value voting can be infinitely more responsible and fair under a post tax schedule than those systems utilizing pre-tax income values. The schedule will ultimately be less exploitable in environments of larger variances in wealth. Fiscal policy is already pivotal in preventing or reversing wealth inequality trends attaching political powers works as an incentive and as an implement. Although regression to a one person one vote systems is impossible in a value voting systems based on post tax values the weighted average can be focused on the middle or median class protecting the franchise of the majority.

Proportions of voting entitlements will almost certainly be more agreeable with the below median income earners paying on average 10% in taxes and above median income earners and the wealthy paying an average flat tax of 35% as evidenced in some of the most regressive income tax schedules employed by democratic nations. Post tax values bend the aggregate values back to the mean but real statistical analysis and modeling will have to be applied to earn solutions where the majority of political power continues to reside in the median-middle classes despite a huge majority of incomes earned exclusively by the top decile of the population.

The schedule would be more appropriate under condition of lower income citizens paying 50% and higher income citizens paying 70-80%. The difference between gross and net amounts are typically smaller in economies with mature progressive tax policies. The median-middle class values are larger proportions of overall demonstrating regression before any statistical modeling is applied. The denizens will already have enough economic and political might to effective argue for their interests and advantage when converting to the post tax based system of representation. The same is not of overwhelmingly regressive systems where the entitlement might contribute to the marginalization of the median and below median income earners.

Excessive imbalances in wealth erode the legitimacy of a political system especially when they are conditioned on incomes or other aspects of wealth. There is no quick and easy solution. It requires improvements in wages and it includes alterations in fiscal policy. The implicit danger is that both wealth and political power will consolidate within a small segment of the population and persist with intractable intent. It must be recognized the contemporary political systems already suffer these insults or threats. Especially those with unregulated campaign finance systems and where institutional imbalances of political power occur between different regions and parties. Nation's with popular representation maintain an opportunity to cure the body politic of the disease but are generally reluctant to exert themselves for a host of reasons. An average can be used to smooth out results and decrease number of potential changes between incomes of different years.

For example, a three year average would make the median incredibly resistant to most non permanent and non significant changes. In politics predictability is almost as important as possibility and utilizing an average will provide the stability a wealth based system of representation needs to protect itself during substantial economic corrections. Any normal event not lasting 2 years or more is unlikely to be expressed in significant terms. Using an average also insulates the wealth based system from dramatic shifts in political power immediate after significant corrections in the economy. It might moderate spontaneous changes but will relent to a popular movement lasting more than 2 or 3 years. Both aspects are important for providing stability – it must be able to resist change but then quickly adapt to it. Most contemporary political system fail in this regard as incumbency protection produce a stiff resistance to change despite environmental conditions.

One negative aspect is the incredible resistance policy architects will have to overcome in order to install a progressive tax policy that restricts the amount of income the individual has access to and then the amount of direct political power they are granted within the system. Although correlating political power with income will discourage support for progressive tax brackets under this system of representation the same population segments would resist the effort anyway. Democratic entitlements are often the product of concessions from economic classes in conflict and it may be possible for a nation to convert to a income based wealth system of representation when attached to tax policies that better guarantee a more equitable distribution of incomes and wealth across the demographic segments and generations.

A more conservative approach would be attaching the post tax income voter entitlement to only one institution in the system as a immediate check to current imbalances in wealth and future imbalances in power. Its presumed that popular representation in the other branches would mitigate the more extreme consequences of an imbalance of power in the chamber utilizing value voting for voter representation. Limiting only one institution or branch to wealth representation also produces a hinge or joint for integration within an allied systems. The two systems can reciprocal representation or equivalent access within each other without completely surrendering political will, ambition, and franchise. Although the application of post tax incomes is rather limited in this respect for those nations already in economic union they can be basis for eventual political incorporation.

The best approach would be assigning voter eligibility based upon post tax income values. The entire population still earns one vote per person but their inclusion in one of the chambers and exclusion from another permits the class differentiation necessary to pronounce political interests in a way that elicits proper responses from the constituents. A Magna Carta or Bolshevik styled rebellion could still result in the enfranchise of one economic class at the expense of the other but most democratic systems are stable enough to avoid the more violent of class struggles typically plaguing autocratic or overly exploitative systems. In these cases, a economic class earns itself representation in a chamber of the legislature or excludes another class from voting in executive or legislative elections producing a positive gradient in political power for themselves. Obviously, these are not the most productive results and it should be expected that the more class balanced systems of wealth representation will outperform them in terms of economic growth and political stability.

Segregated representation where a specific class or income bracket only has access to one legislative chamber or other governmental branch will typically be more dependent on median calculations with progressive income taxes making all chambers less elitist with the majority in representation being earned by lower income earners. Half the population will always be vested in the upper chamber and half the population will always be vested in the lower chamber but the differential in net incomes between both chambers and each chamber will be smaller. The corporate elite and wealthiest will continue to maintain an almost insurmountable advantage in income and captured wealth but are each relegated to only one vote where a much larger proportion of middle class and median class voters will be included within the process.

This will provide a huge counter balance to wealth inequality as the middle class is generally the best educated and most diverse class demographic. They will vote more appropriately for their interests when in direct competition with the wealthy. The lower income voters have a history of voting against their interests after cajoled and coerced and their segregation will force them to focus on their own circumstances and conditions without interloping from the other classes. It will help tremendously when the politicians suffer under identical economic conditions and must accommodate the same solutions and policy remedies.

Specialized chambers with class/income identity permit participants to make more informed decisions based on more precise interests and demands. The populations will identify more with the issues debated within a particular chamber with a numerical superiority expected to be earned by the party more effectively arguing for their interests. The intent is to create the condition where wages aren't outpaced by inflation, where unionization efforts gain protection, and where the more critical aspects of personal finance for the lower class like granting access to healthcare and student loans are more likely to pass the below median chamber. It is expected that the above median income chamber debate wage controls, benefit controls, and unionization controls. The above median income chamber will likely assert themselves to reduce the size of government, retard its regulatory ability, and argue for lower taxes.

Antagonism is present in current politics but they are disguised by a undifferentiated system of representation. Once the chambers are aligned by class more of the population will identify with the expected class incentives. Historic themes of oppression and exploitation may be more readily recognizable and treatable. Due to the lack of identity and lack of transparency a larger segment of the population regularly votes against its interests. Applying business efficiencies to government operation is an incredibly important function of government reform especially to restrain the grosser over-application of government powers. Economy is the most dominant aspect of modern life and business interests deserve influence but over-representation is a dangerous defect that exposes a nation to more extreme political movements and more frequent events.

The fact that the above median income distribution includes a large number of blue collar and professional workers making the chamber more competitive in economic ideology. This is a check against a sizable population in the below median chamber that is expected to vote against their immediate interests for gains in extra-personal issues. The specialization in class earned by both chambers only exacerbates the trends and tendencies already evident in most parties and creates the conditions for more accurate class based representation. It is important to preserve a balance in debate so that the issues are considered in all of the appropriate branches or chambers despite any predispositions to favor one ideological component over another.

Income based representation is not accessible by governments eliminating a useful check and balance of power. In many other facets of wealth representation governments can gain significant representation and influence providing a countervailing force against the accumulated wealth of the leisure class. The only source of income for conventional governments are permanent funds which are structured to remit federal taxes for income tax rather than capital gains. Permanent Funds will be a major component of the public finance systems of more competitive states and nations. There can be no denying that governments with access to more revenues and assets will be more productive at asserting their constituents and residents interests. It is gravely important for a nation's political system to incentivize the creation of permanent funds as nations surrendering their ambitions will find themselves in sovereign poverty and managing only a deficit of opportunities.

More ingenious political architects might construe all of a cities or states tax revenue as income making them eligible for all calculations towards representation in either state or national elections. This can be the main factor in legitimizing a political system premised on income value voting with governments effectively offsetting any wealth inequalities in the general population. The tax revenues within cities and states would tame even the most wildly imbalanced systems with a tally of nearly 20% of all incomes earned conserved within the popular elections. That income is accessible to the lower 80% of the income bracket for use in elections making the overall income distribution for value voting more normally distributed. However, in most balanced political systems leadership will be normally distributed between the parties and most gains will be cancelled out with only a small efficiency remaining for the more popular party.

Many contemporary democracies can convert easily to post tax income based system representation within their legislatures. The **Gaul Republic** makes only two improvements or adjustments to contemporary unitary executive republicans. The first is that the two chambers of the legislature are divided by class and income. Below median income earners vote in one chamber and above median income earners vote in the other. The entire population is represented and the citizens are split evenly between the two the chambers. A median value is used to ensure that exactly half the voting population is represented in the Lower Chamber and exactly half the voting population is represented in the Upper Chamber. If necessary an average in income values over a period of 3-5 years can be used as a means to smooth out the average used in the median calculations.

The second adjustment is made to both chambers' coefficient used to determine the ratio of representatives within population. The Gaul Republic uses gross taxes collected in proportion of part to whole. The tax based representational coefficient discourages abuses in fiscal policy that might otherwise result in exploitation of a class or region. Public sector engineers will have to balance tax liabilities for eligibility for representation in the chambers, the number of representatives each jurisdiction earns, and finally the capital constraints and needs of the nation.

Gaul Republic

Primary Traits;

- Unitary Executive
- Bicameral Legislature divided by income representation
- Appointed Judicial

Advantages;

- Class distinctions are made very obvious by the explicit divide within the two houses of the Congress. This will make obvious the intentions of the constituencies without obfuscating representation through a opaque private campaign finance system.

- Binary opposition within the economic interests of the two classes should average out to produce meaningful, substantial, and reasonable legislation that mitigates the fears and satisfies the aspirations of all segments of the population. There will be a natural check to any gross imbalances in wealth distribution with better representation by both classes – this should install more integrity and stability within both the political system and the economic system helping avoid more economic catastrophes (unnecessary adjustments) and resulting in less severe political changes (violent protests or revolts).

- In order to balance the pronounced differences between the higher and lower chambers of Congress the Executive Branch will remain free of class divisions and the election will continue to be popular without any significant criteria for voting or holding office (other than being a citizen and resident) with public funding of campaigns. It is apportioned a macro-political vote for the exclusive purpose of triangulating passage of legislation between the two chambers of the legislature. It also maintains domain over making judicial appointments although all must be confirmed by the upper chamber. This allocation of powers should mitigate any imbalance of class power within the legislature.

- Both chambers have appointment powers allowing the administration to select the chamber it feels will provide the greatest chance of confirmation. If it fails it can still petition the other chamber.

- Fiscal policy is such a powerful tool for providing funding and for manipulating the voting franchise that both chambers can engineer their own bills and lobby for their passage in both chambers.

- The representational coefficient is based on Gross taxes which will present an incentive for all states to pursue fairer federalist tax policies. Thos regions contributing more gross dollars will have a natural advantage in representation allowing it to protect the allocation and rebate process.

Disadvantages;

- As with any political system that draws a clear distinction between the classes tensions are heightened with an increased possibility that less mature or educated populations will never learn to compromise and navigate the sometimes treacherous arena of political economy making violence more frequent and more severe. The only positive outcome from instability is the accelerated evolution in the political system with a creative-destructive process aiding in the innovation new social and political technologies.

Specifications;

Executive;

- 2.i.iii (Unitary Executive, Elected), 5.a (National), 6.a ii (4 year terms), b.iii (3 maximum concurrent terms), c.i (lifetime maximum), d.i (sum of both elected and appointed), 7.a.i (publicly funded), b.i.x (Presidential), ii.xxxx (One citizen = One vote), c.x (direct elections), 8.v.b. (Citizen), b.i.ii (to hold office and to vote), c.i (exclusive), 10.b (voluntary voting), **14.a (Alpha Macro-political vote – for triangulation with congress)**

Legislature;

- 1.i.xx.z (Bicameral legislature, 1st house), ii.x (Representative), iii.1.2.3.5.7.10 (Laws, Oversight, Treatise, Appropriations, and Taxing), 5.a. (National), 6.a.iii (6 year terms), b.ii (2 terms maximum), c.ii (Intermittent), c.ii (sum of elected only), 7.a.i, b.ii.x, c.x (publicly funded, one citizen = one vote, direct elections), 8.a.v.b (Citizen), **iv.b.1.i.ii.iii.2.d.h (Income from employer, employee, self employed, below median, post tax),** b.i.ii (to vote and to hold office), c.i (exclusive), 10.b (voluntary), 12.a (Jurisdiction), **13.c.i (Representative of Gross Taxes)**

- 1.i.xx.zz (Bicameral legislature, 2nd house), ii.x (Representative), iii.1.3.4.5.7.10 (Laws, Ratification, Appropriations, Appointments, and Taxing), 5.a. (National), 6.a.ii (4 year terms), b.iv (Unlimited), c.ii (Intermittent); c.ii (sum of elected only), 7.a.i, b.ii.x, c.x (publicly funded, one citizen = one vote, direct elections), 8.a.v.b (Citizen), **iv.b.1.i.ii.iii.2.e.h (Income from employer, employee, self employed, above median, post tax),** b.i.ii (to vote and to hold office), c.i (exclusive), 10.b (voluntary), 12.b (Districts), **13.c.i (Representative of Gross Taxes)**

Judicial;

- 3.a.i. (Judicial, circuit), b.i (Judicial powers only), c.ii.x.2 (appointed by executive), 5.a. (National), 6.a.iii (6 year term), b.iii (3 terms maximum), c.i (lifetime maximum); 8.v.b, b.ii (citizen to hold office)

The Unitary Executive remains undifferentiated in representation so that the entire population participates within the same election. This is an implicit check against any criticisms that the nations doesn't satisfy the basic requirements of democracy with a deficit of popular elections. The definition of democracy must be improved to include compound elections where the entire population is represented but only in parts. An example of compound elections is the **Athenian Union.** There is no independent Executive and Judicial branches with all governmental powers conserved within two binary legislative chambers.

Value voting typically benefits the higher income earners in non segregated elections. However, the chambers in this union have eligibility income requirements correcting the imbalance by forcing each cohort into a class of similar wage earners. The wealthiest citizens may maintain a huge advantage but their reach and influence will be limited to the Upper House. In the lower house income are distributed more normally with predicable regression lines and fairer allocations of representation.

Athenian Union

Primary Attributes

- No Executive branch
- No Judicial Branch
- Upper Legislature has above median Income eligibility
- Lower Legislature has below median Income eligibility
- Unicameral Reserve Board

Advantages:

- All of the same advantages that apply to the Binary Legislature apply to this system.
- The Upper Chamber has an above median income eligibility criteria and the Lower is based on below median Income eligibility. Investment income is used to calculate salaries along with retirement stipend incomes, welfare incomes, and pension incomes. Adults with no income don't vote. All incomes used for the value voting are adjusted first by taxes making fiscal policy a part of election regulation – only those revenues taxes as income is included in the calculation.

- The larger disparities in wealth found in most democratic and capitalist nations is accommodated by the split chambers of the legislature. Even with value voting providing the wealth an almost immeasurable advantage that benefit is expressed within the above median income population which is more normally distributed than when the entire income distribution is considered. The lower chamber relies on value voting as well but it is segregated into below median incomes making the proportion much fairer. This should discourage fiscal and economic policies that unnaturally favor the concentration of incomes and wealth within a small population. The middle class maintains the superiority in numbers with incomes more competitive in comparison with the highest income earners.

- The fact that the Reserve Board has triangulation powers with the Lower branch and where the Lower branch will have the numerical advantage in the number of transplants helps correlate the leadership within the government to the more balanced population, more normally distributed incomes with less variance, without completely disenfranchising the professional and leisure class. It should be noted that a huge proportion of the public sector will be staffed by above median income earners and professionals which is the ultimate check against both the lower classes and the leisure classes.

- The Reserve Board is empowered with a Legislative Sub Routine with Triangulation powers allowing it to negotiate the legislation and appointment powers of both chambers of the Binary Legislature. This is another major concession to the lower chamber as its members to the upper houses appointment powers upon retirement. This is a potent benefit in the Binary Legislature structure as it can relegate a party or chamber less relevant for a small number of years until a correction in the election cycle occurs.

- The Reserve Board also maintains the more conventional excising and excommunication powers when super majorities are gained within the institution. Large majorities in the Reserve Chamber bestow incredible powers to the party wielding them but they are checked by the single equivalency on term limits which make it very likely such movements are only temporary.

- Both chambers have Legislative broker properties allowing for some of the more important functions to be consolidated around single individuals for ease in integration and coordination. The increased incomes resulting from the legislative broker properties will not make the politicians eligible for representation in dual chambers. The base income is used for any eligibility calculations.

Disadvantages:

- Politicians might be enticed to leave office prematurely to gain admission to the Reserve Chamber to coordinate majorities and numbers within all three. The Binary Legislatures predisposes use of this strategy by placing intermittent term limits on candidates as after they have exhausted their access they can enter the Reserves and gain access to new eligibilities after their term away.

Specifications;

Executive:

- 2.iii (Abolished Executive), 5.a.b.c (National)

Legislative:

- 1.i.xx.z (Bicameral legislature), ii.x (Representative), iii.1.2.d.e.3.4.b 6.7. (Laws, Oversight on A.G. and Treasury, Ratification, Executive-Presidential and Judicial, Appointments), 5.a (National), 6.a.iii (6 year terms), b.iii (3 terms maximum), c.ii (Lifelong), c.i (sum of elected), **7.a.i (publicly funded), b.ii.xx (value voting),** c.x (direct elections), 8.a.v.b (Citizen), **iv.b.1.i.ii.iii.iv.2.e.h (Income from employer, employee, self employed, above median, post tax),** b.i.ii (to vote and hold office), c.i (exclusive), 10.a (compulsory), 12.a (Jurisdictions), **13.a.i (Representative of Population, by jurisdiction), 13.h (Legislative Broker)**

- 1.i.xx.zz (Bicameral legislature), ii.x (Representative), iii.1.2.b.c.3.4.c.d.5.7.10. (Laws, Oversight on Presidential and Judicial, Executive- domestic and treasury, Appropriations, Appointments, Taxing), 5.a (National), 6.a.ii (4 year terms), b.iii (3 terms maximum), c.i (Lifelong), c.i (sum of elected), **7.a.i (publicly funded), b.ii.xx (value voting),** c.x (direct elections), 8.a.v.b (Citizen), **iv.b.1.i.ii.iii.iv.2.d.h (Income from employer, employee, self employed, below median, post tax),** b.i.ii (to vote and hold office), c.i (exclusive), 10.a (voluntary), 12.a (Jurisdictions), **13.a.i (Representative of Population, by jurisdiction), 13.h (Legislative Broker)**

Judicial:

- 3.iii (Abolished Judicial); 5.a (National)

Reserves:

- 4.i.a.ii (Reserve Board, admitting all retired members), .ii.b (legislative sub routine - b.9 (Triangulation for Laws. Appointments), x.xx.ii.xxx (repealing legislation, excising legislators, excommunication), .iii.b (Unicameral), iv.1.b.2.b (Pool of retired national legislators), v.a (single equivalent terms)

The most glaring deficit in this system is the lack of a voter franchise for adults with no justified income. They are not entitled to a vote within the value voting system. This can easily be mitigated by assigning a lowest common denominator for use in the political system. This factor will be included when calculating the median income values establishing the above and below median eligibility constraints.

Another possible source of imbalance in Reserve representation is the legislative broker power. The more success individual politicians have at consolidating political power around the legislative broker feature the less successful the party will be in the Reserve branch as the number of candidates transferred after lost elections will be lower. It is a sacrifice that the parties and individuals will have to consider when lobbying for those seats. Both branches permit their participants to gain multiple seats which should result in comparable rates of lost representation but the same deficiency over long periods makes the net consequence less predictable.

The separation of executive powers in the Athenian Union is one of the most important improvements in political theory and application. There may be more benefits concentrating the responsibilities in two solitary executives rather than executive committees. The **Bipartite Democracy** accomplishes this reform with one major improvement to previous examples. It tethers its republican upper house to a greek democracy in the lower house. It attempts to harness the creative powers of the population with direct access in a true democratic chamber. Not only is it practical but it maintain more implicit authority. The direct voting in the lower chamber helps legitimize the legislative produce of the republican upper house. This is definitely needed with the more specialized voter franchised attached to the executive branches.

Bipartite Democracy

Primary Traits;

- Bipartite Executive;
- One Presidential-Judicial Executive,
- One Treasurer General and Attorney General
- Appointed Judicial
- Filtered True Democratic Lower Chamber
- Republican Legislature Upper Chamber

Advantages;

- The Presidential Executive has middle and higher income (salary) eligibility requirements for voting.
- The Attorney General and Treasurer General executive branch has lower and middle income requirements for voting.

- The two executive branches are attached by a shared voter entitlement provided to the middle classes. The middle class is typically defined as those citizens earning 25% less than the median and 25% more than the median. They can vote in both executive elections providing the pivot or bond within the electorate. Class tensions can be minimized with the engineered regression toward middle class (median) representation. All candidates will seek for their approval and accommodate the diverse economic stress and political ideologies found within the center of the electorate.

- Upper House is Representative of Gross Tax Liabilities with only citizenship as a pre-requisite for voting. This provides the system more legitimacy despite the fact that voting for the two executive branches is dependent on incomes.

- Lower House is an unfiltered True Democracy which helps diffuse the wealth representation within the Executive branches by virtue of being the most direct interface with constituents citizens.

- The class based franchises can easily be reversed with the middle and lower income gaining access to the Presidential-Judicial branch and the middle and higher income earners gaining more access to the attorney general and treasurer general. There should be no doubt that the two executive branches maintain advantages for all classes and that the disadvantages are interchangeable as well.

Disadvantages;

- The most obvious problem in bifurcating representation based on income is that both classes have access to executives with significant personnel with military training and law enforcement powers. Yes, this is an appropriate distribution on power and a self evident check on each other's power but a long term consequence might be the increase in frequency of events centered on the two divergent executive branches. Current incarnations of executive offices concentrate all of the law enforcement and military personnel within one branch which does mitigate any segment of the population currently at odds with the empowered political party.

Specifications;

Executive;

- 2.ii.x.c (Executive Presidential), 5.a (National), 6.a.ii (6 year terms), b.i (3 terms maximum), c.i (lifetime maximum), d.ii (sum of elected), 7.a.i, b.ii.x, c.x (publicly funded, one citizen = one vote, direct elections), 8.a.v.b (Citizen), **a.iv.b.1.i.ii.iii.iv.2.a.b. (Income from employer, employee, Self employed, and investments, lower quarter, middle half, post tax),** b.i.ii (eligibility for voting and holding office), c.i (exclusive), 10.b (voluntary voting)

- 2.ii.x.cc (Executive Treasury and Attorney General), 5.a (National), 6.a.ii (4 year), b.iiv (Unlimited), c.ii (intermittent maximum), d.ii (sum of elected), 7.a.ii.x.xx.xxx, b.ii.x, c.x (privately funded by citizen, corporations, and governments, one citizen = one vote, direct elections), **a.iv.b.1.i.ii.iii.iv.2.b.c. (Income from employer, employee, Self employed, and investments, upper quarter, middle half, post tax),** b.i.ii (for voting and holding office), c.i (exclusive), 10.b (voluntary voting)

Legislature;

- 1.i.xx.z (Bicameral legislature, 1st house), ii.xx (Representative), iii.1.2.3.5.7.10 (Laws, Oversight, Ratification, Appropriations, Appointments, Taxes), 5.a.b. (National), 6.a.iii (6 year terms), b.ii (2 terms maximum), c.ii (Intermittent), c.ii (sum of elected only); 7.a.ii.x.xx, b.ii.x, c.x (privately funded by citizen, and corporations, one citizen = one vote, direct elections), 8.a.v.b (Citizen), b.i.ii (to vote and to hold office), c.i (exclusive), 10.b (voluntary), 12.a (Jurisdiction), **13.c.ii (Representative of Tax Liabilities, Gross)**

- 1.i.xxxx (True Democratic), 1.a.i (Mono-chamber, Straight vote), 2.a.iii (Referendum monthly), 3.b.ii (confirms legislation bicameral), d. (confirms appointments), e.ii (confirms treaties, bicameral)

Judicial;

- 3.A.i (Judicial, Appointed Hierarchal), B.i (Judicial powers only), c.ii.xx.2 (appointed by executive), 5.a. (National),6.a.iii (6 year term), b.iii (3 terms maximum), c.i (lifetime maximum), 8.v.b, b.ii (citizen to hold office)

The middle class definitely has a voter franchise to protect as they vote in both executive branches. This will provide incentive for the poorer classes and reign in the extra influence of the wealthiest class. The middle class typically contains the most professionals and academics fulfilling the majority of highly specialized roles within business, university, and government and who share a large number of economic stressors with the poor. The middle class should have the most political power because it should contain the most diverse cross section of demographics and identity roles.

The middle class has the overwhelming advantage in the Presidential-Judicial branch as they maintain numerical superiority (66%) over the smaller more wealthy constituents (33%). This makes the entire system more regressive as the lower class has the advantage in numbers with the AG/Treasury branch and the middle class has the advantage in numbers within the Presidential branch. The richest segment does benefit from private campaign finance with a wealth advantage over the middle class and where the lower class may be more susceptible to exploitative ideologies but their lack of representation in the second executive branch checks the extra-representational powers.

Corporate incomes and Corporate personhood will not be treated within this chapter. They will be relegated to another book specializing in corporate based systems of representation. However, corporations can have the same entitlements individuals have in terms of value voting and unit voting and can compete in size and power with even moderately sized cities or states. In periods of darker political economy where imperialism reigns it might contribute to an environment where corporations have unchecked power and con consolidate political powers within their corporate hierarchies. In this respect they can be made compatible with the republican forms of government which take advantage of wealth representation.

Annex

Tax Based
Systems of Representation

Gilt Republic

Executive;

- 2.i (Unitary Executive), 5.a (National) 6.a ii (4 year terms), b.iii (3 maximum concurrent terms), c.i (lifetime maximum), d.i (sum of both elected and appointed) 7.a.i (publicly funded), b.i.x (Presidential), ii.xxxx (One citizen = One vote), c.x (direct elections), 8.a.v.b. (Citizen), b.i.ii (to hold office and to vote), c.i (exclusive), 10.b (voluntary voting)

Legislature;

- 1.i.xx.z (Bicameral legislature, 1st house), ii.x (Representative), iii.1.2.3.5.7 (Laws, Oversight, Ratification, Appropriations, and Appointments), 5.a. (National), 6.a.iii (6 year terms), b.ii (2 terms maximum), c.ii (Intermittent), c.ii (sum of elected only), 7.a.i (publicly funded), b.ii.xxxx (One citizen = One vote), c.x (direct elections), 8.a.v.b (Citizen), b.i.ii (to vote and to hold office), c.i (exclusive), 10.b (voluntary voting), 12.a (Jurisdiction), 13.c.ii (Representative of Net Taxes)
- 1.i.xx.zz (Bicameral legislature, 2nd house), ii.x (Representative), iii.1.2.3.5.10 (Laws, Oversight, Ratification, Appropriations, Taxing), 5.a. (National), 6.a.ii (4 year terms), b.iv (Unlimited), c.ii (Intermittent), c.ii (sum of elected only), 7.a.ii.x.xx.a, (privately funded, citizen and domestic corporations), b.ii.xxxx (One citizen = One vote), c.x (direct elections), 8.a.v.b (Citizen), b.i.ii (to vote and to hold office), c.i (exclusive), 10.b (voluntary), 12.b (Districts), 13.c.i (Representative of Gross Taxes)

Judicial;

- 3.A.i. (Judicial, Circuits), B.i.a (Judicial powers only, general), C.ii.x.1 (Appointed by Unitary President), 5.a.

(National), 6.a.iii (6 year term), b.iii (3 terms maximum), c.i (lifetime maximum), 8.v.b, b.ii (citizen to hold office)

Tax Complex

Executive:

- 2.iii (Abolished Executive); 5.a.b.c (National)

Legislative:

- 1.i.xx.z (Multi-cameral legislature, 1st house), ii.xx (Representative),.iii.4.a.b.c (Presidential Executive Powers); 5.a (National), 6.a.iii (6 year terms), b.iii (3 terms maximum), c.ii (Intermittent); c.ii (sum of elected and appointed); 7.a.ii.xxx (Privately funded by governments); 8.a.v.b (citizen), b.i.ii (to vote and hold office), 10.a (compulsory), 12.a (Jurisdictions), 13.c.i 13.c.ii (Representative of Net Taxes), 13.f (Executive Representation)
- 1.i.xx.zz (Multi-cameral legislature, 2nd house), ii.xx (Representative),.iii.4.b.c (Attorney General Executive Powers); 5.a (National), 6.a.iii (6 year terms), b.iii (3 term maximum), c.ii (Intermittent); c.ii (sum of elected and appointed); 7.a.i (publicly funded), b.ii.xxxx (One citizen = One vote), c.x (direct elections); 8.a.v.b (citizen), b.i.ii (to vote and hold office), c.i (exclusive), 10.a (compulsory), 12.b (Districts), 13.a.i (Representative of Population, by jurisdiction), 13.h (Legislative Broker)
- 1.i.xx.zzz (Multi-cameral legislature, 3rd house), ii.xx (Representative),.iii.4.c (Treasurer General Executive Powers); 5.a (National), 6.a.iii (6 year terms), b.iv (Unlimited), c.ii (Intermittent); c.ii (sum of elected and appointed); 7.a .ii.x.xx (Privately Funded by citizens and corporations), 8.a.v.b (citizen), b.i.ii (to vote and hold office), c.i (exclusive), 10.a (compulsory), 12.b (Districts), 13.c.i (Representative of Gross Taxes)
- 1.i.xx.zzzz (Multi-cameral legislature, 4th house).ii.xx (Representative), 5.a (National), iii.1.5.10 (Laws, Appropriations, and Taxation), 6.a.ii (4 year terms), b.iii (Unlimited), c.i (Lifetime); c.ii (sum of elected and appointed); 7.a.i (publicly funded), b.ii.xxxx (One citizen = One vote), c.x (direct elections); 8.a.v.b (citizen), b.i.ii (to vote and hold office), c.i (exclusive), 10.a (compulsory), 12.a (Ju-

risdictions), 13.a.i (Representative of Population, by jurisdiction), 13.h (Legislative Broker)

- 1.i.xx.zzzzz (Multi-cameral legislature, 5th house).ii.xx (Representative), 5.a (National), iii.1.2.3.5.7 (Laws, Oversight, Treaty Ratification, Appropriations, and Appointments,), 6.a.ii (4 year terms), b.iii (Unlimited), c.i (Lifetime); c.ii (sum of elected and appointed); 7.a.i (publicly funded), b.ii.xxxx (One citizen = One vote), c.x (direct elections); 8.a.v.b (citizen), b.i.ii (to vote and hold office), c.i (exclusive), 10.a (compulsory), 12.b (Districts), 13.c.ii (Net Tax Representation), 13.f (Executive Representation)
- 1.i.xx.zzzzzz (Multi-cameral legislature, 6th house), ii.xx (Representative), iii.6 (Judicial) .5.a (National), 6.a.iii (6 year terms), b.iv (Unlimited), c.i (Lifetime); 7.a.i (publicly funded), b.ii.xxxx (One citizen = One vote), c.x (direct elections); 8.a.vii.x.xx (Judge or Lawyer), v.b (Citizen), b.ii (to hold office), c.i (exclusive), 10.a (compulsory), 12.a (Jurisdictions), 13.a.i (Representative of Population, by jurisdiction)

Judicial

- 3.a.iv (Abolished Judicial); 5.a (National)

Tax Reserve Republic

Executive;

- 2.i.iii (Unitary Executive, Elected), 5.a (National) 6.a ii (4 year terms).b.iii (3 maximum concurrent terms), c.i (lifetime maximum), d.i (sum of both elected and appointed) 7.a.i (publicly funded), b.i.x Presidential) .ii.xxxx (One citizen = One vote), c.x(direct elections); 8.v.b. (Citizen), b.i.ii (to hold office and to vote), c.i (exclusive), 10.a (compulsory voting)

Legislative;

- .i.xx.z (Bicameral legislature, 1st house), ii.xx (Representative), iii.1.2.3.5.7 (Laws, Oversight, Ratification, Appropriations, and Appointments), 5.a. (National), 6.a.iii (6 year terms), b.iv (Unlimited), c.ii (Intermittent); c.ii (sum of elected only); 7.a.i (publicly funded), b.ii.xxxx (One citizen = One vote), c.x (direct elections); 8.a.v.b (citizen), b.i.ii (to vote and to hold office), c.i (exclusive), 10.b (voluntary), 12.a (Jurisdiction), 13.c.i (Representative of Gross Taxes)

- 1.i.xx.zz (Bicameral legislature, 3rd house), ii.xx (Representative), iii.9.b (Triangulation and Laws, Appropriations) 5.a. (National), 6.a.ii (4 year terms), b.iv (Unlimited), c.ii (Intermittent); c.ii (sum of elected only); 7.a.i (publicly funded), b.ii.xxxx (One citizen = One vote), c.x (direct elections); 8.a.v.b (citizen), b.i.ii (to vote and to hold office), c.i (exclusive), 10.b (voluntary), 12.b (Districts), 13.c.ii (Representative of Net Taxes)

Judicial

- 3.i. (Judicial, Hierarchal, Elected); 5.a.(National) 6.a.iii (6 year term), b.iii (3 terms maximum), c.ii (intermittent maximum); d.ii (sum of elected) 7.a.i (publicly funded), b.ii.xxxx (One citizen = One vote), c.x (direct elections); 8.v.b, b.ii (citizen to hold office), 8.vii.a.b.x (public attorneys and judicial experience), c.i (exclusive)

Reserve;

- 4.i.a.ii (Reserve Board, admitting all retired members), .ii.b Bicameral legislative sub routine - 1.2.3.5.7 (Laws, Oversight, Ratification, Appropriations, and Appointments), iv.1.b.2.b (Pool of retired national legislators), v.d (Total equivalent terms)

Tax Liability Based Systems of Representation

Tripartite Tax Republic

Executive;

- 2.ii.x.c (Tripartite Executive Presidential), 5.a (National), 6.a.iii (6 year terms), b.i (1 terms maximum), c.i (lifetime maximum), d.ii (sum of elected), 7.a.i (publicly funded), b.i.x (Presidential) ii.xxxx (One citizen = One vote), c.x (direct elections), 8.a.v.b (Citizen), b.i.ii (eligibility for voting and holding office), c.i (exclusive), 10.b (voluntary voting)
- 2.ii.x.cc (Tripartite Executive Treasury), 5.a (National); 6.a.ii (4 year terms), b.iii (3 terms maximum), c.ii (intermittent maximum), d.ii (sum of elected), 7.a.ii.x.xx.a (pri-

vately funded by citizen and domestic corporations), b.i.x (Presidential), ii.xxxx (One citizen = One vote), c.x (direct elections), 8.a.v.b (citizen), b.i.ii (for voting and holding office), c.i (exclusive), 10.b (voluntary voting)

- 2.ii.x.ccc (Tripartite Executive Attorney General), 5.a. (National), 6.a.iii (6 year terms), b.ii (2 terms maximum), c.i (lifetime maximum), d.i (sum of elected and appointed), 7.a.ii.x.xxx (privately funded by citizen and government), b.i.x (Presidential), ii.xxxx (One citizen = One vote), c.x (direct elections), 8.a.v.b. (citizen), b.i.ii (for voting and holding office), c.i (exclusive), 10.b (voluntary voting)

Legislature;

- 1.i.xx.z (Bicameral legislature, 1st house), ii.x (Representative), iii.1.2.3.5.7 (Laws, Oversight, Ratification, Appropriations, and Appointments), 5.a. (National), 6.a.iii (6 year terms), b.ii (2 terms maximum), c.ii (Intermittent), c.ii (sum of elected only), 7.a.i (publicly funded), b.ii.xxxx (One citizen = One vote), c.x (direct elections), 8.a.v.b (citizen), 8.a.iv.c.i.a.xxxx (Tax Liabilities, above median), ii.e (total liabilities), iii.a (Personal Taxes only), b.i.ii (to vote and to hold office), c.i (exclusive), 10.b (voluntary), 12.a (Jurisdiction), 13.a.i (Representative of Population)
- 1.i.xx.zz (Bicameral legislature, 2nd house), ii.x (Representative), iii.1.2.3.5.10 (Laws, Oversight, Ratification, Appropriations, Taxing), 5.a. (National), 6.a.ii (4 year terms), b.iv (Unlimited), c.ii (Intermittent), c.ii (sum of elected only), 7.a.i (Public Funding), c.x (direct elections), 8.a.v.b (citizen), 8.a.iv.c.i.b.xxxx (Tax Liabilities, below median), ii.e (total liabilities), iii.a (Personal Taxes only), b.i.ii (to vote and to hold office), c.i (exclusive), 10.b (voluntary), 12.b (Districts), 13.a.i (Representative of Population)

Judicial;

- 3.a.i. (Judicial, Circuit), b.i (Judicial powers only), c.ii.x.2 (Appointed by President), 5.a. (National), 6.a.iii (6 year term), b.iii (3 terms maximum), c.i (lifetime maximum), 8.v.b, b.ii (citizen to hold office), c.i (exclusive)

Bipartite Classed Democracy

Executive;

- 2.ii.x.c (Executive Presidential), 5.a (National), 6.a.ii (6 year terms), b.iii (3 terms maximum), c.i (lifetime maximum), d.ii (sum of elected), 7.a.i (publicly funded), b.i.x Presidential) ii.xxxx (One citizen = One vote), c.x (direct elections), 8.a.iv.c.i.b.xxxx (tax liability criteria, below median), ii.e (total taxes), iii.a (Personal taxes only), v.b (Citizen), b.i.ii (eligibility for voting and holding office), c.i (exclusive), 10.b (voluntary voting)
- 2.ii.x.cc.ccc (Executive Treasury and Attorney General), 5.a (National), 6.a.ii (4 year), b.iiv (Unlimited), c.ii (intermittent maximum), d.ii (sum of elected), 7.a.ii.x.xx.a.xxx (privately funded by citizen, domestic corporations, government), b.i.x (Presidential), ii.xxxx (One citizen = One vote), c.x (direct elections), 8.a.v.b (citizen), 8.a.iv.c.i.a.xxxx (tax liability criteria, above median), ii.e (total taxes), iii.a (Personal taxes only), b.i.ii (for voting and holding office), c.i (exclusive), 10.b (voluntary voting)

Legislature;

- 1.i.xx.z (Bicameral legislature, 1st house), ii.x (Representative), iii.1.2.3.5.10 (Laws, Oversight, Ratification, Appropriations, and Taxes), 5.a (National), 6.a.iii (6 year terms), b.ii (2 terms maximum), c.ii (Intermittent), c.ii (sum of elected only), 7.a.i (publicly funded), b.ii.xxxx (One citizen = One vote), c.x (direct elections), 8.a.v.b (Citizen), b.i.ii (to vote and to hold office), c.i (exclusive), 10.b (voluntary), 12.a (Jurisdiction), 13.a.i (Representative of Gross Tax Liabilities), 13.f (Executive Representative)
- 1.i.xx.zz (Bicameral Legislature, 2nd House), ii.xxxx (True Democratic), 1.a.i (Mono-chamber, Straight vote), 2.a.ii (Biweekly), 3.b.ii (confirms legislation, bicameral), d. (confirms appointments), e.ii (confirms treaties, bicameral), 8.v.b (Citizen), b.i (to vote)

Judicial;

- 3.a.i (Judicial, Circuits), b.i (Judicial powers only), c.ii.x.2 (Appointed by the Presidential), 5.a. (National), 6.a.iii (6 year term), b.iii (3 terms maximum), c.i (lifetime maximum), 8.v.b, b.ii (citizen to hold office), c.i (exclusive)

Complex-Tax Reserve

Executive:

- 2.iii (Abolished Executive); 5.a.b.c (National)

Legislative:

- 1.i.xx.z (Multi-cameral legislature, 1st house), ii.x (Representative), iii.4.a. (Unitary Executive Powers), 5.a (National), 6.a.ii (4 year terms), b.iii (Unlimited), c.i (Lifetime), c.ii (sum of elected and appointed), 7.ii.a.x.xxx (Privately funded by citizens and governments), ii.xxxx (One citizen = One vote), c.x (direct elections), 8.a.v.b (Citizen), b.ii (criteria to hold office), 10.b. (voluntary), 12.b (Jurisdictions), 13.a.i (Representative of Population, by jurisdiction)
- 1.i.xx.zz (Bicameral legislature, 2nd house), ii.x (Representative), iii.1.2.3.5.7 (Laws, Oversight, Ratification, Appropriations, and Appointments), 5.a. (National), 6.a.iii (6 year terms), b.ii (2 terms maximum), c.ii (Intermittent), c.ii (sum of elected only); 7.a.i (publicly funded), b.ii.xxxx (One citizen = One vote), c.x (direct elections); 8.a.iv.c.i.a.xxxx (Tax Liabilities, below median), ii.e (total taxes), iii.a (Personal taxes only), 8.a.v.b (citizen), b.i.ii (to vote and to hold office), c.i (exclusive), 10.b (voluntary), 12.a (Jurisdiction), 13.c.i (Representative of Gross Taxes)
- 1.i.xx.zzz (Bicameral legislature, 3rd house), ii.x (Representative), iii.9.a.1.5.10 (Triangulation on Laws, Appropriations, Taxing), 5.a. (National), 6.a.ii (4 year terms), b.iv (Unlimited), c.ii (Intermittent), c.ii (sum of elected only), 7.a.ii.xxxx, c.x (privately funded and open, direct elections), 8.a.v.b (citizen), b.i.ii (to vote and to hold office), 10.b (voluntary), c.i (exclusive), 12.b (Districts), 13.c.ii (Representative of Net Taxes)
- 1.i.xx.zzzz (Multi-cameral legislature, 4th house,), ii.x (Representative), iii.6 (Judicial), 5.a (National), 6.a.iii (6 year terms), b.iii (Unlimited), c.i (Lifetime), c.i (sum of elected and appointed positions), 7.a.i (Public Funding); 8.a.iv.c.i.a.xxxx (Tax Liabilities, above median), ii.e (total taxes), iii.a (Personal taxes only), 8.a.v.b (citizen), b.i (to vote), 8.a.vii.x.xx (Lawyers and judges), a.v.b (citizen),

b.ii (to hold office), 10.a (compulsory), 12.b (Districts), 13.a.i (Representative of Population, by jurisdiction)

Judicial:

- 3.a.iv (Abolished Judicial); 5.a (National)

Reserve:

- 4.i.a (Reserve Board, admitting all retired members, permanent), ii (legislative sub routine - b.1.2.3.5.10 (Laws, Oversight, Treaties, Appropriations, and Taxes), iii.b (Unicameral), iv.1.a.2.b (Pool of retired national legislators), v.d (total equivalent terms)

Binary Tax Legislature

Executive:

- 2.iii (Abolished Executive), 5.a.b.c (National)

Legislative:

- 1.i.xx.z (Bicameral legislature), ii.x (Representative), iii.1.2.d.e.3.4.a 6.7.10 (Laws, Oversight on A,G, Treasury, Ratification, Executive-Presidential, Judicial, Contra Appointments, appropriations, Taxes), 5.a (National), 6.a.iii (6 year terms), b.iii (3 terms maximum), c.ii (Intermittent); c.i (sum of elected), 7.a.i (publicly funded), b.ii.xxxx (One citizen = One vote), c.x (direct elections), 8.a.v.b (Citizen), 8.a.iv.c.i.a.xxxx (tax liability criteria, above median), ii.e (total taxes), iii.a (Personal taxes only), b.i.ii (to vote and hold office), c.i (exclusive), 10.b (voluntary), 12.b (Districts), 13.c.i (Representative of Tax Liabilities, Gross)
- 1.i.xx.zz (Bicameral legislature), ii.xx (Representative), iii.1.2.b.c.3.4.b.c.5.7.10 (Laws, Oversight on Presidential and Judicial, Treatise, Executive- domestic and treasury, Appropriations, Contra Appointments, Taxing), 5.a (National), 6.a.iii (6 year terms), b.iii (3 terms maximum), c.i (Lifelong), c.i (sum of elected), 7.a.i (publicly funded), b.ii.xxxx (One citizen = One vote), c.x (direct elections); 8.a.v.b (Citizen), 8.a.iv.c.i.b.xxxx (tax liability criteria, below median), ii.e (total taxes), iii.a (Personal taxes only), b.i.ii (to vote and hold office), c.i (exclusive), 10.b (voluntary), 12.b (Districts), 13.a.i (Representative of Population, by jurisdiction)

Judicial:

- 3.a.iv (Abolished Judicial), 5.a (National)

Cossack Republic

Executive;

- 2.ii.x.c (Tripartite Executive Presidential), iv.1.9 (Sub routine, Laws, Triangulation), 5.a (National), 6.a.iii (6 year terms), b.i (1 terms maximum), c.i (lifetime maximum); d.i (sum of elected and appointed), 7.a.i (publicly funded), b.i.x (Presidential), ii.xx.ccc (Value Voting, bracket), c.x (direct elections), 8.a.iv.c.ii.e.iii.a.b (tax liability, total, persons and corporate entities), v.b (Citizen), b.i.ii (eligibility for voting and holding office), c.i (exclusive), 10.b (voluntary voting), 14.a (Macro-political Vote, Alpha)
- 2.ii.x.cc (Tripartite Executive Treasury), iv.1.5.9.10 (Sub routine, Laws, Appropriations, Triangulation, Taxation), 5.a (National), 6.a.ii (4 year terms), b.iii (3 terms maximum), c.ii (intermittent maximum), d.ii (sum of elected), 7.a.i (publicly funded), b.i.x (Presidential), ii.xx.ccc (Value voting, bracket), c.x (direct elections), 8.a.iv.c.ii.c.iii.a.b (tax liability, income, personal and corporate entities), v.b (Citizen), b.i.ii (eligibility for voting and holding office), c.i (exclusive); 10.b (voluntary voting), 14.a (Macro-political Vote, Alpha)
- 2.ii.x.ccc (Tripartite Executive Attorney General), iv.1.2.9 (Sub Routine; Laws Oversight, Triangulation), 5.a. (National), 6.a.ii (4 year terms), b.ii (2 terms maximum), c.i (lifetime maximum), d.i (sum of elected and appointed), 7.a.i (publicly funded), b.i.x Presidential), ii.xx.ccc (Value voting, bracket), c.x (direct elections), 8.a.iv.c.ii.b.iii.a (tax liability, property, natural persons only), v.b (Citizen), b.i.ii (eligibility for voting and holding office), c.i (exclusive), 10.b (voluntary voting), 14.a (Macro-political Vote, Alpha)

Legislative;

- 1.i.x.z (Unicameral legislature, 1st house,), ii.x (Representative), iii.6 (Judicial), 5.a (National), 6.a.iii (6 year terms), b.iii (Unlimited), c.i (Lifetime), c.i (sum of elected and appointed positions), 7.a.i (publicly funded), b.ii.xxxx (One citizen = One vote), c.x (direct elections), 8.a.vii.x.

(Lawyers), 8.a.v.b (Citizen), b.ii (to hold office), c.i (exclusive), 10.b (voluntary), 12.b (Districts), 13.a.i (Representative of Population, by jurisdiction), 13.h (Legislative Brokers)

Judicial:

- 3.a.iv (Abolished Judicial), 5.a (National)

GDP Based
Systems of Representation

Producer Republic

Executive;

- 2.ii.x.c (Tripartite Executive Presidential), 5.a (National), 6.a.iii (6 year terms), b.i (1 terms maximum), c.i (lifetime maximum), d.ii (sum of elected), 7.a.i (publicly funded), b.i.x (Presidential), ii.xxxx (One citizen = One vote), c.x (direct elections), 8.a.v.b (Citizen), b.i.ii (eligibility for voting and holding office), c.i (exclusive), 10.b (voluntary voting)
- 2.ii.x.cc (Tripartite Executive Treasury), 5.a (National), 6.a.ii (4 year terms), b.iii (3 terms maximum), c.ii (intermittent maximum), d.ii (sum of elected), 7.a.ii.x.xx.a.xxx (privately funded by citizen, domestic corporations, and government), b.i.x (Presidential), b.ii.xxxx (One citizen = One vote), c.x (direct elections), 8.a.v.b (citizen), b.i.ii (for voting and holding office), c.i (exclusive), 10.b (voluntary voting).
- 2.ii.x.ccc (Tripartite Executive Attorney General), 5.a. (National), 6.a.ii (4 year terms), b.ii (2 terms maximum), c.i (lifetime maximum), d.i (sum of elected and appointed), 7.a.ii.x (privately funded by citizens), b.i.x (Presidential), ii.xxxx (One citizen = One vote), c.x (direct elections), 8.a.v.b. (citizen), b.i.ii (for voting and holding office), c.i (exclusive), 10.b (voluntary voting).

Legislature;

- 1.i.x.z (Unicameral legislature, 1st house), ii.x (Representative), iii.1.2.3.5.7.10 (Laws, Oversight, Ratification, Appropriations, Appointments, Taxation), 5.a. (National), 6.a.iii (6 year terms), b.ii (2 terms maximum), c.ii (Intermittent), c.ii (sum of elected only), 7.a.i (publicly funded), b.ii.xxxx (One citizen = One vote), c.x (direct elections), 8.a.v.b (citizen), b.i.ii (to vote and to hold office), c.i (exclusive), 10.b (voluntary), 12.a (Jurisdiction), 13.b.ii (Representative of GDP, per capita)

Judicial;

- 3.a.i. (Judicial, circuits), b.i (Judicial powers only), c.ii.x.2 (appointed by the President), 5.a. (National), 6.a.iii (6 year term), b.iii (3 terms maximum), c.i (lifetime maximum), 8.v.b, b.ii (citizen to hold office)

Echo-Republic

Executive;

- 2.i.iii (Unitary Executive, Elected), 5.a (National), 6.a ii (4 year terms), b.iii (3 maximum concurrent terms), c.i (lifetime maximum), d.i (sum of both elected and appointed) 7.a.i (publicly funded), b.i.x (Presidential), ii.xxxx (One citizen = One vote), c.x (direct elections), 8.v.b. (Citizen), b.i.ii (to hold office and to vote), c.i (exclusive), 10.b (voluntary voting)

Legislature;

- 1.i.xx.z (Bicameral legislature, 1st house), ii.x (Representative), iii.1.2.3.5 (Laws, Oversight, Ratification, Appropriations), 5.a. (National), 6.a.iii (6 year terms), b.ii (2 terms maximum), c.ii (Intermittent), c.ii (sum of elected only), 7.a.i (publicly funded), b.ii.xxxx (One citizen = One vote), c.x (direct elections), 8.a.v.b (citizen), b.i.ii (to vote and to hold office), c.i (exclusive), 10.b (voluntary), 12.a (Jurisdictions), 13.b.ii (Representative of GDP, Per Capita), 13.h (Legislative Brokers)
- 1.i.xx.zz (Bicameral legislature, 2nd house), ii.xx (Representative), iii.1.3.5.10 (Laws, Ratification, Appropriations, Taxing), 5.a. (National), 6.a.ii (4 year terms), b.iii (3 terms maximum), c.ii (Intermittent); c.ii (sum of elected only), 7.a.i (publicly funded), b.ii.xxxx (One citizen = One vote), c.x (direct elections); 8.a.v.b (citizen), b.i.ii (to vote and to hold office), c.i (exclusive), 10.b (voluntary), 12.a (Jurisdictions), 13.b.i (Representative of GDP, Straight), 13.h (Legislative Brokers)

Judicial;

- 3.a.i. (Judicial, Circuit), b.i (Judicial powers only), c.ii.x.1 (appointed by the Unitary), 5.a. (National), 6.a.iii (6 year term), b.iii (3 terms maximum), c.i (lifetime maximum), 8.v.b, b.ii (citizen to hold office).

Reserve:

- 4.i.a (Reserve Board, admitting all retired members), ii.b.5.7 (legislative sub routine oversight, and appointment), ii.d.x.xx.ii (repealing legislature, excising legislators and judges, and excommunication), iii.b (unicameral), iv.1.a.2.b.c (pool of retired national legislators and judges), v.e (permanent)

Garm Republic

Executive:

- 2.iii (Abolished Executive); 5.a.b.c (National)

Legislature:

- 1.i.xx.z (Multi-cameral legislature, 1st house), ii.xx (Representative), iii.4.a. (Unitary Executive Powers), 5.a (National), 6.a.ii (4 year terms), b.iii (Unlimited), c.i (Lifetime), c.ii (sum of elected and appointed), 7.a.ii.x.xx (privately funded by citizen, corporations), b.ii.xxxx (One citizen = One vote), c.x (direct elections), 8.a.v.b (Citizen), b.ii (criteria to hold office), c.i (exclusive), 10.a (compulsory), 12.b (Jurisdictions), 13.c.ii (Representative of Net Taxes), 13.h (Legislative Broker)
- 1.i.xx.zz (Multi-cameral legislature, 2nd house), ii.x (Representative), iii.1.2.3.5.7.10 (Laws, Oversight, Treaty Ratification, Appropriations, Appointments, Taxes), 5.a (National), 6.a.iii (6 year terms), b.ii (Unlimited), c.ii (Intermittent), c.ii (sum of elected only), 7.a.ii.x.xxx (privately funded by citizen, and government), b.ii.xxxx (One citizen = One vote), c.x (direct elections), 8.a.v.b (Citizen), b.i.ii (to vote and to hold office), c.i (exclusive), 10.b (voluntary), 12.b (Districts), 13.b.i (Representative of GDP, Straight)
- 1.i.xx.zz (Multi-cameral legislature, 2nd house).ii.x (Representative), iii.1.2.3.5.7.10 (Laws, Oversight, Treaty Ratification, Appropriations, Appointments, Taxes), 5.(National), 6.a.iii (6 year terms), b.ii (Unlimited), c.ii

(Intermittent), c.ii (sum of elected only), 7.a.ii.x.xx.a.xxx (Privately funded by citizens, domestic corporations, and governments), 8.a.v.b (Citizen), b.i.ii (to vote and to hold office), c.i (exclusive), 10.b (voluntary), 12.b (Districts), 13.b.ii (Representative of GDP, Per Capita)

- 1.i.xx.zzz (Multi-cameral legislature, 3rd house,), ii.x (Representative), iii.6 (Judicial), 5.a (National), 6.a.iii (6 year terms), b.iii (Unlimited), c.i (Lifetime), c.i (sum of elected and appointed positions), 7.a.i (publicly funded), b.ii.xxxx (One citizen = One vote), c.x (direct elections), 8.a.vii.x. (Lawyers), 8.a.v.b (Citizen), b.ii (to hold office), c.i (exclusive), 10.b (voluntary), 12.b (Districts), 13.a.i (Representative of Population, by jurisdiction), 13.f (Executive Representation)

Judicial:

- 3.a.iv (Abolished Judicial), 5.a (National)

Bond Based Systems of Representation

Bonded Bipartite

Executive;

- 2.ii.x.c (Executive Presidential), 5.a (National), 6.a.ii (6 year terms), b.i (3 terms maximum), c.i (lifetime maximum), d.ii (sum of elected), 7.a.i (publicly funded), b.i.x (presidential), ii.xx.c (value voting, straight), c.x (direct elections), 8.a.v.b (citizen), iv.a.f.2.iii.2 (iv.a.f.2.iii.b (Federal Bonds, Inclusive), b.i.ii (eligibility for voting and holding office), c.i (exclusive), 10.b (voluntary voting)
- 2.ii.x.cc (Executive Treasury and Attorney General), 5.a (National), 6.a.ii (4 year), b.iiv (Unlimited), c.ii (intermittent maximum), d.ii (sum of elected), 7.a.ii.x.xx.a.xxx (privately funded by citizen, domestic corporations, and government), b.i.x (Presidential), ii.xxxx (One citizen = One vote), c.x (direct elections), 8.a.v.b (citizen), b.i.ii (for voting and holding office), c.i (exclusive), 10.b (voluntary voting).

Legislature

- 1.i.x.z (Unicameral legislature), ii.x (Representative), iii.1.2.3.5.7.10 (Laws, Oversight, Ratification, Appropriations, Appointments, and Taxation), 5.a. (National), 6.a.iii (6 year terms), b.iii (3 terms maximum), c.ii (Intermittent), c.ii (sum of elected only), 7.a.i (publicly funded), b.ii.xxxx (One citizen = One vote), c.x (direct elections), 8.a.v.b (citizen), b.i.ii (to vote and to hold office), c.i (exclusive), 10.b (voluntary), 12.a (Jurisdictions), 13.b.i (Representative of GDP, straight)

Judicial

- 3.a.i (Judicial, Circuit), b.i (Judicial powers only), c.ii.x 2 (President appoints judges), 5.a. (National), 6.a.iii (6 year term), b.iii (3 terms maximum), c.i (lifetime maximum), 8.v.b, b.ii (citizen to hold office).

Liability Republic

Executive;

- 2.i.iii (Unitary Executive, Elected), 5.a (National), 6.a ii (4 year terms), b.iii (3 maximum concurrent terms), c.i (lifetime maximum), d.i (sum of both elected and appointed), 7.a.i (publicly funded), b.i.x (Presidential), b.ii.xxxx (One citizen = One vote), b.ii.xx.cc (value voting, ratio) c.x (direct elections); 8.v.b. (Citizen), 8.a.i.xxviii (military enlistment), iv.a.f.2.iii.2 (Federal Bonds, Inclusive), b.i.ii (to hold office and to vote), c.i (exclusive), 10.a (compulsory voting)

Legislature;

- 1.i.xx.z (Bicameral legislature, 1st house), ii.x (Representative), iii.1.2.3.5.7 (Laws, Oversight, Ratification, Appropriations, and Appointments), 5.a. (National), 6.a.iii (6 year terms), b.ii (2 terms maximum), c.ii (Intermittent), c.ii (sum of elected only), 7.a.i (publicly funded), ii.xx.c (Value Voting, straight), c.x (direct elections), 8.a.v.b (Citizen), iv.c.i.c.ii.b (Tax liabilities, straight property tax), b.i.ii (to vote and to hold office), c.i (exclusive), 10.b (voluntary), 12.a (Jurisdiction), 13.c.ii (Representative of Net Taxes)
- 1.i.xx.zz (Bicameral legislature, 2nd house), ii.x (Representative), iii.1.2.3.4.5.10 (Laws, Oversight, Ratification,

Appropriations, Taxing), 5.a. (National), 6.a.ii (4 year terms), b.iv (Unlimited), c.ii (Intermittent), c.ii (sum of elected only), 7.a.ii.xxxx (privately funded), ii.xx.c (value voting, straight), c.x (and open, direct elections), 8.a.v.a.b (resident and citizen), iv.a.f.2.iii.2 (Federal Bonds, Inclusive), 8.a.v.b (Citizen), b.i.ii (to vote and to hold office), c.i (exclusive), 10.b (voluntary), 12.b (Districts), 13.b.i (Representative of GDP, straight)

Judicial;

- 3.a.i. (Judicial, Circuit), b.i (Judicial powers only), c.ii.x.1 (Appointed by the Presidential), 5.a. (National), 6.a.iii (6 year term), b.iii (3 terms maximum), c.i (lifetime maximum), 8.v.b, b.ii (citizen to hold office).

Bonded Binary

Executive:

- 2.iii (Abolished Executive), 5.a.b.c (National)

Legislative:

- 1.i.xx.z (Bicameral legislature), ii.x (Representative), iii.1.2.d.e.3.4.b 6.7. (Laws, Oversight on A,G, Treasury, Ratification, Executive-Presidential, Judicial, Appointments), 5.a (National), 6.a.iii (6 year terms), b.iii (3 terms maximum), c.ii (Intermittent), c.i (sum of elected), 7.a.i (publicly funded), b.ii.xxxx (One citizen = One vote), c.x (direct elections), 8.a.v.b (Citizen), 8.a.i.xxviii (military enlistment), vi.x.c.cc.ccc (emergency professionals and law enforcement from the municipal, state, and national tiers), vii.x.a.b (public attorneys and judges), b.i.ii (to vote and hold office), c.i (exclusive), 10.b (voluntary), 12.b (Districts), 13.a.i (Representative of population, jurisdictions), 13.f (Legislative Broker), 13.h (Executive Representation)
- 1.i.xx.zz (Bicameral legislature), ii.x (Representative), iii.1.2.b.c.3.4.c.d.5.7.10. (Laws, Oversight on Presidential and Judicial, Executive- domestic and treasury, Appropriations, Appointments, Taxing), 5.a (National), 6.a.iii (6 year terms), b.iii (3 terms maximum), c.i (Lifelong), c.i (sum of elected), 7.a.i (publicly funded), b.ii.x (Straight), Numerical), ii.xx.ccc (Bracket for Vote Multiplier), c.x (direct elections), 8.a.v.b (Citizen), iv.a.f.2.iii.2 (Federal

Bonds, Inclusive), b.i.ii (to vote and hold office), c.i (exclusive), 10.b (voluntary), 12.a (Jurisdictions), 13.b.ii (Representative of GDP, per capita)

Judicial:

- 3.iii (Abolished Judicial), 5.a (National)

Land Based
Systems of Representation

Baron Republic

Executive;

- 2.ii.x.c (Tripartite Executive Presidential), iv.1.2 (Sub routine, Laws, Oversight), 5.a (National), 6.a.iii (6 year terms), b.i (1 terms maximum), c.i (lifetime maximum); d.i (sum of elected and appointed), 7.a.i (publicly funded), b.i.x Presidential), ii.xxxx (One citizen = One vote), c.x (direct elections), 8.v.b. (Citizen), b.i.ii (to hold office and to vote), 10.b (voluntary voting), c.i (exclusive), 14.a (Macro-political Vote, Alpha)
- 2.ii.x.cc (Tripartite Executive Treasury), iv.1.2 (Sub routine, Laws and Oversight); 5.a (National); 6.a.ii (4 year terms), b.iii (3 terms maximum), c.ii (intermittent maximum), d.ii (sum of elected), 7.a.i (publicly funded), b.i.x (Presidential) ii.xx.c (Value voting, straight), c.x (direct elections), 8.a.ix.c.i.c.ii.b (tax liability, property), v.b (Citizen), b.i.ii (eligibility for voting and holding office), c.i (exclusive), 10.b (voluntary voting), 14.a (Macro-political Vote, Alpha)
- 2.ii.x.ccc (Tripartite Executive Attorney General), iv.1.2 (Sub Routine; Laws and Oversight), 5.a. (National), 6.a.ii (4 year terms), b.ii (2 terms maximum), c.i (lifetime maximum), d.i (sum of elected and appointed), 7.a.i (publicly funded), b.i.x (Presidential), ii.xxxx (One citizen = One vote), c.x(direct elections), 8.v.b. (Citizen), b.i.ii (to hold office and to vote), 10.b (voluntary voting), c.i (exclusive), 14.a (Macro-political Vote, Alpha)

Legislature;

- 1.i.x.z (Unicameral legislature, 1st house), ii.x (Representative), iii.1.2.3.5.7.10 (Laws, Oversight, Ratification, Appropriations, Appointments, Taxation), 5.a. (National), 6.a.iii (6 year terms), b.ii (2 terms maximum), c.ii (Intermittent), c.ii (Sum of elected only), 7.a.i, c.x (Publicly funded, direct elections), b.ii.xx.c (value voting, straight), 8.a.v.b (citizen), iv.a.f, (Inclusive) 2.ii.2 (Residential Properties), b.i.ii (to vote and to hold office), c.i (exclusive), 10.b (voluntary), 12.a (Jurisdiction), 13.b (Representative of GDP)

Judicial;

- 3.a.i. (Judicial, circuits), b.i (Judicial powers only), c.ii.x.2 (appointed by President) 5.a. (National) 6.a.iii (6 year term), b.iii (3 terms maximum), c.i (lifetime maximum), 8.v.b, b.ii (citizen to hold office), c.i (exclusive)

Binary Magna Legislature

Executive:

- 2.iii (Abolished Executive); 5.a.b.c (National)

Legislative:

- 1.i.xx.z (Bicameral legislature), ii.xx (Representative),.iii.1.2.d.e.3.4.b 6.7. (Laws, Oversight on A,G, Treasury, Ratification, Executive-Presidential, Judicial, Appointments); 5.a (National), 6.a.iii (6 year terms), b.iii (3 terms maximum), c.ii (Intermittent); c.i (sum of elected), 7.a.i (Publicly Funded); b.ii.x (one citizen = one vote), c.x (Direct vote); 8.a.v.b (citizen), iv.a.f, (Inclusive) 2.ii.1 (Residential Real Estate), 8.a.i.xxviii (military enlistment), vi.x.c.cc.ccc (emergency professionals and law enforcement from the municipal, state, and national tiers), vii.x.a.b (public attorneys and judges), b.i.ii (to vote and hold office), c.ii (non -exclusive), 10.a (compulsory), 12.a (jurisdictions), 13.a.i (Representative of Population, by jurisdiction)
- 1.i.xx.zz (Bicameral legislature), ii.xx (Representative),.iii.1.2.b.c.3.4.c.d.5.7.10. (Laws, Oversight on Presidential and Judicial, Executive- domestic and treasury, Appropriations, Appointments, Taxing); 5.a (National), 6.a.iii (6 year terms), b.iii (3 terms maximum), c.i (Lifelong); c.i (sum of elected), 7.a.i (Publicly Funded); b.ii.x (one citizen = one vote), c.x (Direct vote); 8.a.v.b (citizen), b.i.ii (to vote and hold office), c.i (exclusive), 10.a

(compulsory), 12.a (jurisdictions), 13.a.i (Representative of Population, by jurisdiction), 13.f (Legislative Broker)

Judicial:

- 3.iii (Abolished Judicial); 5.a (National)

Real Republic

Executive;

- 2.i.iii (Unitary Executive, Elected), 5.a (National), 6.a ii (4 year terms), b.iii (3 maximum concurrent terms), c.i (lifetime maximum), d.i (sum of both elected and appointed), 7.a.i (publicly funded), b.i.x (Presidential), .ii.xxxx (One citizen = One vote), c.x (direct elections), 8.v.b. (Citizen), b.i.ii (to hold office and to vote), 10.b (voluntary voting), c.i (exclusive)

Legislature;

- 1.i.xx.z (Bicameral legislature, 1st house), ii.x (Representative), iii.1.2.3.5.7 (Laws, Oversight, Ratification, Appropriations, and Appointments), 5.a. (National), 6.a.iii (6 year terms), b.ii (2 terms maximum), c.ii (Intermittent); c.ii (sum of elected only); 7.a.i (publicly funded), b.ii.xxxx (One citizen = One vote), c.x (direct elections); 8.a.v.ab (resident, citizen), iv.a.d.2.ii.2. (Residential Real Estate, above median), b.i.ii (to vote and to hold office), c.i (exclusive), 10.b (voluntary), 12.a (Jurisdictions), 13.a.i (Representative of Population), 13.f (Executive Representation)
- 1.i.xx.zz (Bicameral legislature, 2nd house), ii.x (Representative), iii.1.3.4.5.10 (Laws, Ratification, Appropriations, Taxing), 5.a. (National), 6.a.ii (4 year terms), b.iv (Unlimited), c.ii (Intermittent), c.ii (sum of elected only), 7.a.i (publicly funded), b.ii.xxxx (One citizen = One vote), c.x (direct elections), iv.A.e.2.ii.2. (Residential Real Estate, below median value), b.i.ii (to vote and to hold office), c.i (exclusive), 10.b (voluntary), 12.a (Jurisdictions), 13.a.i (Representative of Population), 13.f (Executive Representation)

Judicial;

- 3.a.ii. (Judicial, Elected, Congressional), b.ii. (Legislative sub routine, Oversight), c.i.x (Elected, Representative), 5.a. (National), 6.a.iii (6 year term), b.iv (Unlimited), c.i (lifetime maximum), d.ii (sum of elected), 7.a.i (publicly funded), b.ii.xxxx (One citizen = One vote), c.x (direct elections), 8.v.b, b.i.ii (citizen to hold office and vote), c.i (exclusive), 10.b (voluntary), 12.b (districts), 13.a.i (Representative of Population)

Equity Based
Systems of Representation

Midgard Republic

Executive;

- 2.i.iii (Unitary Executive, Elected), 5.a (National), 6.a ii (4 year terms), b.iii (3 maximum concurrent terms), c.i (lifetime maximum), d.i (sum of both elected and appointed), 7.a.i (publicly funded), b.i.x (Presidential), ii.xxxx (One citizen = One vote), c.x (direct elections), 8.a.v.b. (Citizen), b.i.ii (to hold office and to vote), c.i (exclusive), 10.a (compulsory voting)

Legislature;

- 1.i.xx.z (Bicameral legislature, 1st house), ii.x (Representative), iii.1.2.3.5.7 (Laws, Oversight, Ratification, Appropriations, and Appointments), 5.a. (National), 6.a.iii (6 year terms), b.ii (2 terms maximum), c.ii (Intermittent), c.ii (sum of elected only), 7.a.i (publicly funded), b.ii.xxxx (One citizen = One vote), c.x (direct elections), 8.a.v.b (Citizen), b.i.ii (to vote and to hold office), c.i (exclusive), 10.b (voluntary), 12.a (Jurisdiction), 13.a.i (Representative of Population)
- 1.i.xx.zz (Bicameral legislature, 2nd house), ii.x (Representative), iii.1.2.3.4.5.10 (Laws, Oversight, Ratification, Appropriations, Taxing), 5.a. (National), 6.a.ii (4 year terms), b.iv (Unlimited), c.ii (Intermittent), c.ii (sum of elected only), 7.a.ii.xxxx, (privately funded and open), b.ii.xxxx (One citizen = One vote), c.x (direct elections), 8.a.v.b (Citizen), b.i.ii (to vote and to hold office), c.i (exclusive), 10.b (voluntary), 12.b (Districts), 13.a.i (Representative of Population)
- 1.i.xx.zz (Unicameral legislature, 3rd house), ii.x (Representative), iii.9 (Triangulation), 5.a. (National), 6.a.iii (6

year terms), b.ii (4 terms maximum), c.i (lifelong limit), c.ii (sum of elected only), 7.a.ii.x.xx.c (privately Funded, individuals and domestic corporations), ii.xx (Asset value Voting), c.x (direct elections); 8.a.v.b (Citizen), 8.a.iv f.2.i.1.2.3 (Equity Asset, Inclusive, Governmental), c.i (exclusive), 10.b (voluntary), 12.a (Jurisdiction), 13.a.i (Representative of Population), 13.h. (Executive Representation)

Judicial;

- 3.A.i. (Judicial, Appointed, Hierarchal), B.i (Judicial powers only); 5.a. (National) 6.a.iii (6 year term), b.iii (3 terms maximum), c.i (lifetime maximum); 7.d.x.2.i (Tyrant, appointed by Presidential Executive); 8.v.b, b.ii (citizen to hold office), c.i (exclusive).

Mandrake Union

Executive:

- 2.i.iii (Unitary Executive, Elected), 5.a (National), 6.a ii (4 year terms), b.iii (3 maximum concurrent terms), c.i (lifetime maximum), d.i (sum of both elected and appointed), 7.a.ii.xxx.cc (privately Funded, domestic governments), b.ix.ii.xx (Presidential, Asset value Voting), c.x (direct elections), 8.a.v.b (Citizen), 8.a.iv f.2.i.1.2.3 (Equity Asset, Inclusive, Governmental), b.i.ii (to hold office and to vote), c.i (exclusive), 10.a (compulsory voting)

Legislative:

- 1.i.x.z (Unicameral legislature), ii.x (Representative), iii.1.2.3.5.7.10 (Laws, Oversight, Ratification, Appropriations, Appointments, Taxing), 5.a. (National), 6.a.iii (6 year terms), b.ii (4 terms maximum), c.i (lifelong limit), c.ii (sum of elected only), 7.a.ii.x.xx.c.xxx.cc (privately Funded, domestic governments), ii.xx (Asset value Voting), c.x (direct elections), 8.a.v.b (Citizen), 8.a.iv f.2.i.1.2.3 (Equity Asset, Inclusive, Governmental), c.i (exclusive), 10.b (voluntary), 12.a (Jurisdiction), 13.a.i (Representative of Population)

Judicial:

- 3.a.i. (Judicial, Appointed, Hierarchal), b.i (Judicial powers only), c.ii.x.2 (Appointed by the President), 5.a.(National)) 6.a.iii (6 year term), b.iv (unlimited), c.i (lifetime maximum), 8.vii.a.b (legal and judicial experience), v.b (Citizen)

Reserve:

- 4.i.a.ii (Reserve Board, admitting all retired members, permanent), .ii.b (legislative sub routine - 1.2.3.7 (Laws, Oversight, Treaties, Appointments), .iii.b (Unicameral), iv.1.a.2.b.c (Pool of retired national legislators and judges), v.d (total equivalent terms)

Industrial Republic

Executive;

- 2.ii.x.c.ccc (Bipartite Executive Presidential- Attorney General), 5.a (National), 6.a.ii (6 year terms), b.ii (2 terms maximum), c.i (lifetime maximum), d.ii (sum of elected), 7.a.i, b.x, c.x (publicly funded, presidential, direct elections), 8.a.v.b (Citizen), b.i.ii (eligibility for voting and holding office), 10.a (compulsory voting)
- 2.ii.x.cc (Bipartite Executive Treasury,); 5.a (National); 6.a.ii (4 year terms), b.iii (3 terms maximum), c.i (lifetime), d.ii (sum of elected), 7.a.ii.x.xx.c.xxx.cc (privately Funded, citizens, domestic corporations, domestic governments), b.ix.ii.xx (Presidential, Asset value Voting), c.x (direct elections), 8.a.v.b (Citizen), 8.a.iv f.2.i.1.2.3 (Equity Asset, Inclusive, Private, Commercial, Governmental), b.i.ii (eligibility for voting and holding office); c.i (exclusive), 10.b (voluntary voting),

Legislature;

- 1.i.xx.z (Bicameral legislature, 1st house), ii.x (Representative), iii.1.2.3.5.7.10.11 (Laws, Oversight, Ratification, Appropriations, Appointments (Confirm), Appointments (Direct), Taxing), 5.a. (National), 6.a.iii (6 year terms), b.ii (4 terms maximum), c.i (lifelong limit), c.ii (sum of elected only), 7.a.i, c.x (publicly funded, direct elections), 8.a.v.b (Citizen), b.i.ii (to vote and to hold office), c.i (exclusive), 10.b (voluntary), 12.a (Jurisdiction), 13.a.i (Representative of Population, by jurisdiction)
- 1.i.xx.zz (Bicameral legislature, 2nd house), ii.x (Representative), iii.2.5.10 (Oversight. Appropriations, and Taxing), 5.a (National), 6.a.iii (6 year terms), b.ii (4 terms maximum), c.i (lifelong limit), c.ii (sum of elected only);

7.a.ii.x.xx.c.xxx.cc (privately Funded, citizens, domestic corporations, domestic governments), b.i.x, ii.xx (Presidential, Asset value Voting), c.x (direct elections); 8.a.v.b (Citizen), 8.a.iv f.2.i.1.2.3 (Equity Asset, Inclusive, Private, Commercial, Governmental), b.i.ii (to vote and to hold office), c.i (exclusive), 10.b (voluntary), 12.a (Jurisdiction), 13.c.ii (Representative of Tax Liabilities, Net)

Judicial;

- 3.a.i (Judicial, Appointed, Hierarchal), b.i (Judicial powers only), c.ii.xx (appointed by primary legislature), 5.a. (National) 6.a.ii (4 year term), b.iii (3 terms maximum), c.i (lifetime maximum); d.ii (sum of elected)

Commercial Complex

Executive:

- 2.iii (Abolished Executive), 5.a.b.c (National)

Legislative:

- 1.i.xx.z (Multi-cameral legislature, 1st house), ii.xx (Representative), iii.4.a. (Unitary Presidential Executive Powers), 5.a (National), 6.a.iii (6 year terms), b.iii (3 terms maximum), c.ii (Intermittent), c.ii (sum of elected and appointed), 7.a.ii.xxx.cc (privately Funded, domestic governments), ii.x (Asset value, Numerical per stock), c.x (direct elections), 8.a.v.b (Citizen), iv f.2.i.3 (Equity Asset, Inclusive, Governmental), c.i (exclusive), 10.a (compulsory), 12.a (Jurisdictions), 13.c.ii (Representative of Tax Liabilities, Net), 13.h (Executive Representation)
- 1.i.xx.zz (Multi-cameral legislature, 2nd house), ii.xx (Representative), iii.4.b (Unitary Attorney General Executive Powers), 5.a (National), 6.a.iii (6 year terms), b.iii (3 term maximum), c.ii (Intermittent), c.ii (sum of elected and appointed), 7.a.i (publicly funded), ii.xx (value voting, straight), c.x (direct elections), 8.a.v.b (Citizen), iv.A.f.2.iii.a (Federal Bonds, Inclusive), b.i.ii (to vote and hold office), c.i (exclusive), 10.b (voluntary), 12.a (Jurisdictions), 13.b (Representative of GDP), 13.f (Legislative Broker),
- 1.i.xx.zzz (Multi-cameral legislature, 3rd house), ii.xx (Representative), iii.4.c (Unitary Treasurer General Executive Powers), 5.a (National), 6.a.iii (6 year terms), b.iv

(Unlimited), c.ii (Intermittent), c.ii (sum of elected and appointed), 7.a.ii.x.xx.c.xxx.cc (privately Funded, citizens, domestic corporations, domestic governments), ii.x (Asset value, Numerical per stock), c.x (direct elections), 8.a.v.b (Citizen), iv f.2.i.2.3 (Equity Asset, Inclusive, Commercial, Governmental), c.i (exclusive), 10.a (compulsory), 12.b (Districts), 13.a.i (Representative of Population, by jurisdiction)

- 1.i.xx.zzzz (Multi-cameral legislature, 4th house), ii.xx (Representative), 5.a (National), iii.1.3.4.5.10 (Laws, Treaty Ratification, Appropriations, and Taxation), 6.a.ii (4 year terms), b.iii (Unlimited), c.i (Lifetime), c.ii (sum of elected and appointed), 7.a.i (publicly funded), b.ix.ii.xx (Presidential, value voting), 8.a.v.b (Citizen), iv.A.f.2.iii.a (Federal Bonds, Inclusive), b.i.ii (to vote and hold office), c.i (exclusive), 10.b (voluntary), 12.a (Jurisdictions), 13.b (Representative of GDP), 13.f (Legislative Broker)
- 1.i.xx.zzzzz (Multi-cameral legislature, 5th house).ii.xx (Representative), 5.a (National), iii.1.2.3.4.5.7 (Laws, Oversight, Treaty Ratification, Appropriations, Appointments, and Taxation), 6.a.ii (4 year terms), b.iii (Unlimited), c.i (Lifetime), c.ii (sum of elected and appointed), 7.a.ii.xxx.cc (privately Funded, domestic governments), ii.x (Asset value, Numerical per stock), c.x (direct elections), 8.a.v.b (Citizen), iv f.2.i.2.3 (Equity Asset, Inclusive, Commercial, Governmental), c.i (exclusive), 10.a (compulsory), 12.b (Districts), 13.c.ii (Representative of Tax Liabilities, Gross)
- 1.i.xx.zzzzz (Multi-cameral legislature, 6th house,), ii.x (Representative), iii.6 (Judicial), 5.a (National), 6.a.iii (6 year terms), b.iii (Unlimited), c.i (Lifetime); c.i (sum of elected and appointed positions), 7.a.i (Public Funding), c.x (direct elections), 8.a.vii.x. (Lawyers), v.b (Citizens) b.ii (to hold office), c.i (exclusive), 10.b (voluntary voting 12.b (Districts), 13.a.i (Representative of Population, by jurisdiction)

Judicial:

- 3.iii (Abolished Judicial), 5.a (National)

Pre-Tax Income Based Systems of Representation

Lion Republic

Executive;

- 2.ii.x.c (Tripartite Executive Presidential), 5.a (National), 6.a.iii (6 year terms), b.i (1 terms maximum), c.i (lifetime maximum), d.i (sum of elected and appointed), 7.a.i (publicly funded), b.i.x (Presidential), ii.xxxx (One citizen = One vote), c.x (direct elections), 8.v.b. (Citizen), b.i.ii (to hold office and to vote), c.i (exclusive), 10.b (voluntary voting), 14.a (Alpha Macro-political vote – for Veto)
- 2.ii.x.cc (Tripartite Executive Treasury), 5.a (National), 6.a.ii (4 year terms), b.ii (4 terms maximum), c.ii (intermittent maximum), d.ii (sum of elected), 7.a.i (publicly funded), b.i.x Presidential), ii.xxxx (One citizen = One vote), c.x (direct elections), 8.v.b. (Citizen), b.i.ii (to hold office and to vote), c.i (exclusive), 10.b (voluntary voting), 14.a (Alpha Macro-political vote – for Veto)
- 2.ii.x.ccc (Tripartite Executive Attorney General), 5.a. (National), 6.a.ii (4 year terms), b.ii (2 terms maximum), c.i (lifetime), d.ii (sum of elected), 7.a.i (publicly funded), b.i.x Presidential), .ii.xxxx (One citizen = One vote), c.x (direct elections), 8.v.b. (Citizen), b.i.ii (to hold office and to vote), c.i (exclusive), 10.b (voluntary voting), 14.a (Alpha Macro-political vote – for Veto)

Legislature:

- 1.i.xx.z (Bicameral legislature, 1st house), ii.x (Representative like House), iii.1.2.3.5.10 (Laws, Oversight, Ratification, Appropriations, and Taxes), 5.a. (National), 6.a.ii (4 year terms), b.iii (3 terms maximum), c.ii (Intermittent), c.ii (sum of elected only), 7.a.i, b.ii.x, c.x (publicly funded, one citizen = one vote, direct elections), 8.a.v.b (Citizen), iv.b.1.i.ii.iii.iv.w.d.g (Income from employer, employee, and self employed, below median, pre-tax), b.i.ii (to vote and to hold office), c.i (exclusive), 10.b (voluntary), 12.a (Jurisdiction), 13.b (Representative of GDP)
- 1.i.xx.zz (Bicameral legislature, 2nd house), ii.xx (Representative like House), iii.1.2.3.5.10 (Laws, Oversight, Ratification, Appropriations, and Taxes), 5.a. (National),

6.a.iii (6 year terms), b.ii (2 terms maximum), c.ii (Intermittent), c.ii (sum of elected only), 7.a.i, b.ii.x, c.x (publicly funded, one citizen = one vote direct elections); 8.a.v.b (Citizen), iv.b.1.i.ii.iii.iv.w.e.g (Income from employer, employee, and self employed, above median, pre-tax), b.i.ii (to vote and to hold office), c.i (exclusive), 10.b (voluntary), 12.a (Jurisdiction), 13.c.i (Representative of Gross Taxes)

Judicial;

- 3.a.i (Judicial, Circuit), b.i (Judicial powers only), c.ii.x.2 (appointed by President), 5.a. (National) 6.a.ii (4 year term), b.iii (3 terms maximum), c.i (lifetime maximum); d.ii (sum of elected)

Reserve:

- 4.i.a. (Reserve Board, all retired officials), ii.b.1.5.9.a.7.10 (legislative sub routine, appointments, triangulation over legislation, appropriations, and taxes), ii.d.x.xx.i.ii (Repealing, Excising Legislators and Executives), iii.b (Unicameral), iv.1.a.2.b.c (Pool of retired national legislators and justices), v.c (total equivalent terms)

Wealth Complex

Executive:

- 2.iii (Abolished Executive), 5.a.b.c (National)

Legislature:

- 1.i.xx.z (Multi-cameral legislature, 1st house), ii.x (Representative), iii.4.a. (Unitary Executive Powers), 5.a (National), 6.a.ii (4 year terms), b.iii (Unlimited), c.i (Lifetime), c.ii (sum of elected and appointed), 7.a.i (publicly funded), b.ii.xx (value voting), c.x (direct elections); 8.a.v.b (Citizen), iv.b.1.i.ii.iii.2.d.g (Income from employer, employee, and self employed, in below median, pre tax), c.i (exclusive), 10.b (voluntary), 12.b (Jurisdictions), 13.c.i (Representative of Tax Liabilities, Gross)
- 1.i.xx.zz (Multi-cameral legislature, 2nd house), ii.x (Representative), iii.1.2.3.7 (Laws, Oversight, Treaty Ratification, Appointments), 5.(National), 6.a.iii (6 year terms), b.ii (Unlimited), c.ii (Intermittent), c.ii (sum of elected only), 7.a.i (Public Funding), b.ii.x (one citizen = one vote), c.x (direct elections), 8.a.v.b (Citizen), iv.b.1.i.ii.iii.2.d.g

(Income from employer, employee, and self employed, in below median, pre tax), b.i.ii (to vote and to hold office), c.i (exclusive), 10.b (voluntary 12.b (Districts), 13.a.i (Representative of Population, by jurisdiction)

- 1.i.xx.zzz (Multi-cameral legislature, 3rd house).ii.x (Representative), iii.1.5.10 (Laws, Appropriations, Taxes), 5.(National), 6.a.iii (6 year terms), b.ii (Unlimited), c.ii (Intermittent), c.ii (sum of elected only), 7.a.i (Public Funding), b.ii.x (one citizen = one vote), c.x (direct elections), 8.a.v.b (Citizen), iv.b.1.i.ii.iii.2.e.g (Income from employer, employee, and self employed, above median, pre tax), b.i.ii (to vote and to hold office), c.i (exclusive), 10.b (voluntary), 12.b (Districts), 13.a.i (Representative of Population, by jurisdiction)
- 1.i.xx.zzzz (Multi-cameral legislature, 4th house), ii.x (Representative), iii.6 (Judicial), 5.a (National), 6.a.iii (6 year terms), b.iii (Unlimited), c.i (Lifetime), c.i (sum of elected and appointed positions), 7.a.i (Public Funding), b.ii.x (one citizen = one vote), c.x (direct elections), 8.a.vii.x. (Lawyers), b.ii (to hold office), c.i (exclusive), 10.b (voluntary), 12.b (Districts), 13.a.i (Representative of Population, by jurisdiction)

Judicial:

- 3.iii (Abolished Judicial), 5.a (National)

Charlemagne Republic

Executive:

- 2.iii (Abolished Executive); 5.a.b.c (National)

Legislative:

- 1.i.xx.z (Bicameral legislature), ii.x (Representative), iii.1.2.d.e.3.4.b.6.7 (Laws, Oversight on A,G, Treasury, Ratification, Executive-Presidential, Judicial, Appointments), 5.a (National), 6.a.iii (6 year terms), b.iii (3 terms maximum), c.ii (Lifelong); c.i (sum of elected), 7.a.i, b.ii.x, c.x (publicly funded, one citizen = one vote, direct elections), 8.a.v.b (Citizen), 8.iv.b.1.i.ii.iii.2.e.g (Income from employer, employee, self employed, above median, pre tax), b.i.ii (to vote and hold office), c.i (exclusive), 10.b (voluntary), 12.a (Jurisdictions), 13.b (Representative of GDP), 13.f (Executive Representation)

- 1.i.xx.zz (Bicameral legislature), ii.x (Representative), iii.1.2.b.c.3.4.c.d.5.7.10 (Laws, Oversight on Presidential and Judicial, Executive- domestic and treasury, Appropriations, Appointments, Taxing), 5.a (National), 6.a.ii (4 year terms), b.iii (3 terms maximum), c.i (Lifelong), c.i (sum of elected), 7.a.i, b.ii.x, (publicly funded, one citizen = one vote), c.x (direct elections), 8.a.v.b (Citizen), iv.b.1.i.ii.iii.2.d.g (Income from employer, employee, self employed, below median, pre tax), b.i.ii (to vote and hold office), c.i (exclusive), 10.b (voluntary), 12.a (Jurisdictions), 13.a.i (Representative of Population, by jurisdiction), 13.h (Legislative Broker)

Judicial;

- 3.a.i (Judicial, Circuit), b.i (Judicial powers only), c.ii.x.2 (appointed by President), 5.a. (National) 6.a.ii (4 year term), b.iii (3 terms maximum), c.i (lifetime maximum); d.ii (sum of elected)

Reserves:

- 4.i.a.ii (Reserve Board, admitting all retired members), .ii.b (legislative sub routine - b.9 (Triangulation for Laws. Appointments), x.xx.ii.xxx (repealing legislation, excising legislators, excommunication), iii.b (Unicameral), iv.1.a.2.b (Pool of retired national legislators), v.a (single equivalent terms).

Spartan Union

Executive:

- 2.ii.x.c (Tripartite Executive Presidential), iv.1.9 (Sub routine, Laws, Triangulation), iv.; 5.a (National); 6.a.ii (6 year terms), b.ii (2 terms maximum), c.i (lifetime maximum); d.i (sum of elected and appointed), 7.a.ii.xxx (Privately Funded by Governments), b.ii.xx (value voting), c.xxxx (Coalition of State level executives), 8.a. iv.b.1.vi (Tax Revenue), 8.a.v.b (Citizen), b.i.ii (eligibility for voting and holding office); c.i (exclusive), 10.a (compulsory voting), 14.a (Macro-political Vote, Alpha),
- 2.ii.x.cc (Tripartite Executive Treasury), iv.1.5.9.10 (Sub routine, Laws, Appropriations, Triangulation, Taxation); 5.a (National); 6.a.ii (4 year terms), b.iii (3 terms maximum), c.ii (intermittent maximum); d.ii (sum of elected),

7.a.i (Publicly Funded);b.ii.x (one citizen = one vote), 8.a.v.b (citizen), b.i.ii (to vote and hold office), c.i (exclusive), 10.a (compulsory voting), 14.a (Macro-political Vote, Alpha)

- 2.ii.x.ccc (Tripartite Executive Attorney General), iv.1.2.9 (Sub Routine; Laws Oversight, Triangulation); 5.a. (National); 6.a.ii (4 year terms), b.iii (3 terms maximum), c.i (lifetime maximum); d.i (sum of elected and appointed), 7.a.ii.xxx (Privately Funded by Governments), b.ii.xx (value voting), c.xxxx (Coalition of State level executives), 8.a.iv.b.1.vi (Tax Revenue), v.b. (citizen), b.i.ii (for voting and holding office); c.i (exclusive), 10.a (compulsory voting), 14.a (Macro-political Vote, Alpha)

Legislative;

- 1.i.x (Unicameral Legislature), ii.xxxx. (Democratic legislature), 1.a.i (Monochamber, straight vote), 2.a.iii (Referendum, monthly votes), 3.b.ii (Laws by triangulation with the tripartite executives), e.iii (Treaties by unicameral process), v.b (Citizen), b.i (to vote), 10.b (voluntary)

Judicial:

- 3.a.i. (Judicial, Circuit), B.i (Judicial powers only), C.ii.x.2 (appointed by President), 5.a. (National), 6.a.iii (6 year term), b.iii (3 terms maximum), c.i (lifetime maximum), 8.v.b, b.ii (citizen to hold office), c.i (exclusive)

Post-tax Income Based Systems of Representation

Gaul Republic

Executive;

- 2.i.iii (Unitary Executive, Elected), 5.a (National), 6.a ii (4 year terms), b.iii (3 maximum concurrent terms), c.i (lifetime maximum), d.i (sum of both elected and appointed), 7.a.i (publicly funded), b.i.x (Presidential), ii.xxxx (One citizen = One vote), c.x (direct elections), 8.v.b. (Citizen), b.i.ii (to hold office and to vote), c.i (exclusive), 10.b (voluntary voting), 14.a (Alpha Macro-political vote – for triangulation with congress)

Legislature;

- 1.i.xx.z (Bicameral legislature, 1st house), ii.x (Representative), iii.1.2.3.5.7.10 (Laws, Oversight, Treatise, Appropriations, and Taxing), 5.a. (National), 6.a.iii (6 year terms), b.ii (2 terms maximum), c.ii (Intermittent), c.ii (sum of elected only), 7.a.i, b.ii.x, c.x (publicly funded, one citizen = one vote, direct elections), 8.a.v.b (Citizen), iv.b.1.i.ii.iii.2.d.h (Income from employer, employee, self employed, below median, post tax), b.i.ii (to vote and to hold office), c.i (exclusive), 10.b (voluntary), 12.a (Jurisdiction), 13.c.i (Representative of Gross Taxes)
- 1.i.xx.zz (Bicameral legislature, 2nd house), ii.x (Representative), iii.1.3.4.5.7.10 (Laws, Ratification, Appropriations, Appointments, and Taxing), 5.a. (National), 6.a.ii (4 year terms), b.iv (Unlimited), c.ii (Intermittent); c.ii (sum of elected only), 7.a.i, b.ii.x, c.x (publicly funded, one citizen = one vote, direct elections), 8.a.v.b (Citizen), iv.b.1.i.ii.iii.2.e.h (Income from employer, employee, self employed, above median, post tax), b.i.ii (to vote and to hold office), c.i (exclusive), 10.b (voluntary), 12.b (Districts), 13.c.i (Representative of Gross Taxes)

Judicial;

- 3.a.i. (Judicial, circuit), b.i (Judicial powers only), c.ii.x.2 (appointed by executive), 5.a. (National), 6.a.iii (6 year term), b.iii (3 terms maximum), c.i (lifetime maximum); 8.v.b, b.ii (citizen to hold office)

Athenian Union

Executive:

- 2.iii (Abolished Executive), 5.a.b.c (National)

Legislative:

- 1.i.xx.z (Bicameral legislature), ii.x (Representative), iii.1.2.d.e.3.4.b 6.7. (Laws, Oversight on A.G. and Treasury, Ratification, Executive-Presidential and Judicial, Appointments), 5.a (National), 6.a.iii (6 year terms), b.iii (3 terms maximum), c.ii (Lifelong), c.i (sum of elected), 7.a.i (publicly funded), b.ii.xx (value voting), c.x (direct elections), 8.a.v.b (Citizen), iv.b.1.i.ii.iii.iv.2.e.h (Income from employer, employee, self employed, above median, post tax), b.i.ii (to vote and hold office), c.i (exclusive),

10.a (compulsory), 12.a (Jurisdictions), 13.a.i (Representative of Population, by jurisdiction), 13.h (Legislative Broker)

- 1.i.xx.zz (Bicameral legislature), ii.x (Representative), iii.1.2.b.c.3.4.c.d.5.7.10. (Laws, Oversight on Presidential and Judicial, Executive- domestic and treasury, Appropriations, Appointments, Taxing), 5.a (National), 6.a.ii (4 year terms), b.iii (3 terms maximum), c.i (Lifelong), c.i (sum of elected), 7.a.i (publicly funded), b.ii.xx (value voting), c.x (direct elections), 8.a.v.b (Citizen), iv.b.1.i.ii.iii.iv.2.d.h (Income from employer, employee, self employed, below median, post tax), b.i.ii (to vote and hold office), c.i (exclusive), 10.a (voluntary), 12.a (Jurisdictions), 13.a.i (Representative of Population, by jurisdiction), 13.h (Legislative Broker)

Judicial:

- 3.iii (Abolished Judicial); 5.a (National)

Reserves:

- 4.i.a.ii (Reserve Board, admitting all retired members), .ii.b (legislative sub routine - b.9 (Triangulation for Laws. Appointments), x.xx.ii.xxx (repealing legislation, excising legislators, excommunication), .iii.b (Unicameral), iv.1.b.2.b (Pool of retired national legislators), v.a (single equivalent terms)

Bipartite Democracy

Executive;

- 2.ii.x.c (Executive Presidential), 5.a (National), 6.a.ii (6 year terms), b.i (3 terms maximum), c.i (lifetime maximum), d.ii (sum of elected), 7.a.i, b.ii.x, c.x (publicly funded, one citizen = one vote, direct elections), 8.a.v.b (Citizen), a.iv.b.1.i.ii.iii.iv.2.a.b. (Income from employer, employee, Self employed, and investments, lower quarter, middle half, post tax), b.i.ii (eligibility for voting and holding office), c.i (exclusive), 10.b (voluntary voting)
- 2.ii.x.cc (Executive Treasury and Attorney General), 5.a (National), 6.a.ii (4 year), b.iiv (Unlimited), c.ii (intermittent maximum), d.ii (sum of elected), 7.a.ii.x.xx.xxx, b.ii.x, c.x (privately funded by citizen, corporations, and governments, one citizen = one vote, direct elections),

a.iv.b.1.i.ii.iii.iv.2.b.c. (Income from employer, employee, Self employed, and investments, upper quarter, middle half, post tax), b.i.ii (for voting and holding office), c.i (exclusive), 10.b (voluntary voting)

Legislature;

- 1.i.xx.z (Bicameral legislature, 1st house), ii.xx (Representative), iii.1.2.3.5.7.10 (Laws, Oversight, Ratification, Appropriations, Appointments, Taxes), 5.a.b. (National), 6.a.iii (6 year terms), b.ii (2 terms maximum), c.ii (Intermittent), c.ii (sum of elected only); 7.a.ii.x.xx, b.ii.x, c.x (privately funded by citizen, and corporations, one citizen = one vote, direct elections), 8.a.v.b (Citizen), b.i.ii (to vote and to hold office), c.i (exclusive), 10.b (voluntary), 12.a (Jurisdiction), 13.c.ii (Representative of Tax Liabilities, Gross)
- 1.i.xxxx (True Democratic), 1.a.i (Mono-chamber, Straight vote), 2.a.iii (Referendum monthly), 3.b.ii (confirms legislation bicameral), d. (confirms appointments), e.ii (confirms treaties, bicameral)

Judicial;

- 3.A.i (Judicial, Appointed Hierarchal), B.i (Judicial powers only), c.ii.xx.2 (appointed by executive), 5.a. (National),6.a.iii (6 year term), b.iii (3 terms maximum), c.i (lifetime maximum), 8.v.b, b.ii (citizen to hold office)

Made in the USA
Monee, IL
04 November 2026

67383316R00187